More Critical Praise for Danny

for *In Search of the Lost Chord*

"A legendary steward of the hip musical world . . . Goldberg plunges into a thorough, panoramic account of the culture, politics, media, music and mores of the year to demolish the idea that it was trivial. He has researched and interviewed widely—his section on underground newspapers is impressively detailed—and he's been there with many of the principals through all these years . . . Goldberg's deep purchase on his subject and his storytelling ease make it fresh . . . Personal asides give the account intimacy . . . [The book proves] that so much activism and passion can be crowded into barely more than a single year. When Goldberg was writing his book, that might have been a useful message. Today, in Trump's America, with a fueled and gathering resistance, it is a potentially mirroring one."   —*New York Times Book Review*

"Goldberg's book is what one might call a survey of the period. His narrative skillfully weaves the music, the drugs, the politics, and the spiritual searching of the hippie counterculture into a tale that moves quickly and smoothly . . . What Goldberg has achieved in *In Search of the Lost Chord* is laudable. Not only has he provided his contemporaries with a very readable and fairly wide-ranging look at an important time in their youth, he has also given today's younger readers a useful and well-told historical survey of a subculture and time they hear about quite often."   —*CounterPunch*

"Goldberg, a longtime music industry executive and journalist, takes the reader through the history of the year 1967 and the social transformations that led up to it. The book is full of names and references and tales that stir memories of the time . . . The book is a tribute to a time gone by that helps us better understand who we are today."
          —*Progressive*, A Top Book of 2017

"This wide-ranging, deeply personal narrative by journalist and music executive Danny Goldberg subjectively and perspicaciously explores the ongoing relevance of the political and counter-cultural movements that emerged in the pivotal year 1967."
          —*Big City Rhythm & Blues* magazine

"In his new book *In Search of the Lost Chord: 1967 and the Hippie Idea*, author Danny Goldberg interviewed dozens of people who were touched by that summer." —*AARP* magazine

"[Goldberg] explores how the political, mystical, psychedelic, and musical fused to create that memorable year." —*Toronto Star*

"A neat compendium." —*New York Journal of Books*

"Entertainment industry executive and raconteur Danny Goldberg's new book tackles 1967, the most promising but confusing year of that era, straight on. It's a veritable literary head rush, and he delivers some tasty and tantalizing details along the way. The Vietnam War, race relations, psychedelic rock, LSD, the first Be-In, various counterculture groups: All get plenty of attention, and Goldberg's personal connection to several key figures allows him to get quotes and new thoughts on the era, 50 years later." —*Capital & Main*

"Though the dream appeared to end, what Goldberg describes as a 'mystical experience' for many participants continues to reverberate a half century later in everything from the environmental movement to the push for organic food." —*Shepherd Express* (Milwaukee)

"*In Search of the Lost Chord* takes a refreshing new look at 1967, offering up a unique perspective and personal analysis of the counterculture era itself." —*Night Flight*

"Long a gloried mover and shaker in the music industry, Danny Goldberg knows whereof he speaks in his iconoclastic history of American popular culture . . . Based on his own exhaustive research, including interviews with luminaries ranging from Allen Ginsberg to Baba Ram Dass (aka Richard Alpert), the book drills deeply into sex, drugs and rock 'n' roll, and much else besides." —*Jewish Journal*

"Danny Goldberg is a relentless tracker of people. However elusive this Lost Chord may be, Danny G. searches it out and nails it to the tree flesh. Eternity now! 1967 forever!" —Wavy Gravy

"Danny Goldberg's deeply personal and political history of 1967 and the hippie idea weaves together rollicking, rousing, wonderfully colorful and disparate narratives to remind us how the energies and aspirations of the counterculture were intertwined with protest and reform.

There is a direct line from many of the events, movements, and people of 1967 to our times. Goldberg draws the line for us with mesmerizing storytelling, characters, and conversations."
—Katrina vanden Heuvel, *The Nation*

"Danny Goldberg has written a lively, well-researched, kaleidoscopic account—at once openhearted and levelheaded—of a spiritual, pharmacological, political, and musical supernova whose reverberations are still strongly felt a half-century later." —Hendrik Hertzberg

"Hippie 101—a kaleidoscopic snapshot of the Big Bang fifty years ago, three parts social and musical history, one part personal memoir, a sweeping overview that also manages to be up close and personal. Bravo." —Joel Selvin, author of *Altamont: The Rolling Stones, the Hells Angels, and the Inside Story of Rock's Darkest Day*

"Danny Goldberg is probably one of the purest, most reasonable guides you could ask for to 1967." —Andrew Loog Oldham, author of *Rolling Stoned*

"Danny Goldberg has done something I could not have thought possible: with diligent research, sharp prose, a clear mind, and an open heart, he has rescued a period of history from the clichés that had previously defined it. I began this book thinking hippies ridiculous. I ended it with a far more complex view, and one that showed me how little I had known or understood—a truly impressive achievement."
—Eric Alterman, author of *The Cause: The Fight for American Liberalism from Franklin Roosevelt to Barack Obama*

"This extraordinary book transports us back to a 'moment' when, as Goldberg writes, the phrase '"peace and love" was not meant or taken ironically.' Beginning at sixteen, Goldberg was a participant in the rise and cresting of the hippie movement, the hippie ideal, which has been trivialized and disparaged in later decades. He cuts through the obfuscation and recreates the sense of magic, wonder, intimacy, and community that was in the air and you could breathe it in. If you want to know, or remember, what it was like to be alive and part of that historic wave, I can think of no better guide than *In Search of the Lost Chord*."
—Sara Davidson, author of *Loose Change: Three Women of the Sixties*

"In a time of the harshest dissonance, Danny Goldberg's *In Search of the Lost Chord* arrives like soma from a heaven that is still up there if you look hard enough. One the great gambits of the rightist culture has been to paint the 1960s, and the hippie movement in particular, as some stammering, slothful stoner movie. As an eyewitness, I can testify it was much, much more. Danny Goldberg's highly informative missive from that long, strange trip not only reminds veterans of the glorious possibilities of the age but also serves as an excellent primer to onward generations."   —Mark Jacobson, author of *The Lampshade*

for *Bumping into Geniuses*

"Goldberg reminds us that the recording industry was remade in the late sixties and seventies by businessman-hippies seeking not just profit but proximity to artists they admired and a role in the countercultural ferment. It is one of many insights in this surprisingly excellent book, an engaging, droll, and . . . largely demystifying look at the evolution of the rock trade from Woodstock to grunge."
                —*New York Times Book Review*

"An insightful behind-the-scenes view of the music industry from 1969 through 2004 . . . like having a laminated backstage pass to the music business, intertwined with a juicy slice of countercultural history."
                —Paul Krassner, *Los Angeles Times Book Review*

"Danny Goldberg chronicles the phases of his career—rock journalist, record-company president, manager to musicians ranging from Kurt Cobain to Warren Zevon—with the sort of candor few record-biz execs would attempt . . . Admirably blunt, but also spiked with tart humor."
                —*Entertainment Weekly*

"A behemoth in the rock and roll industry."   —*Vanity Fair*

"Since I first met Danny Goldberg in 1970, he has had an honest re-lationship with the music business. He believes in the transcendent beauty and power of rock and roll, and at the same time has a unique perspective on the business which has presented and preserved it. Danny writes about rock and roll with his characteristic mix of intelligence, reverence, and humor."   —Patti Smith

"Inside the industry for almost four decades, Goldberg now looks back at those he bumped into during his rise from rock writer to public rela-tions to personal management, plus heading three major record companies . . . Goldberg summons up some fascinating anecdotes as he writes about these performers with much honesty and compassion, bringing it all back home." —*Publishers Weekly*

"Goldberg tells of his adventures in the music business with insight, humor, and compassion." —*Seattle Times*

for *Dispatches from the Culture Wars*

"The Democratic Party has two choices: get a clue or die. Danny Goldberg's new book is a stirring, brilliant, last-chance plea to Democrats that if they are unwilling to do their job—be a voice for working people, young people, women, the elderly, the poor, and people of color (in other words, for the MAJORITY of the country)—then their days as a party are numbered. Years from now, if the Democrats have long faded from American memory, anthropologists and historians will ask, *Didn't any of them read this book by Danny Goldberg?*" —Michael Moore

"Goldberg authoritatively dissects the disconnect between progressive politics and younger voters." —*Time Out New York*

"An affecting memoir of Goldberg's experiences within the clash of popular culture and politics . . . The great value of his book is as an insider's tour of American cultural life from the sixties to the present." —*Library Journal*

"Danny Goldberg's searing insights and straightforward recommendations for the future of the left should be required reading for anyone concerned with the state of democratic politics in this country. This book exemplifies the notion that the pen truly is mightier than the sword." —Reverend Jesse L. Jackson Sr.

"Rock, rap, reactionaries, and liberals all get a thrashing in Goldberg's insightful *Dispatches from the Culture Wars*." —*Vanity Fair*

"Lively and intelligent . . . Goldberg reminds us once again how the battle for freedom of expression needs to be refought every day." —Eric Alterman

"Danny Goldberg's memoir contains the powerful reflections of the most progressive activist in the recording industry. His candor, vision, and sense of humor are infectious." —Cornel West

IN SEARCH OF THE LOST CHORD

IN SEARCH OF THE LOST CHORD

1967 AND THE HIPPIE IDEA

DANNY GOLDBERG

BROOKLYN, NEW YORK, USA
BALLYDEHOB, CO. CORK, IRELAND

Published by Akashic Books
Original hardcover edition published by Akashic Books in 2017
©2017, 2018 Danny Goldberg

Period photographs by Peter Simon
Author photograph by Peter Cunningham

ISBN: 978-1-61775-668-9
Library of Congress Control Number: 2016953889
First printing

Akashic Books
Brooklyn, New York, USA
Ballydehob, Co. Cork, Ireland
Twitter: @AkashicBooks
Facebook: AkashicBooks
E-mail: info@akashicbooks.com
Website: www.akashicbooks.com

For Paul Krassner, Wavy Gravy, and Ram Dass

TABLE OF CONTENTS

INTRODUCTION

"There is a mysterious cycle in human events," my parents' idol Franklin Delano Roosevelt proclaimed in the speech in which he also said that their generation had a "rendezvous with destiny." The mystery that informed my own adult life revolves around a different rendezvous several decades after Roosevelt's speech. I was sixteen and wide-eyed and there really was a moment when "peace and love" was not meant or taken ironically. In terms of mass popular American culture, that moment peaked in 1967. Where did it come from? Where did it go?

The hippie movement that swept through the Western world was like a galloping horse in the wild. A few dozen people were able to ride it for a while, some even steering it for a brief period, but no one—no philosopher, no spiritual figure, no dope dealer, no songwriter or artist, and certainly no political leader—ever controlled it. It was the original "open source." From the influence of psychedelics to a widespread rebellious ethos that resisted any kind of authority within various countercultures, the era can only be understood through a collection of disparate, sometimes contradictory narratives.

David Crosby, Paul Kantner, and Robin Williams are among those who have been credited with the saying, "If you remember the sixties, then you weren't really there." The quote is usually deployed as a laugh line, as if anyone truly immersed in hippie culture would have been so stoned that they would have forgotten it all.

On the other hand, perhaps some *chose* not to talk about certain nuances that seemed too fragile to survive in the public air. In *The Varieties of Religious Experience*, William James suggests that one quality of a mystical experience is the impossibility of describing it. Yet hints can be found.

"The sixties" is a hybrid of the civil rights and antiwar movements combined with a mystical spirit that worked through some extremely fallible humans. Allen Cohen, a founder and editor of the San Francisco countercultural newspaper the *Oracle*, referred to hippies as "a prophetic community." But they were not, for the most part, formally religious or even well behaved. There is no doctrine, just thousands of stories, and a lingering vibe.

I graduated from Fieldston High School in New York City in 1967, and the sixties had a lasting influence on me and many of my closest friends from that time. I attended the University of California, Berkeley, briefly (*very* briefly), and by the end of 1968 had begun my career in the rock-and-roll business, an industry that itself owes much of its success to sixties culture.

I refer to a "lost chord" in the title of this book because whatever "it" was in 1967 was the result of dozens of separate, sometimes contradictory "notes" from an assortment of political, spiritual, chemical, demographic, historical, and media influences that collectively created a unique energy. It should go without saying that no two people perceived the late sixties in the same way, and that the space limitations of a single volume and my own myopia require me to leave out far more than I include.

This is a subjective and highly selective history, an attempt at trying to remember the culture that mesmerized me, to visit the places and conversations I was not cool enough to have been a part of.

My perspective is that of a straight white male New Yorker from a mostly secular Jewish family. I did very little research on countercultural developments outside of London, California, and New York, the places that fired my imagination at the time. I had little awareness of many vibrant cultural spheres including art, literature, and fashion, limitations that are obvious in my narrative.

Political struggles both on the street and in the corridors of government were central to the era. However, I disagree with numerous left-wing historians who view the "hippie" phenomenon as a secondary sideshow revolving around escapism that did more harm than good to what they regard as the "serious" aspects of the sixties. This conventional lefty wisdom ignores the mystical aspects of the counterculture that were intertwined with protest and reform.

Yet, even though many of us were a lot more into LSD than SDS, the overwhelming shadow of the military draft affected tens of millions of young men and their families. There was a widespread loss of faith in authorities who advocated obedience to a Cold War foreign policy. The cauldron of social readjustments for both blacks and whites in the wake of a long overdue dismantling of racist Jim Crow laws was intense. (Needless to say, many Americans of other ethnicities, including Latinos, Native Americans, and Asians, had their own challenges and journeys, but in the cultures of 1967 that reached my teenage brain it was the black/white relationship that predominated.)

The lost chord I am seeking had many other notes in it as well. After all, men in the United Kingdom were not called upon to fight in Vietnam; notwithstanding its colonial karma, the UK did not have racial tensions comparable to America's. Yet there is no version of "the sixties" in which British rockers like the Beatles, Cream, and Donovan, radical therapists like R.D. Laing, writers like Bertrand Russell, and fashion icons like Mary Quant, were not integral figures. Millions of European, Australian, Canadian, and American teenagers felt they had more in common with each other than they did with anyone else.

In talking to dozens of people of my generation who were affected by the hippie idea, there is a near universal recollection of a period of communal sweetness. There was an instant sense of tribal intimacy one could have even with a stranger. The word that many used was "agape," the Greek term that distinguishes universal love from interpersonal love.

One personal story I like to tell about the sixties took place in the San Francisco airport in 1967 when I was trying to get on a plane back to New York to see my family for Thanksgiving. I was barefoot and was told by an unpleasant airline employee that I could not board without shoes. With little time to spare, I scanned the airport and made a beeline toward a young guy with long hair who looked cool to me. I explained my predicament and asked if he would lend me his shoes for the flight, and gratefully accepted them when he agreed without a moment's hesitation. I am still not sure what is more remarkable, the fact that he gave his shoes to a stranger or that I had the certainty that he would do so. I am equally certain that this would not have been possible a year later.

The word "hippie" morphed from a brief source of tribal pride to a cartoon almost immediately. Ronald Reagan, who began his first term as governor of California in 1967, said, "A hippie is someone who looks like Tarzan, walks like Jane, and smells like Cheetah."

Most of the mainstream liberal establishment of the time was almost as dismissive. In August of 1967, Harry Reasoner delivered a report for the CBS Evening News in which he referred to the Haight-Ashbury section of San Francisco as "ground zero of the hippie movement." After an interview with members of the Grateful Dead, Reasoner questioned the premise that hippies were doing anything to make the world a better place: "They, at their best, are trying for a kind of group sainthood, and saints running in groups are likely to be ludicrous. They depend on hallucination for their philosophy. This is not a new idea, and it has never worked. And finally, they offer a spurious attraction of the young, a corruption of the idea of innocence. Nothing in the world is as appealing as real innocence, but it is by definition a quality of childhood. People who can grow beards and make love are supposed to move from innocence to wisdom."

A similar disdain was prevalent in most liberal circles

in Washington. After Timothy Leary and Allen Ginsberg testified in front of the US Senate Subcommittee on Juvenile Delinquency, Thomas Dodd, the Democratic committee chair, denounced them as "pseudo-intellectuals who advocate the use of drugs in search for some imaginary freedoms of the mind and in search of higher psychic experiences."

Fifty years later, reading those sanctimonious putdowns reminds me of the revulsion I had for such "respectable" men. For many of us, the idea of breaking the addiction to climbing the ladder of officially sanctioned "success" was not an "imaginary freedom" but a reason to live. None of us felt, individually, that we were "saints," but we did believe that there was a growing subculture that could come up with a better value system than the one we were born into. We didn't see "innocence" and "wisdom" as mutually exclusive, and we bitterly resented it when unhappy authority figures insisted on this false choice.

There was indeed a danger from indiscriminately using hallucinogens, but we also knew that for most people they were nowhere near as dangerous as the corrosive effects of legal drugs like beer and gin and tonics, or tranquilizers like Librium, which were inexplicably accepted by many of the same people who were so down on pot and acid—the criminalization of which further eroded the credibility of their authority for many of us.

As for Senator Dodd's condescending use of the word "pseudo-intellectuals," he was among the majority of Democrats who sided with the supposedly wise Ivy League "intellectuals" in the Kennedy and Johnson administrations who were responsible for the escalation of the Vietnam War.

I first used the phrase "the hippie idea" after Gil Scott-Heron died. Gil was one of the great R&B/jazz poets of the seventies and eighties and considered one of the progenitors of hip-hop. But I first met him in 1964 when we were in the same tenth-grade English class. Gil's mother was strict enough that he wasn't taking acid with us in high school. A lot of his identity in those days revolved around being a jock—the center on the basketball team and a wide receiver on the football team.

But Gil also befriended "heads" like me and breathed the air of the hippie idea along with the rest of us. (A "head" was someone who smoked dope. "Straight" in the pre–gay liberation era meant someone who didn't get high.) Gil joined several pickup rock bands and sang contemporary hits like "Wooly Bully" and "Like a Rolling Stone." He was always up for a conversation about the meaning of life and already had the seeds of a leftist radical critique of racism and the ugly side of capitalism that would inform his extraordinary body of work. Shortly after we graduated, Gil released the classic song "The Revolution Will Not Be Televised." For decades the song was used in film montages of protests and riots. Yet a year before he died, Gil did an interview where he sardonically explained that the lyrics were often misunderstood: "It meant that the revolution is inside you." (As this book was being written, the song was repurposed over the opening credits in the sixth season of the Showtime series *Homeland*.)

What I mean by "the hippie idea" is the internal essence of the tribal feeling separate and apart from the external symbols which soon became overused, distorted, co-opted, and thus, understandably, satirized. The conceit is that if you subtract long hair, hip language, tie-dyed clothing, beads, buttons, music, demonstrations, and even drugs, there was still a distinctive notion of what it meant to be a happy and good person, and a sense of connection to others was the invisible force *behind* those things. It included the moral imperative to fight for civil rights and against the war, and the spiritual notion that there were deeper values than fame and fortune. Peace and love.

The derisive term for what one *didn't* like was "plastic." At the same time, the hippie idea was also a joyous contrast to pessimistic postwar existentialists and Marxist intellectuals. They wore black. Hippies liked colors.

To some, the counterculture offered an alternative to organized religions that too often seemed preoccupied with rules and conformity, especially on sexual matters. (One reason Eastern religious traditions resonated with many hippies was because they carried no American family baggage.) But for millions like me, it was a deeply felt rejection of the secular religion of fifties and early sixties America: *Mad Men* materialism, along with Ayn Rand's social Darwinism and, to some extent, the Freudian doctrine that reinforced it. Much of the "established" world seemed removed from the deepest aspects of human consciousness.

Martin Luther King Jr.'s devotion to Christianity, Muhammad's Ali commitment to Islam, Timothy Leary's reverence for *The Tibetan Book of the Dead*, the connection to Buddhism and Hinduism that inspired Allen Ginsberg and many of the other beats, the fascination of the Beatles with meditation and the Hare Krishna movement, the metaphysical metaphors in many Bob Dylan songs, the guitar solos of Jimi Hendrix, the ripple effect of John Coltrane, and millions of individual psychedelic experiences framed the counterculture of the sixties with a level of mysticism far more intense and meaningful than had been prevalent in the previous postwar era. (Atheists and agnostics fit right into the hippie idea as long as they were cool. As Grateful Dead manager Rock Scully said, the Dead had one cardinal rule: "Do not impose your trip on anyone else.")

American bohemianism went back at least as far as Emerson and the transcendentalists and reemerged in the fifties in beatnik literature, a few anarchic comedians, and the folk and jazz scenes. But these were all marginalized subcultures, dwarfed in most of America by network TV, pop radio, sports, advertising, money, and mainstream religion.

The distinguishing characteristic of the sixties that emerged after the assassination of President Kennedy was that ideas which had previously been quarantined to a few avant-garde enclaves and ghettos now collided with a giant and prosperous "baby boomer" generation. Allen Ginsberg said that when he heard Bob Dylan's song "A Hard Rain's A-Gonna Fall," he wept, because the bohemian torch of illumination and self-empowerment had been passed on to a new generation.

In 1967, previously esoteric ideas burst briefly into the center of mass culture, influencing the thoughts of millions more people than any American counterculture before or since. Changes in the technology of stereo recordings (and a newly portable ability to hear them), FM radio, and the mimeograph machine fostered "underground" media at an unprecedented level. The sheer magnitude of the baby boomer generation, coupled with advertisers' hunger for the young demographic, created a climate of mainstream media in which the counterculture made good copy and got high ratings.

1967 was the year of Be-Ins and the Summer of Love, when tens of thousands of teenagers flocked to the small hippie neighborhood of Haight-Ashbury in San Francisco. LSD had been made illegal in California in October 1966, with the rest of the country soon to follow. The antidrug laws, like other forms of prohibition, immediately increased the demand and use of acid, dwarfing the previous interest in and availability of it.

1967 was the year of the Monterey International Pop Festival, which introduced Jimi Hendrix, Otis Redding, Ravi Shankar, and Janis Joplin to a big American rock audience. Hendrix, Joplin (as part of Big Brother and the Holding Company), Pink Floyd, the Velvet Underground, Country Joe and the Fish, the Doors, the Grateful Dead, and Sly & the Family Stone all released their debut albums that year. Among the year's classic singles were Van Morrison's "Brown Eyed Girl," the Turtles' "Happy Together," Procol Harum's "A Whiter Shade of Pale," Scott McKenzie's "San Francisco (Be Sure to Wear Some Flowers in Your Hair)," and the Youngbloods' hit version of "Get Together" with the chorus, *Come on people now, smile on your brother, everybody get together, try to love one another right now.*

It was also the year in which the Beatles released the singles "All You Need Is Love" (introduced via the world's first global satellite TV transmission) and "Strawberry Fields Forever," in addition to the album *Sgt. Pepper's Lonely Hearts Club Band*. *Rolling Stone* began publishing in 1967 and "underground rock radio" started broadcasting.

Rhythm and blues (increasingly called "soul music") was growing on a parallel track through the minds of geniuses like Smokey Robinson, Marvin Gaye, and Aretha Franklin, while at the same time there was a cluster of jazz musicians who dove into the hippie ocean and greatly affected it, including Ornette Coleman, Sun Ra, and Pharoah Sanders.

It was the year that Richard Alpert, who had helped popularize LSD, first went to India, met his guru, and was renamed Ram Dass. It was also the year that the Beatles met the Maharishi, putting the word "meditation" on the front pages of newspapers around the world.

Many pivotal political moments took place in 1967. In the spring, Muhammad Ali refused induction into the army, and Martin Luther King Jr. parted company with mainstream civil rights leaders and publicly denounced the Vietnam War.

In October there was an antiwar march in Washington in which some hippies fancifully insisted they would levitate the Pentagon. That same month, Huey P. Newton got arrested for murder in Oakland, elevating the Black Panther leader to international celebrity status. Stokely Carmichael and Charles V. Hamilton published *Black Power*. The summer produced the worst race riots in American cities since the Civil War. (The word "riot" itself was, and remains, a source of controversy. Many activists prefer "revolt" or "rebellion.")

1967 was to be the last full year of power for Lyndon B. Johnson. Allard K. Lowenstein searched for an anti-war Democrat to run against Johnson, and Senator Eugene McCarthy stepped into that role. Che Guevara was killed in Bolivia and overnight became a left-wing icon. Israel won the Six-Day War.

Yet, for all that happened in this pivotal year, my focus is on the feeling, not on the calendar, and there are moments integral to the story that occurred both before and after 1967. Nevertheless, 1968, taken as a whole, was much darker—Martin Luther King Jr. and Robert Kennedy (who joined the presidential race early in the year) were both assassinated, and that year's primary political legacy was the violent police reaction to protests outside of the Democratic National Convention, and the subsequent election of Richard Nixon.

Forces in the government and corporate America conspired to crush the cultural rebellions, but they were aided by infighting on the political left, a syndrome which, legend has it, led Che Guevara to quip that if you asked American leftists to form a firing squad, they'd get into a circle.

Hubris and/or paranoia distorted the behavior of would-be leaders, while in many corners of the subculture there developed smug, hip parochialism that grew rancid over time. Too often, "heads" looked down on "straights," which caused more polarization than brotherhood.

By 1968, heroin and speed were ubiquitous in hippie culture. An assortment of lowlife parasites rushed in to exploit the explosive hippie scene and virtually erased the fragile, intense meaning the word "hippie" had embodied just a year earlier. Undercover FBI agents could grow their hair long and wear brightly colored clothes.

The market for products that hippies liked created a class of hip capitalists who had varying degrees of commitment to ethical and spiritual ideals. The shallower aspects of Hollywood started to take their toll. Words like "cool" and "groovy" and sitar riffs could all be dumbed down to support sitcom gags and could be appropriated by superficial bullshit artists.

As the decades passed, the music of the period would prove to be the most resilient trigger of authentic memories, but even some of the songs of the era were gradually drained of meaning by repetitive use in TV shows, movies, and commercials, all trying to leverage nostalgia. Nostalgia for what?

The efforts of millions of peace activists were sometimes overshadowed by the destructive, violent acts of a few dozen delusional radicals. An earnest spiritual movement became obscured to most observers by stoned, pontificating buffoons. No wonder the punk movement that began in the midseventies detested the cartoon distortion of hippies.

Even so, every other belief system has had its pretenders. If one extends the religious metaphor to the hippie idea, it's not really surprising that its existence didn't eliminate most of the darkness of the world. Neither did Christianity nor the Enlightenment. But the counterculture did broaden the idea of what it is to be a human being in the Western world.

There is a direct line from many of the leaders of 1967 to contemporary figures such as Steve Jobs, Mark Zuckerberg, Bernie Sanders, Judd Apatow, and Oprah

Winfrey, all of whom acknowledge important influences from the figures I am writing about. The environmental movement, which is a direct offshoot of hippie ideas, continues to be a major social force, and "mindfulness" and yoga are even more prevalent in the United States of 2017 than veggie burgers.

Researching 1967 has been a roller coaster ride for me. Sometimes it rekindles the "lost chord" and inspires me. At other moments I yearn to go back in time and warn my heroes that they are about to walk down a path they will regret.

As I explored the forgotten intricacies of 1967, the hippie idea that entranced me as a teenager still seems like an alchemy that produced something unique and special out of the energies and aspirations of dozens of disparate, intense, and cantankerous people, many of them deeply damaged, all of them in one way or another very far out.

That line—if you remember the sixties, you weren't really there—does have some truth to it. In addition to hallucinogens, the drug of fame often led to fanciful mythmaking. Some stories have been repeated so many times that they have taken on a life of their own. Even close friends have different versions of well-known events. The underground press, whose writers were often the only public witnesses to countercultural activities, had little or no fact-checking capabilities. I have done my best to get it right, but apologize in advance for any faulty assumptions.

Examined up close, there were dozens of separate subcultures, each of which felt it *owned* the late sixties. San Francisco and Los Angeles rock-and-roll people were deeply suspicious of each other. The Beatles lived in their own world. New York hip life was more intellectual. Black nationalism, the nonviolent civil rights movement led by Dr. King, Muhammad Ali, and the Nation of Islam had fierce disagreements with each other, and they all had different views of the antiwar movement. Student radicals, the old left, liberal antiwar Democrats like Bobby Kennedy and Gene McCarthy, and anarchists often detested each other. Beatniks, psychedelic evangelists, and mystics were often on separate planets.

Yet to many teenagers at the time, this collection of energies somehow harmonized and created a single feeling, the lost chord that lasted briefly, but penetrated deeply into the minds and hearts of those who could hear it. I admired something about all of them. I never felt aligned with just one faction but with the ephemeral collective vibe that permeated the culture. Time was so compressed that many of the signature events of 1967 happened within hours or days of each other. Often they were intertwined. My fascination is with the whole, not merely its parts. However, if I could time travel back to 1967, there is no question that I would begin in the Haight-Ashbury section of San Francisco.

CHAPTER 1
BEING IN

The precursor to the brief cycle in which Haight-Ashbury was the biggest counterculture magnet in the Western world is generally thought to have begun in the summer of 1965 at the Red Dog Saloon in Virginia City, Nevada—just across the border from Northern California—where a rock band called the Charlatans played for several months. They took a lot of acid and created some of the first light shows and psychedelic concert posters. They wore Edwardian clothing, conveyed a weird nostalgia for idealized prenuclear America, and revered Native Americans. Although the Charlatans never developed the national following of other San Francisco bands, they were integral to many of the big rock events in the Bay Area in the late sixties. (Dan Hicks of the Charlatans would go on to form Dan Hicks & His Hot Licks.)

By the end of 1965, the Charlatans had moved to the racially integrated Haight-Ashbury neighborhood of San Francisco. It was near several university campuses and had become a center for artists, beatniks, and other bohemians, primarily because of its cheap rents. There were many large Victorian houses, which had up to six bedrooms and cost as little as $120 a month. By the end of 1966, the twenty-five square blocks had a distinctive culture. One could see mandalas made of yarn and drawings from Native American and Eastern religious traditions in many windows. A group of merchants with names like God's Eye Ice Cream and Pizza Parlor had sprung up to service the new residents. Members of the new psychedelic rock bands Jefferson Airplane, the Grateful Dead, and Big Brother and the Holding Company all moved into the neighborhood.

On January 3, 1966, the Psychedelic Shop opened on 1535 Haight Street, signaling a turning point in the growth of the area as a countercultural center. The store sold books on Eastern religion and the occult, records of Indian music, beads, incense, posters, pipes, and other paraphernalia. It would be the prototype for hundreds of "head shops" that would open up across America in the coming years. A couple of weeks later, the Trips Festival attracted what was at the time a staggeringly high number of people—six thousand over the course of a weekend—to the Longshoreman's Hall in San Francisco. Many of the attendees drank fruit punch spiked with LSD while watching performances by popular local bands.

By the end of the summer of 1966, several thousand hippies were living in the Haight, and in the fall a new publication called the *San Francisco Oracle* appeared. During its brief but glorious eighteen months of existence, the *Oracle* was as definitive a document as would ever exist of the messianic aspirations of the Haight-Ashbury scene. (Tattered individual copies regularly sell for hundreds of dollars on eBay.) The paper was conceived by editor Allen Cohen and art director Michael Bowen. Cohen said he had a dream of a newspaper with rainbows on it that was read all over the world. Both of the *Oracle* founders were acidheads. Cohen sold some of famed LSD maker Augustus Owsley Stanley III's earliest tablets, and Bowen had been arrested with LSD pioneer Timothy Leary in Millbrook, New York.

The initial $500 investment for the *Oracle* came from Ron Thelin, who ran the Psychedelic Shop with his brother Jay. The *Oracle* featured brightly colored psychedelic art and essays by and about counterculture luminaries. In its first issue it had a manifesto with a founding-fathers-on-acid declaration: "When in the course of human events it becomes necessary for people to cease [obeying] obsolete social patterns which have isolated man from his consciousness . . . we the citizens of the earth declare our love and compassion for all hate-carrying men and women."

The *Oracle* regularly printed articles by and interviews with luminaries like Allen Ginsberg, Gary Snyder, Alan Watts, Richard Alpert, and Timothy Leary. Within a few months the *Oracle* could be found in nascent hip communities in every region of the United States and many other parts of the world. With typical grandiosity Leary stated, "If the Buddha were alive, he would read the *Oracle*."

However, the *Oracle* did not speak for most political radicals and it certainly did not represent the vibe of the Diggers, an American collective who took their name from a group of seventeenth-century British radicals opposed to the Church of England and the British Crown.

The sixties Diggers delighted in tormenting brothers and sisters in the hippie and radical political communities for being insufficiently pure. The Diggers did not believe in money or any external measure of accomplishment. They berated head shop owners, concert promoters, and others in San Francisco who made money from the culture, and they detested media coverage of the scene.

The Diggers had emerged from the avant-garde San Francisco Mime Troupe and were more about performance art than politics. On the streets of Haight-Ashbury, the Diggers sometimes wore animal masks, held up traffic, passed out joints to people on the street, and gave away fake dollar bills printed with winged penises. They also organized a lot of the free concerts that helped cohere the Haight-Ashbury community. They got ahold of a mimeograph machine and began printing and distributing a newsletter under the name the Communication Company. One of their flyers read: "To show Love is to fail. To love to fail is the Ideology of Failure. Show Love. Do your thing. Do it for FREE. Do it for Love. We can't fail."

The Diggers also felt a moral imperative to address the day-to-day realities of poor people. They made "Digger stew" from day-old food gathered from local markets and gave away hundreds of meals a week. They also briefly operated a "free store" in Haight-Ashbury that gave away donated clothing.

Emmett Grogan of the Diggers was an intense twenty-four-year-old from Brooklyn with movie-star good looks and a fierce vision of cultural revolution. In his memoir *Ringolevio*, Grogan expressed Digger thinking at the time, railing against "the pansyness of the SF *Oracle* underground newspaper, and the way it catered to the new, hip, moneyed class by refusing to reveal the overall grime of Haight-Ashbury reality." He detested the "absolute bullshit implicit in the psychedelic transcendentalism promoted by the self-proclaimed, media-fabricated shamans who espoused the turn-on, tune-in, drop-out, jerk-off ideology of Leary and Alpert." Grogan wrote that he "immediately dismissed as ridiculous the notion that everything would be all right when everyone turned on to acid."

The other best-known Digger was the twenty-five-year-old Peter Cohon, who would soon change his name to Peter Coyote and in the decades that followed have a successful career as an actor in dozens of Hollywood films including E.T.

One person who was equally at home in the worlds of the beatniks, radicals, acidheads, and rock and roll was Allen Ginsberg. In addition to his explorations of psychedelics, he was an unrelenting critic of militarism. In 1966, he wrote a poem called "Wichita Vortex Sutra," which mocked Secretary of Defense Robert McNamara, who had described one of his errors in escalating the war in Vietnam as a "bad guess." The poem included some of the very few public references to the allegedly closeted homosexuality of J. Edgar Hoover and Cardinal Spellman of New York, who was also one of the biggest cheerleaders for the war in Vietnam: "How big is Cardinal Vietnam? / How little the prince of the FBI, unmarried all these years!"

I worked with Ginsberg on his last recordings in the early nineties and asked him if he knew that Hoover was gay. The poet nodded. Why had he not been more outspoken about Hoover's sexuality at a time when the FBI director was wreaking havoc on the lives of so many decent people? Ginsberg told me he had a friend when he was a college student at Columbia who regularly had sex with Cardinal Spellman and who asked the prelate if he weren't worried that his career would be ruined if his propensity for having sex with young men was ever made public. Spellman supposedly laughed and said defiantly, "Who would believe it?" Ginsberg explained to me that in the context of the repressive power of the establishment at the time, the words of the poem were as far as he felt he could safely go.

Allen Ginsberg

"Wichita Vortex Sutra" also made clear Ginsberg's antipathy to Soviet-style communism, which, among its many moral shortcomings, was repressive in the arts.

> *Black Magic language,*
> *formulas for reality—*
> *Communism is a 9 letter word*
> *used by inferior magicians*
> *the wrong alchemical formula for transforming earth into gold*

With his black horn-rimmed glasses, long black beard, and white Indian shirt, Ginsberg, despite being forty years old at a moment when youth was ascendant, was one of the most recognizable figures of the counter-culture. Although he was often profane, was openly gay, and was an unapologetic left-winger, Ginsberg's literary brilliance and flair for self-promotion had propelled him to a level of celebrity rarely found in bohemian history. Unique among the beat writers, Ginsberg had embraced sixties rock and roll and the hippie culture. He had taken LSD with Tim Leary *and* Ken Kesey, and had been befriended by the Beatles *and* Bob Dylan.

Known primarily for poetry, advocacy of free speech in the arts, and mysticism, Ginsberg was also a peace activist and had withheld a percentage of his taxes as a form of protest against the war. The IRS notified him at some point that they would seize $182.71 from his *Howl and Other Poems* royalties, which, among other things, was a testament to how little compensation there was in being America's most famous poet.

When the editors of the *Oracle* wanted to get the

counterculture to the next level in early 1967, Allen Ginsberg was the indispensable man to help them do so.

GATHERING OF THE TRIBES

Ginsberg would later say that the Be-In in San Francisco in early 1967 was "the last purely idealistic hippie event," but at the time the notion that the spiral of sixties countercultural growth and euphoria was peaking would have seemed absurd to those involved. There were more "heads" every single day.

Organizing an event with self-proclaimed revolutionaries, radicals, and cosmic explorers had not been easy. The very term "Be-In" was a mocking hippie twist on the civil rights movement's term "sit-in" and the Vietnam War protest's "teach-in." The phrase was also a pun—another way of saying "being," as in "human being." (Like much hip language, the device had a short shelf life before going mainstream. An NBC network prime-time comedy show called *Rowan & Martin's Laugh-In* would debut in September 1968.)

There were intense factions whose conflicts with each other were at the center of day-to-day life at the center of the hippie storm. Hence the subtitle of the 1967 San Francisco Be-In: "A Gathering of the Tribes." Tribes, plural.

The Be-In sprang from the minds of the *Oracle*'s Allen Cohen and Michael Bowen. Cohen saw the counterculture in glorious terms. Years later he would write, "The beat and hippie movements brought the values and experiences of an anarchistic, artistic subculture, and a secret and ancient tradition of transcendental and esoteric knowledge and experience, into the mainstream of cultural awareness . . . [It] gave us back a sense of being the originators of our lives and social forms, instead of hapless robot receptors of a dull and determined conformity."

A few months earlier, a police shooting of a black youth on September 27, 1966, led to riots in the Hunters Point neighborhood and a curfew was imposed in San Francisco. Bowen put up posters telling hippies to stay inside. Emmett Grogan, on the other hand, posted signs saying, *Disobey the Fascist Curfew*. Each took down the other's signs. The two men ran into each other at a telephone pole, and they began an argument which would persist throughout 1967.

"The Diggers were . . . passionately critical of the commercialization of the Haight," wrote Cohen. "Generally, the atmosphere around the Diggers was desperate, dark, and tense, while at the ordinary hippie pad, it was light, meditative, and creative, with a mixture of rock and raga music, Oriental aesthetics, and vegetarian food." Maybe so, but at their peak the Diggers were providing five hundred free meals a week to people in the community, which brought them a lot of credibility on the street.

If Cohen and Bowen were going to be successful in pulling off the Be-In as a true "gathering," they needed to avoid a torrent of negativity from the Diggers, who initially saw it as a gimmick created by an organization of head shops and a loose conglomeration of "hip stores" called the Haight Independent Proprietors (HIP). The Diggers were suspicious that HIP was hoping to attract national publicity so that they could sell "hippie products" to chain stores and at the same time attract more tourists to Haight-Ashbury.

While it's impossible to know the inner motivation of every Haight merchant of the time, the Digger theory does seem to have been an unfair characterization of Ron Thelin, whose shop was part of HIP. Thelin soon thereafter told the *Oracle*, "The direction I see it taking is getting back to the land and finding out how to take care of ourselves, how to survive, how to live off the land, how to make our own clothes, grow our own food, how to live in a tribal unit." (In October 1967 the Psychedelic Store would close and Thelin would move to Marin County, where for the rest of his life he worked as a cab driver, a mason, and a carpenter.) At the *Oracle*, Cohen and his colleagues lived hand-to-mouth and avoided the kinds of tabloid stories that drove up the circulation of typical "underground" newspapers; they rejected sleazy ads as well.

Cohen got HIP to agree that Haight stores would all be closed on the day of the Be-In so at least there wouldn't be immediate profit from those who came in the name of idealism. The Diggers scored an additional agreement with a different kind of capitalist, Augustus Owsley Stanley III (known mostly as "Owsley" or his nickname "Bear"), who agreed to give three hundred thousand tablets of "White Lightning" LSD to the Diggers to distribute free to attendees of the Be-In. Owsley also provided the seventy-five turkeys from which free sandwiches would be made. Although Grogan would later mock the spiritual aspirations of the Be-In, the Diggers stuck to a commitment not to bad-mouth it beforehand.

Cohen also had to reassure the San Francisco rock musicians who had emerged as key thought leaders in the community. The musicians were a generation younger than the beatniks. Bob Weir of the Grateful Dead was nineteen; Janis Joplin was twenty-three; Jerry Garcia and Marty Balin were twenty-four; Jefferson Airplane's new singer, Grace Slick, was twenty-seven. The Airplane, the Dead, and Joplin all had houses in the Haight within a few blocks of each other. Their primary concern was maintaining a vibe that fostered creativity.

Jefferson Airplane

British folk-rock singer Donovan had followed in Bob Dylan's footsteps and had gone electric in 1966 with the album *Sunshine Superman*, which included the song "The Fat Angel," the chorus of which paid homage to the Haight rockers: *"Fly Jefferson Airplane, gets you there on time."* The Airplane was the first local band to get a record deal (with RCA). Grace Slick had not been a member on their first album but joined in late 1966. Two songs on which she sang lead on the band's second album, "Somebody to Love" and "White Rabbit" (which she also wrote), both became massive hits in 1967, the first emanations of the Haight culture to go mainstream.

Yet another "tribe" in the counterculture who initially resisted participation in the Be-In were the Berkeley radicals who by 1967 were primarily focusing on trying to end the Vietnam War. The weekly underground paper across the Bay, the *Berkeley Barb*, centered far more on radical politics and far less on spirituality than the *Oracle*.

Cohen explained, "Bowen and I had become concerned about the philosophical split that was developing in the youth movement. The antiwar and free-speech movement in Berkeley thought the hippies were too disengaged and spaced out, and that their influence might draw the young away from resistance to the war. The hippies thought the movement was doomed to endless confrontations with the establishment that would recoil with violence and fascism . . . In order to have a Human Be-In, we would have to have a powwow."

The meeting took place at Bowen's pad at the corner of Haight and Masonic. The Berkeley radical contingent included Max Scherr, who was the publisher of the *Berkeley Barb*, and antiwar activists Michael Lerner and Jerry Rubin. Rubin was a twenty-eight-year-old native of Cincinnati who had enrolled in the University of California, Berkeley, in time to witness the Free Speech Movement in 1964. Later that year he was among a group of American students who traveled illegally to Cuba and met with Che Guevara. In 1965, he was one of the organizers of the Vietnam Day Committee—a small group who tried to block trains filled with GIs who were ultimately headed for Vietnam. Rubin and fellow radicals

Mario Savio and Stew Alpert served short jail sentences after being convicted of "public nuisance."

Rubin and his girlfriend Nancy Kurshan had recently met with then-unknown Eldridge Cleaver, who had been released from prison in late 1966 and would soon join the Black Panther Party, eventually becoming their Minister of Information. In an introduction to Rubin's book *Do It!* Cleaver recalled, "Thinking back to that evening in Stew's pad in Berkeley, I remember the huge poster of W.C. Fields on the ceiling, and the poster of Che on the wall . . . This was our first meeting. We turned on and talked about the future." Now the question was whether Rubin could relate equally well to the San Francisco hippies.

While Rubin tried to soak up the hippie ethos, his comrade Michael Lerner earnestly asked the group, "What are your demands?" The hippies and musicians were amused. "Man, there are no demands! It's a fucking *Be-In!*" Still, it was agreed that Rubin could make a short speech.

Ginsberg said that the Be-In would be "a gathering together of younger people aware of the planetary fate that we are all sitting in the middle of, imbued with a new consciousness, and desiring of a new kind of society involving prayer, music, and spiritual life together rather than competition, acquisition, and war."

Bowen and Cohen consulted Gavin Arthur, a philosopher and astrologer who was the grandson of US President Chester Arthur. According to Gene Anthony's *The Summer of Love*, Arthur said that January 14 was the day "when communication and society would be most favored for a meld of positive communication for the greatest good." He also claimed it was "a time when the population of the earth would be equivalent in number to the total of all the dead in human history."

The *Oracle* cover story about the upcoming Be-In said, "A new nation has grown inside the robot flesh of the old . . . Hang your fear at the door and join the future. If you do not believe, please wipe your eyes and see." The issue featured a centerfold with an ornate trippy drawing by Rick Griffin in which the faces of ancient mystics emerged from hookahs. In its center was a heart-shaped depiction of a lecture Ginsberg had given to Unitarian ministers in Boston the previous November called "Renaissance or Die," in which he associated his philosophy with that of Thoreau and Emerson and then urged everyone over the age of fourteen to try LSD at least once. The *Barb* also ran an announcement on their front page.

A poster designed by psychedelic artist Stanley Mouse was put up in Marin County, Berkeley, and the Peninsula, as well as around Haight-Ashbury. It featured a trippy drawing of an Indian sadhu with a third eye, and the typeface used stylized art nouveau lettering that required a great deal of concentration to read.

Saturday, January 14, 1967, 1–5 p.m.
A Gathering of the Tribes for a Human Be-In
Allen Ginsberg, Timothy Leary, Richard Alpert, Michael
Mclure [sic], *Jerry Ruben* [sic], *Dick Gregory, Gary*
Snyder, Jack Weinberg, Lenore Kandel
ALL SF ROCK GROUPS
At the Polo Field, Golden Gate Park
FREE
Bring food to share, bring flowers, beads, costumes,
feathers, bells, cymbals, flags

* * *

It was just past dawn on the morning of the Be-In and Allen Ginsberg wasn't really worried about the rumors, but he wanted to sanctify the gathering anyway. The day before, word had spread through San Francisco that a satanic cult had put some sort of a curse on Polo Field where the Be-In was scheduled to take place. A couple of hippies who lived near the park had found some chopped-up pieces of meat and bones in the field. In a community with a lot of mystics, many of them high on psychedelics, it hadn't taken long for the paranoid theory to reach the ears of some of the "elders" who had been planning the event. Suzuki Roshi, founder of the San Francisco Zen Center, had given a blessing, but many in Haight-Ashbury were still a bit unnerved. Ginsberg, who had spent a lot of time in India the previous year, knew just what to do.

It had been an unusually rainy winter in the Bay Area but the sun was shining with barely a cloud in the sky and the temperature was around fifty degrees. Shortly after sunrise, Ginsberg, along with fellow poet Gary Snyder and a few of their close friends, performed a Hindu ritual called "Pradakshina," which consisted of a slow, solemn walk around the field (which was 480 feet wide by 900 feet long) while reciting sacred prayers. This, the poets explained, was crucial for ensuring that the Be-In would be a *mela*—a pilgrimage gathering—and not just a big stoned party.

A dozen years earlier at the Six Gallery, which was just five miles away on Fillmore Street, Ginsberg had read his groundbreaking epic poem "Howl" for the first time. (The famous first line of the poem is, "I saw the best minds of my generation destroyed by madness," but the poet's own mind, no matter how far out he got, was as sharp as a razor.) Along with his friend Jack Kerouac's novel *On the Road*, Ginsberg's poem expressed a radically different vision of sexual morality, art, and the very meaning of life than that which characterized the prevailing ethos at the peak of the Eisenhower era, which was still under the dark shadow of McCarthyism. In the succeeding decades, Ginsberg and Kerouac became beacons of light for thousands of marginalized smart kids. One of those was Jerry Garcia of the Grateful Dead, who said in the late sixties, "I can't separate who I am now from what I got from Kerouac . . . I don't know if I would ever have had the courage or the vision to do something outside with my life—or even suspected the possibilities existed—if it weren't for Kerouac opening those doors." Ironically, Kerouac hated the hippies; he just couldn't connect with the next generation. But Ginsberg had dived fully into the heart of the hippie movement.

The posters that had been put up around the Bay Area said that the Be-In would start at one in the afternoon, so Ginsberg was pleasantly surprised when dozens of people were already arriving by nine in the morning, just as the Pradakshina was ending. They kept coming and coming and coming. Previously, the biggest hippie gathering had been six thousand at the Trips Festival a year earlier. Before the afternoon was done, at least thirty thousand had shown up "to be." Where the fuck had they all come from?

Although there were various theories about the best way to take LSD, there was no question that the drug created a powerful inner experience only some aspects of which lent themselves to verbal explanations. Experiences in which small groups of friends discussed the various theories of the meaning of life were not necessarily the same "trips" as those of people doing the same things in different homes, in different neighborhoods. So the idea of a "tribe" did not merely refer to high-profile clusters of hip celebrities like the bands or the Diggers or Ken Kesey's Merry Pranksters or the Free Speech Movement veterans of Berkeley. It applied to hundreds of small groups with varying notions of community and inner experiences.

One of the reasons the external manifestation of tens of thousands of freaks felt so extraordinary was because of the notion so vividly held at the Be-In that an integrated matrix of hundreds of tribes could function as the nucleus of a new society. Looking back, it is not at all surprising that this turned out not to be the case. What was remarkable was that it ever *felt* that way on such a mass scale, even for a moment.

Many at the Be-In brought cameras, and within weeks, photos would be seen in magazines and newspapers around the world of the massive crowd, which included barefoot young women in madras saris, folk singers, self-proclaimed shamans, and motorcyclists. Some of the men dressed in Victorian clothes, Edwardian jackets, and velvet cloaks, with stovepipe or porkpie hats. Others looked more like cowboys, or Native Americans, and a few, like Ginsberg, like well-fed sadhus. There were lots of feathers, drums, esoteric flags, soap bubbles, and balloons.

Hundreds of the men had really long hair, way past

their shoulders, longer than that of the Beatles. Many of the women wore long dresses, while others wore mini-skirts and see-through tops; there were also quite a few mothers with small children. Some had masks and body paint; there were astrologers, jugglers, and a couple with shining eyes passing out tarot cards. But these were the veterans of earlier hippie gatherings. The bulk of this expanded community was still in jeans and khakis and wouldn't have looked out of place at a folk festival.

Although Haight-Ashbury was a relatively integrated neighborhood, the hip community in the Bay Area at that moment was mostly white. Dick Gregory was the only scheduled African American speaker and he bailed at the last minute to attend a protest at Puget Sound. Jazz virtuosos Dizzy Gillespie and Charles Lloyd, who sat in on a couple of Airplane and Grateful Dead songs, were the only black musicians to perform.

A group of Krishna devotees with their distinctive shaved heads and single braids danced. On the periphery, a sole Christian evangelist with a bullhorn vainly tried to argue that hell and damnation awaited those who followed the lead of the speakers. The hippies smiled sweetly at him as they sauntered by.

Adding to the surreal feeling in the huge crowd was the fact that its transcendental craziness was happening adjacent to apparent normality. Golden Gate Park is one of the largest parks in an American city and a rugby game was being played on the other end of the vast field. A few local cops on horseback surveyed the crowd, but didn't make any busts. For the moment, it was live and let live.

The sheer sense of a newly expanded community,

collectively tripping out to an inchoate notion of universal love, and the feeling that the ideas, fashions, vibes, and music would spread and spread and spread, was in and of itself the main memory that many in the crowd would have. But there was a "program" that tried to shape and enhance the energy.

It started, as scheduled, at 1 p.m. sharp with the blowing of a conch shell by poet Gary Snyder, who had lived at a Japanese monastery for about ten years before his recent return to Northern California. He had longish brown hair and a beard and was wearing a dark turtleneck and a darker vest with a single string of beads around his neck and an earring in one ear (very far out for a man in those days). Sitting next to Snyder on the stage was Ginsberg, who chanted a Hindu mantra in his earnest off-key voice and then switched to English: "Peace in America, peace in Vietnam, peace in San Francisco, peace in Hanoi, peace in New York, peace in Peking. *Hari Om Nama Shivaya.*"

Although a few people strolled on the periphery, where the weak sound system didn't reach, the bulk of the crowd sat attentively, straining to take in every word. Several minutes into Ginsberg's chant, a beautiful blond woman wearing a short black dress with mirrored circles on it rose and danced sensuously to the rhythm of the poet's hand cymbals. Ginsberg gently nudged the crowd: "You also need to sing." He explained that the Hindu deity Shiva was, among other things, the god of hash smokers.

Michael McClure had recently written a play called *The Beard* about a sexually charged fictitious meeting between Jean Harlow and Billy the Kid. (It had been closed down by the cops in San Francisco at one point because of its depiction of cunnilingus.) McClure played a quirky song while accompanying himself on the autoharp, with a lyric that ended, *"It is all perfect, this really is."*

Lenore Kandel was a local poet with long brown braids who had met Jack Kerouac earlier in the decade and was later immortalized by him as Romana Swartz, "a big Rumanian monster beauty," in his novel *Big Sur*. She had recently published *The Love Book*, a collection of erotic poetry, which had also been the subject of a local obscenity prosecution. (She was convicted after a five-week trial in which she was supported by numerous literary figures, but the case would be thrown out on appeal on First Amendment grounds.) Kandel earnestly told the crowd, "The Buddha will reach us all through love—not through doctrine, not through teachings, but through love. And looking at all of you—all of us—I feel more and more that Maitreya is not this time going to be born in one physical body but born out of all of us." (Theosophists believed Maitreya to be the messiah of the future.)

Then it was Jerry Rubin's turn. He had a Trotsky-ite handlebar mustache and tufts of his midlength hair were blowing above his head in the breeze. He too wore a white shirt. "Boy, I'm happy to be here. This is a beautiful day. I wish today that all of America could be here." Despite his best efforts to keep it mellow, an outraged tone crept into his voice. "The police, like the soldiers in Vietnam, are both victims and agents. I just came from the old world, here to the new world. The old world are places like jails—structures where a person cannot feel like a human being." He asked members of the crowd to contribute to the bail fund for arrested protesters and awkwardly ended, "Our smiles are our political banners and our nakedness is our picket sign." Despite his effort to fit in, Rubin retained an unmistakable whiff of self-righteous lefty hysteria. Jerry Garcia would later say, "I remember being at [the] Be-In and Jerry Rubin got up on stage and started haranguing the crowd. All of a sudden it was like everyone who had ever harangued a crowd. It was every asshole who told people what to do. The words didn't matter. It was that angry tone. It scared me. It made me sick to my stomach." After the Be-In, the Grateful Dead often avoided associations with radical politics.

The last of the speakers was Timothy Leary, who mirrored Ginsberg's holy man uniform, wearing a white shirt and pants. For the last several years, Leary had been the highest-profile American advocate of LSD, but he was based on the East Coast. The Be-In was his first public appearance in San Francisco. Leary had a yellow flower behind each of his ears and was barefoot. "We have to get Western man out of the cities and back into tribes and villages. The only way out is in." He finished by solemnly intoning, "Turn on, tune in, drop out," a phrase he had unveiled in New York a few months earlier. Ginsberg, who was sitting beside publisher/poet Lawrence Ferlinghetti on the stage, leaned over and whispered, "What if we're all wrong?"

Then came the rock and roll. After the power line was cut during a Quicksilver Messenger Service song, it was quickly repaired, and thereafter the stage and electric generator were guarded by Chocolate George, a member of the Hells Angels who was so nicknamed because of his fondness for chocolate milk.

Timothy Leary

Two years later there would be a now-infamous violent incident involving the Angels at the Altamont Festival, but at the Be-In they were in perfect harmony with their surroundings. (Lenore Kandel was married to an Angel named Sweet William.)

At one of Ken Kesey's events in 1966, Ginsberg had given many of the local Angels LSD, and for that moment they had been on the same page as the hippies. One of the reasons for naive optimism about the effects of LSD in the community was that incongruous bonding of a gay Jewish poet with members of the outlaw motorcycle gang who had not so long before beaten up antiwar protesters. (In August, when Chocolate George was killed in a motorcycle accident on Haight Street, the Grateful Dead and Big Brother and the Holding Company played at his wake, and Grogan and Coyote of the Diggers also attended.)

The Angels' appeal to the Diggers, Coyote explained to me, was that they were fellow anarchists who resisted conventional authority. During my brief time of living in the Bay Area in 1967–68, I shared that romance about the Angels. The fact that I knew people who were close to some of them gave me the same kind of illusion of protection that kids who grew up playing with the offspring of Mafia families had in some urban neighborhoods. In retrospect, I feel that nonviolence means nothing unless it applies to everyone, including people who otherwise seem very cool.

The bands who played at the Be-In had developed a passionate local following with little or no connection to the music business. Only the Airplane had released an album, but most of the others would be signed to major record companies within the year.

The coin of the realm for bands in the San Francisco scene was the ability to play extended semi-improvised solos and jams which sounded especially good when the listener was high. No one did this more effectively than the Grateful Dead, who were the last band to play, ending with a psychedelicized version of the Motown song "Dancing in the Street," to which Ginsberg danced ecstatically as Jerry Garcia sang, *"It doesn't matter what you wear just as long as you are there,"* followed by a long, trippy guitar solo. Jim Morrison and the other members of the Doors (who were in San Francisco for a gig at the Fillmore) did not play at the Be-In, but wandered around Polo Field cheerfully tripping on Owsley's acid.

At some point during the Dead's set a parachutist who'd jumped from a small plane floated down into the middle of the celebration and was greeted by many stoned *oohs* and *aahs*. Not long afterward, Ginsberg took the microphone again, gently cradling a four-year-old boy, and said, "If the parents are here for this child— please come and take him."

The music was fun and served as a magnet for the crowd. San Francisco rock was at its innocent peak. But the day was still permeated by an elusive but palpable sense of nondenominational cosmic purpose that made it very different from a regular party or concert. The main point was for members of the crowd to experience each other. There were so many freaks! It was like the straight world had just melted away.

As the afternoon drew to a close, Allen Cohen repeated three times, "You are your own salvation, man!" He continued, "I have had one of the fullest days of my life. In that day, there was much good. There was also bad. But my day was full. I am thankful that each and every person here came to share this day with each and every person here . . . I would ask you to, at this moment, realize that the sun is setting and our day is at an end. I would ask you to turn and face the sun, and Allen Ginsberg, along with Gary Snyder, will chant the night . . . Thank you for sharing the day with all the people here, and please, please take it home and realize the beauty that can come forth . . . I would say this to all the members of the establishment—we are happy and proud to have you in our brave new world."

Ginsberg chanted, *"Om Jai Maitreya, Om Jai Maitreya."* Dozens of people, some holding paisley flags and the rest holding hands, danced in a circle on the periphery of the crowd. Ginsberg ended with a request for civic responsibility: "Now that you have looked up at the sun, look down at your feet and practice a little kitchen yoga after this first American *mela*. Please pick up any refuse you might see around you. *Shanti*."

Present throughout the day was Leary's protégé Richard Alpert, who was then thirty-five. Alpert had been among the elite in the American psychedelic scene for the last five years and his name had appeared on the Be-In posters. On the surface Alpert seemed optimistic and ecstatic, but in the days that followed he would start to talk and write a lot about "the problem of coming down."

Robbie Conal was an artist from New York, a "red-diaper baby" whose schoolteacher dad was followed by the FBI during the blacklisting era. He began attending San Francisco State and lived in Haight-Ashbury starting in 1963, so he had watched the whole scene unfold. Conal stayed in college as long as he could without graduating to retain a draft deferment, but says of the time, "I was taking psychedelics and smoking dope. I was as far away from politics as I'd ever been." He was in Golden Gate Park almost every day, but the Be-In touched him deeply. "What stayed with me was Ginsberg. You don't get to see a guy like that very often."

Also among the attendees in San Francisco were James Rado and Gerome Ragni, who shortly thereafter wrote the musical *Hair*, which premiered in New York the following year, by which time much of the essence of the culture they were exploiting had dispersed. Most early hippies viewed the musical as a dumbed-down version of their evanescent culture, but over the years, millions of people have professed to having picked up shards of light from it. The spirit moved in mysterious ways.

In the early evening following the Be-In, Bowen hosted a party at his place. Around eighteen people squeezed into his meditation room, including Ginsberg, Snyder, Leary, and two local TV cameramen. The *New Yorker*'s Jane Kramer hung out with the effusive Ginsberg. "I thought it was very Eden-like today, actually," he told her. "Kind of like Blake's vision of Eden. Music. Babies. People just sort of floating around having a good time and everybody happy and smiling and touching and turning each other on. A lot of groovy chicks all dressed up in their best clothes."

One of the TV guys interrupted him to ask, "But will it last?"

Ginsberg shrugged. "How do I know if it will last? And if it doesn't turn out, who cares?" Once was enough.

Around nine that night, a crowd assembled on Haight Street and cops said they were blocking buses. Twenty-five people were arrested for causing a nuisance. Nonetheless, the scale and colorful nature of the crowd that had gathered during the day created a significant impression. Photos of the Be-In appeared in newspapers and magazines around the world.

McClure would later write, "The Be-In was a blossom. It was a flower. It was out in the weather. It didn't have all its petals. There were worms in the rose. It was perfect in its imperfections. It was what it was—and there had never been anything like it before."

Of course, to a huge part of the country, the Be-In was of no particular consequence. Far more Americans paid attention the next day, January 15, when the Green

Bay Packers beat the Kansas City Chiefs 35–10 at Los Angeles Memorial Coliseum in the first Super Bowl.

Meanwhile, the Diggers were worried that the publicity from the Be-In would change people's heads in the hip community for the worse, so they held their own event called "The Invisible Circus at the Glide Church." It took place in San Francisco a month later, on February 24, with no posters or advertising that the media would notice, just word of mouth. It went all night and had more nudity, sex, and intense drug use than the Be-In had (and nary a Hindu chant).

NEW YORK: LOWER EAST SIDE

New York City's Lower East Side was Haight-Ashbury's psychic cousin. At times it seemed like they were two pieces of the same puzzle, but there were differences. The Lower East Side was economically poorer and more crime ridden, and in New York the hippies had a lot more competition for possession of the cultural zeitgeist.

Greenwich Village, which was just a few blocks west and north of the Lower East Side, had been a haven for rebel culture at least as far back as the beginning of the twentieth century. Even though Bob Dylan had taken a lot of the air out of the folk world (no one could compete with his brilliance), the folk scene that spawned him was still there, and so, on occasion, was Dylan himself. There was a revolutionary art world that included Andy Warhol, and a fierce literary community that included the likes of Paul Goodman, James Baldwin, George Plimpton, and Norman Mailer.

Harlem had its own vast energy and many of the jazz

geniuses of the age—such as Ornette Coleman, Miles Davis, Dizzy Gillespie, and Thelonious Monk—were still in their prime. John Coltrane, whose 1965 master-piece *A Love Supreme* was as influential a musical/spiritual opus as any rock record, would die of cancer at the age of forty in July of 1967.

Most record companies at the time were based in New York (although Los Angeles was rapidly expand-ing and would soon be an equal music business center), which was also the American home of Broadway as well as avant-garde theater, most notably the Living Theatre.

Ed Sanders, a native of Missouri, had moved to the city to attend New York University, from which he grad-uated with a degree in Greek. An impassioned supporter of the peace movement, he was arrested at a protest near a nuclear submarine when he was twenty-two years old in 1961 and wrote his first poem in jail. Shortly there-after, Sanders started an avant-garde literary magazine called *Fuck You: A Magazine of the Arts.*

In 1964, Sanders and beatnik poet Tuli Kupferberg started a rock band called the Fugs, named after the eu-phemism Norman Mailer had invented to substitute for the word "fuck" in his classic World War II novel *The Naked and the Dead.* The Fugs combined literary sophis-tication with profane, hip rage. They set William Blake poems to music, but would follow them with songs like "Coca Cola Douche" and "My Baby Done Left Me" (the chorus of which had the brokenhearted narrator sing-ing, "*I feel like homemade sh—*").

The Fugs also had a political side and participated in numerous anti–Vietnam War rallies. They wrote "Kill for Peace," which they performed at Carnegie Hall at a

"Sing-In for Peace" that also featured Pete Seeger, Phil Ochs, and civil rights hero Fannie Lou Hamer.

In 1965, Sanders opened the Peace Eye Bookstore at 383 East 10th Street, which became one of the key meeting places in the Lower East Side hip community. At the grand opening the Fugs and the hippie/bluegrass band the Holy Modal Rounders played. (The Rounders wrote a new verse to the jug band standard "Hesitation Blues" in which they said they were wearing "psychedelic shoes.") Andy Warhol gave Sanders three large silkscreen prints of flowers for the walls. Among the literati who attended were Allen Ginsberg, George Plimpton, William Burroughs, and best-selling novelist James A. Michener, who arrived in a limo.

Sanders had a mimeograph machine at the bookstore to continue publishing *Fuck You* as well as the prolegalization *Marijuana Newsletter*. On January 1, 1966, police raided the Peace Eye Bookstore and charged Sanders with obscenity.

Ginsberg was in Los Angeles at the time and held a benefit poetry reading in Hollywood to raise money for initial legal fees. The ACLU quickly stepped in to defend Sanders, which limited future costs.

In Tom Wolfe's book *The Electric Kool-Aid Acid Test*, he quotes Ken Kesey telling him in 1966, "No offense but New York is about two years behind [California]." By 1967 this was no longer the case. It had become easy to get LSD in New York and both Greenwich Village and the Lower East Side had proud bohemian traditions. New York's counterparts to the *Oracle* were the late-night shows on WBAI-FM, a radio station that created a similar sense of a psychedelic/revolutionary community.

WBAI was part of the small, feisty, and noncommercial Pacifica Network, which had been created in the late 1940s by a pacifist named Lewis Hill. The first affiliated stations were KPFA in Berkeley and KPFK in Los Angeles. In 1960 Pacifica was given WBAI in New York. (In later years, Pacifica added stations in Houston and Washington, DC.) The idea of "listener-sponsored" radio, without commercials, was a novelty (National Public Radio wasn't founded until 1970), and the audiences for Pacifica stations were passionate and engaged. The stations offered a combination of classical music and public affairs programming with a pronounced left-wing tilt.

Among WBAI's virtues was an extremely strong signal that reached up to Westchester where my parents lived. The station published monthly programming folios for donors. A glance at the first week of programming from March 1967 gives an idea of the cultural footprint WBAI had in the New York area.

In keeping with the sensibilities of the FM radio audience of the time, they broadcast a large sampling of classical music, including Clementi piano music, Carl Orff's adaptation the thirteenth-century poem "Carmina Burana," Schubert's "Octet in F Major," sacred compositions by Benjamin Britten, and Beethoven string quartets. Other highbrow programming included *Shakespeare with a Difference*, hosted by Alfred Rothschild, the editor of Bantam Classics' Shakespeare editions, a recording of a full performance of the Bard's *Measure for Measure*, a program dedicated to Indian music played by Ravi Shankar, and a jazz show hosted by *Downbeat* editor Ira Gitler.

Weekly programming included *Commentary*, a production of the New York chapter of SDS, a review of the Soviet press, satirical shows by Paul Krassner and Hugh Romney, and a panel discussion by the board of the Ethical Culture Society (a religion created by rationalist Jews earlier in the century who had founded Fieldston, the high school I attended). Specials during the first week of March included one on the trials in Newark of African American poet LeRoi Jones, another on the "police harassment" of Timothy Leary in Millbrook, and a conversation between antiwar congressman William Fitts Ryan (whose district included Manhattan's Upper West Side) and former army general David Shoup, who had turned against the war. WBAI also offered new, original reporting from Vietnam (they had sent reporter Chris Koch there as early as 1965), and later in the year the Pacifica stations broadcast a live interview with Che Guevara a few months before he was killed.

I had a limited appetite for this well-intentioned but often dull programming, yet WBAI's late-night offerings rocked my world. From Monday through Friday, Bob Fass broadcast from midnight to four a.m. On Saturday and Sunday, it was Steve Post. Together, they created a sense of a secret, hip world, totally remote from the tedium of school and work. Bob Dylan often showed up in the wee hours of the morning to play a new song or exchange cynical cosmic observations with Fass, and regular guests on these shows included such luminaries as Paul Krassner, editor of the *Realist* and Lenny Bruce's autobiography.

Fass decided to try to find out how many engaged listeners he actually had and suggested that they all come to JFK Airport on the night of February 11 for a "Fly-In."

Despite the fact that it ended up being the coldest night of the year with temperatures near zero, several thousand bleary-eyed WBAI listeners (whom Fass affectionately referred to as "the cabal") showed up.

The next month, on Easter Sunday, there was a daytime Be-In in Central Park's Sheep's Meadow. Paul Williams and Jim Fouratt were the primary organizers. Williams was a precocious eighteen-year-old who had started *Crawdaddy*, the first magazine to write about rock and roll with the intellectual gravitas previously reserved for jazz, folk, and classical music. He had written all of the articles in the first ten-page issue, but the mimeographed magazine attracted enough attention in the blossoming rock world that other brilliant writers soon flocked to him, including Jon Landau, who would later become Bruce Springsteen's manager, and Paul Nelson, who would sign the New York Dolls during a brief stint at Mercury Records. (Williams was a visionary but a terrible businessman. Both Landau and Nelson left *Crawdaddy* by the end of 1967 to write for a new San Francisco–based rock magazine called *Rolling Stone*.)

I would meet Fouratt a few years later, by which time he was the "Company Freak" (this was his actual title!) at CBS Records, where, among other tasks, he was the primary liaison with Janis Joplin. He was also a central figure in the gay liberation movement that emerged from the Stonewall Riots in 1969.

But in 1967, Fouratt, having spent time with the Diggers in San Francisco, was calling himself Jimmy Digger. He brought the Diggers' anti-elite sensibility to the New York Be-In. "We really wanted not to have an audience and a stage and performers in an active/passive situation. We wanted to make people figure out how to relate in real time." Thus there were no speakers and no music. It was a pure vehicle for the community to come together and "be."

New York's biggest alternative weekly, the *Village Voice*, founded in 1955, had been dominated by grimly grounded New York lefties who were invested in the civil rights movement, the antiwar movement, and off-Broadway. The *Voice* had initially been dubious about the hippie scene but that was about to change.

Howard Smith wrote a column called "Scenes" in the *Voice*, and he saw himself as an activist as well as a journalist. "Howard called me one day and said that the *Voice* was throwing out a Gestetner machine because they'd gotten a new one," Jim Fouratt recalls. This was the same kind of mimeograph machine that the Diggers used in San Francisco. It was capable of printing tens of thousands of flyers in a few hours. Fouratt convinced some kids to pick it up on the street outside of the *Voice*'s office. At the time there were plenty of high school students hanging around the Lower East Side, some of whom went to private schools like Dalton. The students would steal reams of paper from their schools that would eventually become flyers for the upcoming New York Be-In.

Pop artist Peter Max created a psychedelic graphic for free and printed up thousands of handouts, but the flyer had his name on it; Fouratt was incensed. "I told Peter that we didn't want any individual having visibility and he was very good about it. He destroyed the first printing and gave us thousands more without his name. We tried to remain anonymous. People would ask who was organizing it, and we would give them a Be-In button and tell them, *You are!*" Another distinguishing fact of the New York Be-In was that the words on the posters and flyers were in both English and Spanish—as a result, thousands of Puerto Ricans showed up.

In the week leading up to the Be-In, Fouratt was on the Bob Fass show, *Radio Unnameable*, virtually every night "anonymously" exhorting listeners to come to the event. As had been the case in San Francisco, a hip community which had previously never been known to exceed a couple thousand people had increased tenfold, seemingly overnight. The New York Be-In attracted roughly twenty thousand celebrants. Some had Easter Parade hats and others wore psychedelic robes. Many painted their faces in wild designs and colors ranging from chalk white to glowing lavender; they often included a dot, a tiny mirror, or a prism disk pasted on the forehead. One man was dressed in a suit of long, shaggy strips of paper. A tall man, his face painted white, wearing a silk top hat adorned with straw flowers, wandered ethereally through the Be-In holding aloft a tiny sign that simply read, *LOVE*.

Abbie Hoffman, then thirty years old, would not emerge as a media figure until later in the year, but he and his soon-to-be wife Anita were in attendance. Hoffman was a native of Worcester, Massachusetts, and had a thick New England accent, long dark hair, and a big Jewish nose. (Although Hoffman described himself as an atheist, he was proud of having been born Jewish and frequently mentioned it.) He had graduated from Brandeis and had gotten involved in the civil rights movement.

A few months earlier Hoffman had opened a "Freedom Store" on East 13th Street that sold products made by civil rights workers in the South. Unfortunately, the store did not do well. At the Be-In, Hoffman's mind raced with ideas about how to synthesize the disparate cultural and political elements that were exploding before his eyes. He had become enamored with Marshall McLuhan's book *Understanding Media,* and as much as he enjoyed the Diggers' intensity and creativity, going forward he would have no interest in anonymity.

Anita Hoffman described the scene in a roman à clef called *Trashing,* written under the pseudonym Ann Fettamen. "Someone gave us some orange and a chocolate. It was mind-blowing to be offered a poem or a daffodil by someone you'd never seen before. In New York you'd usually never speak to a total stranger."

Among those mingling with the hippie kids were leaders of the pacifist Fellowship of Reconciliation and Group Image artistic commune. Also flowing with the crowd were a number of New York jazz and rock musicians, including Ornette Coleman, and Ed Sanders and Tuli Kupferberg of the Fugs.

The cops at the Be-In were cool. A police car arrived around six forty-five in the morning, and the few hundred people already gathered rushed the car and pelted it with flowers, yelling, "Daffodil power!" There were no arrests, not even of people who stripped and ran around naked, nor of those few couples who had sex out in the open. "The police were beautiful," remembers Fouratt. "It was really strange and it freaked them out, but they were beautiful."

Under Smith's influence the *Voice* abandoned its lefty

cynicism in their coverage of the Be-In the following week: "Laden with daffodils, ecstatic in vibrant costumes and painted faces, troupes of hippies gathered . . . Rhythms and music and mantras from all corners of the meadow echoed in exquisite harmony, and thousands of lovers vibrated into the night. It was miraculous . . . Layers of inhibitions were peeled away and, for many, love and laughter became suddenly fresh."

LOS ANGELES

Hippie energy was spreading in Los Angeles as well. On weekends, teenage longhairs would crowd the Sunset Strip in Hollywood, causing the local merchants to complain. Eventually, the Los Angeles Police Department announced a curfew.

On Saturday, November 12, 1966, a demonstration was held to protest the curfew outside the popular Pandora's Box nightclub on the corner of Sunset and Crescent Heights boulevards. The ten p.m. curfew would effectively shutter Pandora's Box and other nightclubs frequented by teenagers. A thousand young people demonstrated and the LAPD overreacted and declared it a riot, beating and handcuffing many of the participants.

Stephen Stills, a twenty-one-year-old guitarist and singer for the new rock group Buffalo Springfield, wrote "For What It's Worth" about the Sunset Strip "riots," and the band recorded it on December 5, 1966. The song would later be used in countless movie montages of antiwar protests, but had been written to celebrate the simple idea of teenagers expressing themselves.

On the same Easter Sunday in 1967 that the New York Be-In took place, a Love-In occurred in Downtown LA in

Elysian Park, near where the Dodgers played. The psychedelic posters urged people to "bring incense, bells, flowers, and joy." The turnout was around twenty thousand, roughly ten times as big as the hippie dances and events in Los Angeles during the preceding year.

Elliot Mintz, then twenty-one years old, had a talk show on the Los Angeles Pacifica station KPFK. Someone at the station had decided they should reach out to younger audiences and Mintz had sent in his resume at the right time. He was the youngest person on the radio in LA and was making it up as he went along.

Around the same time, Peter Bergman and Philip Proctor, who would soon form the underground comedy group the Firesign Theatre, were creating trippy audio montages for the station. "I was intimidated," remembers Mintz. "I had no knowledge of how to edit in sound effects or write conceptually the way [Bergman and Proctor] did." Instead, Mintz initially played an eclectic blend of music until he found his métier as an interviewer of young musicians, actors, writers, and hip philosophers.

"I talked the Love-In up every night and gave driving directions, parking info, and kept reminding people it was free." Mintz and Peter Bergman played the roles of a very laid-back masters of ceremonies, introducing the bands who played.

The LA Love-In was neither as minimalist as the New York Be-In nor as structured as the one in San Francisco. There was a stage where local LA rock bands played—including the Strawberry Alarm Clock, the Peanut Butter Conspiracy, and Clear Light—but there were no poems, political speeches, or spiritual ceremonies. (Noting the magnitude of the newly expanded scene, the bigger LA rock bands—the Byrds, the Doors, Love, and Buffalo Springfield—showed up and played for free at subsequent Love-Ins in Griffith Park later in the year.)

Among those in the swarm of mostly teenage hippies were Micky Dolenz and Peter Tork of the TV band the Monkees. The group was dismissed by many "serious" rock fans, but the guys in the band were determined to bond with the hippie community. (Tork had recently "invested" $5,000 in the *Oracle*.)

Also in attendance was Peter Fonda—the twenty-seven-year-old son of Hollywood icon Henry Fonda—who had started a minor acting career of his own. In August of 1965, the Beatles had rented a house on Benedict Canyon Drive in Beverly Hills, and Fonda had taken LSD there, along with John Lennon and Ringo Starr. At one point while tripping, Fonda announced, "I know what it's like to be dead." Lennon used the phrase in the song "She Said She Said," which appeared on *Revolver*, an album the band released in August 1966. Fonda had been among those roughed up by cops at the Sunset Strip "riots." He had grown his hair long, which prevented him from getting most acting jobs for the moment, but he and his friends Jack Nicholson and Dennis Hopper were convinced that the same hippie energy that was transforming rock and roll would soon come to Hollywood. Later in the year, Fonda starred in a low-budget film written by Nicholson called *The Trip*, playing a TV commercial director who takes LSD. Hopper played the dealer. Encouraged by the experience, Fonda and Hopper wrote a more serious movie about the hippie scene called *Easy Rider* (cowritten with Terry Southern) which would be released in 1969, and would achieve massive commercial success, ushering in the era of what was called "the new Hollywood."

Another attendee at both the San Francisco Be-In and LA's Love-In was eighteen-year-old Pamela Miller, who would soon become well-known as "Miss Pamela" of the GTOs, a band signed to Frank Zappa's label, and eventually became even more famous for the memoirs she wrote as Pamela Des Barres about her experiences with numerous legendary rock musicians. She recalls hitchhiking to the San Francisco Be-In: "I was a hippie turning into a flower child before I turned into a freak." In San Francisco, she made out with Bobby Beausoleil, then a good-looking nineteen-year-old aspiring rock singer and actor. (Later that year Beausoleil would meet Charles Manson when he was released from prison and moved to Haight-Ashbury; in 1970 Beausoleil would be convicted of a murder said to be made at Manson's behest.)

Miss Pamela came to the LA Love-In with a friend. They'd made dozens of cupcakes to give away. "They were taken and eaten immediately," she says with a laugh. Soon after, she met Jimi Hendrix, and appeared in a "short film" (what would now be called a music video) made for "Foxy Lady." She fell in love with her first serious boyfriend, Noel Redding, the bass player of the Jimi Hendrix Experience; in the 1970s she went on to marry rock singer Michael Des Barres.

As at the other Be-Ins, the crowd brought lots of balloons, flutes, and tambourines. Many wore flowers in their hair and had drawings on their faces. Hippies were dancing, playing conga drums, looking through kaleidoscopes, flying kites, and blowing soap bubbles. Miss Pamela warmly remembers people "tangled up in each other's daisy chains and making out with strangers." There was at least one couple actually having public sex. But her primary memory is a "sharing atmosphere with kindred souls. I was so thrilled that I was actually a part of it." By the following year, Miss Pamela and her friend Sparky (also in the GTOs) were pictured on a poster advertising the next Easter Sunday Love-In. "It was in all the head shops. I was half-naked in a dress I'd made out of a tablecloth and Sparky was holding a gigantic stuffed bunny."

The main drug at the event was marijuana, and although the LA cops were more confrontational than those in San Francisco or New York, there were only around a dozen arrests. There were several large hand-painted signs with the Egyptian ankh symbol on it and a colorful banner for the Brotherhood of Eternal Love, and the big acid dealers in Orange County gave out samples of their wares, although not in the quantity that Owsley had distributed in San Francisco.

Sweep-In

Back in New York, Abbie Hoffman felt that the "Fly-In" and "Be-In" had been too self-involved and that the community should do something with a "good purpose like cleaning up junk on the Lower East Side." So, on the day after Easter on Fass's WBAI show, they announced a "Sweep-In" where they asked the people who had attended the other events to come clean up the block on the Lower East Side where Paul Krassner lived (7th Street between avenues C and D), which was usually strewn with garbage. (Some accounts of the Sweep-In say that it was Emmett Grogan's idea.)

It was essentially at this moment that Hoffman emerged as a public figure, and his sense of humor and fearless defiance in the face of all forms of authority made him an instant hip celebrity—exactly the kind of thing the Diggers had sworn they would prevent from emerging. Grogan himself had moved to the Lower East Side and became a bitter critic of Hoffman, accusing him, among other things, of leading a bunch of self-aggrandizing suburban white kids into poor neighborhoods without respecting the needs of the minority communities there.

Hoffman and Fass planned the Sweep-In for April 8, 1967, and word of the upcoming spring-cleaning quickly reached New York's sanitation department. Apparently embarrassed by the idea of dirty hippies doing their work for them, city trucks were dispatched in the wee hours to clean the block from top to bottom, an unprecedented occurrence.

Fass was undeterred. When a thousand people arrived armed with brooms, mops, sponges, and cleaning solutions—only to discover that the original mission had already been accomplished—he directed them to 3rd Street and they started scrubbing there. The *New York Times* reported that a sizable group of participants were kids who came in from Westchester County and Long Island. I was one of them.

A new culture was being born, but like all births, it had originated somewhere else.

CHAPTER 2
BEFORE THE DELUGE (1954–1966)

FIFTIES CULTURE

L ater in his life Timothy Leary often said, "If you want to understand the sixties, you need to understand the fifties." He was, for the most part, talking about the early experiments with psychedelics by psychiatrists, artists, and the United States government, as well as the oppressive shadow of McCarthyism and cultural and political orthodoxy.

When the Beatles' animated film *Yellow Submarine* was released in 1968, it depicted the enemies of joy as "the blue meanies." Some saw the cartoon villains simply as cops, but to a lot of us the blue meanies were a metaphor for materialists, racists, warmongers, repressive religious fanatics, and those who wished to censor artists. We imagined shadowy conservative white men wearing business suits who had won far too many of the arguments after World War II.

In the eyes of the counterculture, the "establishment" had created a materialistic and inhibited society that trapped many of our parents, a society which we, with the help of the Beatles, were determined to change for the better. All sixties change-agents, famous or obscure, owed a debt to the many who blazed progressive paths in the far less hospitable fifties.

Starting in 1952, *Mad* magazine satirized the materialistic advertising culture. In the early sixties, waiting for puberty to take hold, I used to read every word of every issue as if the contents were manna from sarcastic heaven. At the same time, older baby boomers were enjoying subversive comics like Mort Sahl, Lenny Bruce, Hugh Romney (who later renamed himself Wavy Gravy), Dick Gregory, and Lord Buckley as mind-expanding alternatives to the borscht belt humor of the vaudeville era. I loved the comedy routine *2,000 Year Old Man*, which was recorded as a series of albums in the 1960s. Straight man Carl Reiner asks the ancient protagonist played by Mel Brooks what mankind's earliest religion was. Brooks responds: "At first we worshipped Phil. He was the biggest and strongest among us and we worshipped him and we feared him. Then one day a bolt of lightning struck Phil and killed him. And we looked at each other and we said to each other, *There's something bigger than Phil.*"

Elvis Presley and others created the first wave of mass-appeal rock and roll, which helped loosen sexual repression and forged a musical culture that was shared by whites and blacks. American music culture of the fifties also spawned a deeper and edgier jazz, and, in the early sixties, a feisty, liberal folk music boom that included Joan Baez's mixture of vocal purity and pacifist politics and Bob Dylan's early albums, which had several "protest" songs.

Hollywood gave the world antiheroes played by Marlon Brando, James Dean, and Montgomery Clift, and the sexuality of Marilyn Monroe, Jayne Mansfield, and Kim Novak.

The American intellectual community of the fifties and early sixties included radical thinkers such as Paul Goodman, James Baldwin, and Norman Mailer. J.D. Salinger's novel *Catcher in the Rye* inspired millions of teenagers to mock "phonies." (Salinger's subsequent book, *Franny and Zooey*, has extensive references to mystical Christianity, Zen Buddhism, and Hindu Advaita Vedanta, and influenced the "new age" movement in future decades.)

The most radical white cultural expression came from the beatniks, most notably from Jack Kerouac's novel *On the Road* and Allen Ginsberg's poem "Howl," which among its many lasting effects on Western culture began a decades-long process of defeating censorship in the arts.

It can be argued that the fifties ended in November 1960 when John F. Kennedy was elected president of the United States. He was twenty-seven years younger than his predecessor Dwight D. Eisenhower. The following February, a month after he had taken office, President Kennedy crossed an American Legion picket line to see the film *Spartacus*, written by formerly blacklisted screenwriter Dalton Trumbo. The new president effectively ended the blacklist that had excluded hundreds of left-wing writers, actors, and directors from working in Hollywood films and network television, thereby creating the space for a more rebellious and diverse mass culture.

Ideas about sex were changing too. After World War II, Alfred Kinsey, a zoologist at the University of Indiana, researched the sex lives of thousands of Americans and published two books on his findings: *Sexual Behavior in the Human Male* in 1948, and *Sexual Behavior in the Human Female* in 1953. In addition to stimulating more honest conversations about heterosexual sex, Kinsey's works were among the first to bring information about homosexuality into mainstream culture.

1960 was also the year that birth control pills were introduced for mass consumption, a development that dramatically changed how everyone thought about sexual activity.

CIVIL RIGHTS

In May 1954 the United States Supreme Court issued the *Brown v. Board of Education of Topeka* decision that outlawed racial segregation in public schools. That lawsuit was filed by the National Association for the Advancement of Colored People (NAACP), which had been formed in 1909 to combat racial discrimination and in the ensuing years had become the "establishment" civil rights organization with the most conventional political clout.

The Montgomery bus boycott from December 1955 to December 1956 succeeded in ending segregation on the city's buses and propelled Dr. Martin Luther King Jr. into international fame, and further popularized nonviolent civil disobedience, a tactic which the NAACP had eschewed. (Dr. King formed his organization, the Southern Christian Leadership Conference, or SCLC, shortly after the boycott.)

For the next several years, further progress was stymied by white segregationists. While the NAACP and Dr. King maintained leading roles, new more militant organizations also sprung up, including the Congress of Racial Equality (CORE) and the Student Nonviolent Co-ordinating Committee (SNCC).

By 1960, Malcolm X had emerged as a prominent spokesman for the Nation of Islam (NOI) and as a new militant black voice who was outspoken in his contempt for Dr. King's use of nonviolence. Malcolm X grew to greater renown when he befriended Cassius Clay shortly before Clay upset Sonny Liston for the World Heavyweight Boxing Championship on February 25, 1964. Clay's wit and poetry (he composed doggerel predicting the results of his fights) were a dramatic contrast to the mob-connected, glowering, inarticulate Liston, and at the age of twenty-two, Clay was the youngest man ever to win the heavyweight championship.

Dr. Martin Luther King Jr.

Immediately after the Clay/Liston fight the new champion announced that he was a Muslim and changed his name to Muhammad Ali. Every kid I knew loved Ali, so many of us experienced cognitive dissonance while reading the laments of older sports writers who compared the new outspoken champion unfavorably to Joe Louis, the black boxing hero of the older generation, who had always been polite outside the ring.

Malcolm X would not benefit from the champ's explosion of popularity because on March 8, Malcolm publicly broke with Elijah Muhammad, the leader of the Nation of Islam. Ali, who overnight had become one of the most popular black Americans, remained loyal to the NOI.

In 1961, CORE began freedom rides to integrate buses and interstate bus terminals in the South; the group later expanded to voter registration. On June 21, 1964, CORE workers James Chaney, Michael Schwerner, and Andrew Goodman disappeared. Their bodies were later found—they had been murdered in Philadelphia, Mississippi.

That same year, in response to the blatant voter suppression of blacks in Mississippi, civil rights activists, including Fannie Lou Hamer, formed the Mississippi Freedom Democratic Party (MFDP). The group sent sixty-eight representatives to the Democratic Convention that August in Atlantic City, New Jersey, and demanded to be seated as delegates. President Lyndon B. Johnson orchestrated a "compromise" that offered the MFDP a mere two nonvoting seats at the convention while retaining the all-white "official" Mississippi delegation. Hamer and her MFDP colleagues were outraged.

The sense of betrayal would fuel an increased militancy in many quarters of the civil rights movement in years to come.

After Malcolm X left the NOI, he converted to Sunni Islam, made a pilgrimage to Mecca, returned with a more nuanced view of race relations, and was tragically killed, allegedly by members of NOI, on February 21, 1965. A month later, on March 21, 1965, after a couple of failed attempts, Dr. King led the Selma-to-Montgomery March for Voting Rights in Alabama.

THE ROAD TO VIETNAM

During this same period, there was a subculture of Americans who objected to the Cold War foreign policy that had taken hold after the death of Franklin Roosevelt. My parents were among this minority who felt that President Harry Truman had betrayed many of Roosevelt's ideas, particularly with regard to the Soviet Union. They had volunteered for Henry Wallace's ill-fated, anti–Cold War third-party campaign in 1948. Like the parents of many of the baby boomers who would become my friends in the sixties, they were appalled by Senator Joseph McCarthy and his "ism." They felt that McCarthy wildly exaggerated the threat of American Communists and used the ensuing hysteria to ostracize non-Communist liberals and Socialists who had been part of Roosevelt's New Deal.

The Korean War started on June 25, 1950, nine days before I was born, at the peak of the American baby boom that would be at the cultural center of the late sixties.

The protests against the war in Vietnam in the sixties would be driven by resistance to the military draft, but there had been a draft fifteen years earlier for the Korean War, and many of the arguments that were used against the Vietnam War applied to Korea as well. Yet there had been no mass resistance to the Korean War. What had changed in America between 1950 and 1965 to create the space for such a dramatically different response just one generation removed?

One factor was that the Korean War itself left an unsatisfying aftertaste to much of the American public. More than 36,000 American soldiers died in the war, but it did not produce an emotionally satisfying victory like World War II had. Instead there was a negotiated settlement, the benefit of which was at best an abstract concept to many Americans.

"Pacifist" is another word like "hippie" and "Socialist" that was supposedly unacceptable for serious people. Yet many Americans felt that pacifists like Britain's Lord Bertrand Russell, who had vainly opposed World War I and who was outspoken until his death in 1970, had been vindicated by history. Among these were two Quaker organizations, the American Friends Service Committee and the War Resisters League, which brought a quiet, spiritual fervor to the peace movement.

The oldest person integral to the peace movement of the sixties, Abraham Johannes "A.J." Muste, was born in 1885 and began his career as a minister of the Dutch Reformed Church. A believer in nonviolence, Muste opposed America's participation in World War I. During the 1920s he switched his focus to the labor movement, but by the thirties he had renewed his commitment to pacifism, for which he would be known for the rest of his life. Muste also opposed US involvement in World War II and said in 1940, "If I can't love Hitler, I can't love at all," which he meant as a spiritual belief consistent with many religious teachings but which reinforced his outsider status in the American political world including most of the left.

Nonetheless, as chairman of the Fellowship of Reconciliation, A.J. Muste was a mentor to many who would lead the nonviolent civil rights movement in the fifties and sixties, including James Farmer, Bayard Rustin, and Martin Luther King Jr. An unrelenting critic of the Cold War, Muste led various efforts to stop nuclear proliferation and was later among the first to criticize the war in Vietnam.

Muste never particularly related to the counterculture. In an obituary of Albert Camus for *Liberation* magazine, he favorably contrasted the French existentialist with beatniks, whom Muste claimed "stupidly give up the search for meaning." Yet in the context of the antiwar movement of the midsixties, Muste, by then in his early eighties, had a unique status. Although physically frail, he had a spectral presence and exuded a moral purity that made him the elder statesman of the pacifist side of the movement. Asked for his motivation at a candlelight vigil outside the White House to protest the Vietnam War, he said, "I don't do this to change the country. I do this so the country won't change me."

Dave Dellinger was thirty years younger than Muste, but as a fifty-year-old in 1965 when the Vietnam protests began, he too was a pacifist elder in the movement. Dellinger had refused to fight in World War II, and was sentenced to a term in jail where he was punished for not recognizing racially segregated seating. In 1956, Dellinger, Muste, and others started *Liberation* magazine, which became an important voice of the non-Communist left.

The nuclear arms race accelerated over the course of the fifties. The level of American paranoia increased markedly between the winter of 1959, when the Cuban Revolution led by Fidel Castro overturned the US-backed government, and the spring of 1961, when the Soviet Union launched a satellite with a pilot named Yuri Gagarin into outer space, the first time a human being escaped the force of gravity.

"There was the constant sense of doom," recounts Joel Goodman, my best friend in high school. In Barry Alexander Brown and Glenn Silber's film *The War at Home*, an antiwar activist recalls being given a copper dog tag at his public school in New York so he could be identified if a nuclear bomb destroyed the city.

I remember reading a pamphlet that had a graphic showing the impact of a five-megaton nuclear bomb, through a series of concentric circles. At the center was the area in which everyone would be immediately vaporized or otherwise killed. A few miles beyond that people would die from radiation poisoning within twenty-four hours. A few miles beyond that people would die within the year. Of course, New York City was considered one of the most likely targets; the suburb where my family lived was in that terrifying third circle.

In my last couple of years of elementary school, a business had grown in America around the building and selling of fallout shelters. The theory was that these structures would prevent radioactive contamination in the event that the Chinese or Soviets dropped nuclear weapons on us. I was torn between jealousy of my friends who had one and a growing sense that it was an absurd scam.

In 1961, Dagmar Wilson, a children's book illustrator who lived in Virginia with her family, became upset after reading about the arrest of Bertrand Russell at a London demonstration against nuclear testing. She and a few friends formed Women Strike for Peace to support Russell's agenda.

Barry Commoner, a biologist and professor at Washington University in St. Louis, suspected that the radioactive fallout from atmospheric tests could endanger the health of children exposed to the cancer-causing isotope strontium-90. Commoner's research led him to believe that the radiation would contaminate the soil and grass, which would be eaten by cows. Those same cows would go on to produce milk that would be consumed by children whose growing bodies were particularly vulnerable.

As a college student at the University of Wisconsin, Cora Weiss had organized recall petitions against Senator Joseph McCarthy for his anti-Communist witch hunt. Several years later, now the mother of three young daughters, Weiss joined Women Strike for Peace. She organized a project for Commoner in which mothers around the country sent the professor young children's baby teeth. "We gave them to the tooth fairy first so the kids could get their five cents," Weiss recalls.

Commoner published the "Baby Tooth Survey" in a November 1961 edition of *Science*. It showed that levels of strontium-90 in children had risen steadily in those born in the 1950s, with those born later showing the most increased levels.

Women Strike for Peace were not doctrinaire pacifists. Weiss explains, "It was close enough to the
memory of World War II that some of us believed in
the concept of a just war." Yet they saw nothing just
about atmospheric nuclear testing. Wilson, Weiss, and
Bella Abzug (who would later be elected to Congress)
were among a small group that organized fifty thousand
women to march at various locations across the country,
calling for an end to atmospheric nuclear testing. Weiss
focused on the opinion of Middle America. "We wore
hats and white gloves. I wanted to make sure it was safe
for Mommy and Daddy and little children, so we insisted
on no civil disobedience and no unruly behavior."

Cora Weiss

President Kennedy was said to have been deeply
troubled by reports of radioactive contamination of milk,
and in August 1963 the United States, Great Britain, and
the Soviet Union signed the Limited Nuclear Test Ban

Treaty, which banned testing in the atmosphere and in the oceans. Weiss remembers fifty members of Women Strike for Peace gathering outside the White House in support of the signing, which took place in Moscow.

Jacqueline Kennedy personally delivered coffee and donuts to the women. "We were all young enough then that we ate the donuts," Weiss says wistfully. "We were told by one of his aides that President Kennedy wanted to acknowledge the role that Women Strike for Peace had played in creating public opinion supportive of the treaty."

This Cold War peace movement was the context in which I first crossed paths with Joel Goodman. We met on my first day at Fieldston, in seventh grade, in the fall of 1962. Joel's father was Percival Goodman, a prominent New York architect best known for his innovative designs of postwar Jewish synagogues. Percy was also a radical intellectual and the older brother of the celebrated writer Paul Goodman, a pacifist who had recently published a critique of modern American society called *Growing Up Absurd*, which became an ur-text for many sixties radicals.

Although seven years apart in age, the brothers were close. Multiple copies of Paul's books were stacked in Joel's parents' apartment on the Upper West Side. Percy was twenty years older than my father and was a remote figure to me and I suspect to Joel. When I would have dinner at their apartment during sleepovers, Percy, Paul, and Joel's mother Naomi would be occupied in their world of intellectual discourse while we "kids" had our own coded conversations which we were sure had much more relevance to the world.

Yet, at the same time, we internalized the political values of our parents. Joel's cousin Matty (Paul's son) was a year older than him and had refused to participate in air-raid drills at the Bronx High School of Science the year before. Joel suggested to me that we should have our own protest. (Although we thought we were alone on the cutting edge, Dorothy Day of the Catholic Worker movement had been arrested for protesting air-raid drills in 1955; Joan Baez had refused to participate in an air-raid drill at Palo Alto High School in 1958; Norman Mailer and Paul Krassner first met at an anti–air raid drill demonstration in 1961.)

The Cuban Missile Crisis occurred in October 1962, six weeks into the school year, increasing our sense of urgency. Our message was that air-raid drills were not only pointless, but they added to an atmosphere that normalized the idea of nuclear war. My parents approved. The sign I made with a black marker said, *Don't Prepare for War, Prevent It.*

It was a liberal school so we were not expelled. (The alumnus Fieldston boasted most about was J. Robert Oppenheimer, the physicist who helped develop the American nuclear bomb. Oppenheimer later turned against the arms race and was subsequently ostracized by many in the military and political establishments.) We were suspended for a day and Fieldston quietly stopped having air-raid drills.

The pre–Vietnam War peace movement was richly expressed in the late fifties and early sixties folk music scene, particularly by the previously blacklisted Pete Seeger, and by Baez, who released her first album at the age of nineteen in 1960.

In the early 1950s, folk singer Ed McCurdy, who had been known for recording bawdy Elizabethan songs, wrote and released the peace song "Last Night I Had the Strangest Dream"—"*Last night I had the strangest dream I'd ever dreamed before. I dreamed the world had all agreed to put an end to war.*" The song would be translated into seventy-six languages and recorded by dozens of artists, including Seeger, Baez, Johnny Cash, Garth Brooks, and Simon & Garfunkel on their debut album, *Wednesday Morning, 3 AM,* which was released in 1964.

"Where Have All the Flowers Gone?" written in 1955 and recorded by Seeger in 1962, is a pacifist lament about the costs of war. It was later recorded by Peter, Paul and Mary, the Kingston Trio, Marlene Dietrich, Roy Orbison, Dolly Parton, the Four Seasons, Earth, Wind & Fire, Olivia Newton-John, and Flatt & Scruggs, among others. In 1963, peace songs on popular folk albums included Bob Dylan's "Masters of War," which he quickly followed with another antiwar classic, "With God on Our Side," which appeared on 1964's *The Times They Are a-Changin'*. Also released in 1964 was Buffy Sainte-Marie's "Universal Soldier," which Donovan covered the following year; 1965 saw the release of Phil Ochs's album *I Ain't Marching Anymore.*

However, in 1965, pop radio was still the only way most American kids could hear new music. Barry McGuire, a former member of the pop folk group the New Christy Minstrels, had a number one hit record with *Eve of Destruction*. Written by P.F. Sloan, the lyrics were a despairing depiction of the American political culture. It referenced the civil rights struggle in Selma, the Vietnam War, and, implicitly, the assassination of President Kennedy. It was much more radical than anything that had previously been heard on Top 40 radio.

A few months later the promilitary song "Ballad of the Green Berets" by Sergeant Barry Sadler, which was widely perceived as an affirmation of the rationale for the Vietnam War, also went to number one. It is hard to imagine a single human being who would have been a fan of both songs. Polarization was at hand.

Several movies added to the sense of potential apocalypse. In 1959, *On the Beach*, starring Gregory Peck, Ava Gardner, and Fred Astaire, dramatized the horrible aftermath of a nuclear war. Two films in 1964 showed how an American military could be drawn into such a war: *Fail Safe*, starring Henry Fonda, and my favorite, *Dr. Strangelove*, in which Peter Sellers played three different characters. In 1967, the Academy Award for Best Documentary went to *The War Game*, written and directed by British filmmaker Peter Watkins. A docudrama about the devastation caused by a nuclear war, it was originally produced for British television but the BBC refused to air it because "the effect of the film has been judged by the BBC to be too horrifying for the medium of broadcasting."

Young people were primed to weigh in. Students for a Democratic Society (SDS) was created in 1960 at the University of Michigan. At its first convention in 1962, SDS issued a new American left-wing manifesto called the Port Huron Statement, primarily written by twenty-two-year-old Tom Hayden, who was SDS president at the time. Hayden was brought up in Detroit, where his Irish-Catholic family were members of a church presided over by Father Charles Coughlin, who had been a controversial conservative critic of President Roosevelt in the 1930s and was also a notorious anti-Semite. Hayden met Martin Luther King Jr. on a picket line protesting segregation at the 1960 Democratic Convention in Los Angeles. He then joined the Freedom Riders and was arrested and beaten in Mississippi and Georgia. For the rest of his life, Hayden approached activism through the prism of the nonviolent civil rights movement.

SDS agreed with the peace movement's critique of the Cold War and the nuclear arms race. It supported the civil rights movement, and criticized major political parties and labor unions for complacency about poverty. Even so, SDS was critical of what they called "the old left" because of its factionalism and its top-down decision-making hierarchies. SDS advocated "participatory democracy" and supported civil disobedience to help achieve these goals.

To the extent that there was an American left that had any political influence in the fifties and early sixties, it had vigorously denounced communism in response to the pressure of McCarthyism. SDS rejected this liberal orthodoxy and invited a representative from the Progressive Youth Organizing Committee, a Communist group, to attend their convention as an observer. This, in turn, freaked out many older Socialists who had walked a very thin line in the preceding years, most notably Michael Harrington, whose book *The Other America* was one of the catalysts for President Johnson's War on Poverty programs. Harrington, who was part of a leftist group called the League for Industrial Democracy (LID), was intent on distinguishing between Socialist programs/ideology and the totalitarian repression of existing Communist governments. To the "new left" exemplified by SDS, the "old left" was hobbled by memories of the late forties and early fifties, and there was also a suspicion among many students that the self-styled lefty elders were merely being protective of their turf. (A.J. Muste agreed with Hayden about inclusivity and the old pacifist addressed SDS conventions in 1964 and 1965.)

In an article for the *Nation* in 2002 about the fortieth anniversary of the Port Huron Statement, Hayden still sounded pissed: "While the draft Port Huron Statement included a strong denunciation of the Soviet Union, it wasn't enough for LID leaders like Michael Harrington. They wanted absolute clarity, for example, that the United States was blameless for the nuclear arms race . . . In truth, they seemed threatened by the independence of the new wave of student activism . . ."

During the early part of his career, when he was best known for political protest songs, Bob Dylan seemed to share Hayden's irritation with the old left. In late 1963, when Dylan was presented with the Tom Paine Award by the Emergency Civil Liberties Committee, which had been formed in the early fifties to oppose McCarthyism, he made a contrarian speech that signaled his independence from any political dogma. Shortly thereafter, Dylan briefly visited the SDS National Council meeting and told SDS leader Todd Gitlin that he had been turned off by "these bald-headed potbellied people sitting out there in suits." (It was around this time that the phrase "generation gap" became a useful part of understanding certain conflicts.)

The role of the student left increased dramatically after August 7, 1964, shortly before the Democratic National Convention, when President Johnson pressured the US Congress into passing the Gulf of Tonkin Resolution that set the stage for escalation of the war in Vietnam, without a formal declaration of war. Only two senators, Wayne Morse of Oregon and Ernest Gruening of Alaska, opposed it. President Johnson had the good fortune of being opposed in the 1964 election by the conservative Republican Senator Barry Goldwater, whose rhetoric was so extreme (including the suggestion that he would use nuclear weapons in Vietnam) that Johnson was able to run as the "peace" candidate. Nonetheless, disappointment by civil rights activists about the Democratic Convention, anxiety about the Cold War, and the SDS critique of American-style capitalism fostered activism to the left of the Democratic Party on many college campuses.

In October 1964, the Free Speech Movement was launched at the University of California, Berkeley, when a former graduate student named Jack Weinberg was arrested while manning a CORE table, defying university rules against political activism on campus. A series of campus protests ensued and students were supported by numerous activists, including Joan Baez. On November 3, President Johnson defeated Senator Goldwater in a landslide, but this had no effect on the underlying issues at Berkeley. On December 2, 1964, the most prominent of the student leaders, Mario Savio, made a famous speech on the steps of Sproul Hall that concluded, "There's a time when the operation of the machine becomes so odious, makes you so sick at heart, that you can't take part! You can't even passively take part! And you've got to put your bodies upon the gears and upon the wheels, upon the levers, upon all the apparatus, and you've got to make it stop!"

Almost immediately after Johnson's reelection, he ordered an escalation of the war. Opposition, led by the peace groups, immediately grew. The antiwar movement initially focused on the academics and other experts who had the background to contradict the rationales advanced by the policy intellectuals of the Johnson administration. SDS organized the first major teach-in at the University of Michigan, Ann Arbor, on March 24 and 25, 1965. The event was attended by about 3,500, and consisted of debates, lectures, movies, and musical events aimed at protesting the war.

Not to be outdone, Berkeley radicals created the Vietnam Day Committee (VDC) and produced their own thirty-six-hour teach-in beginning May 21, 1965, which attracted 30,000 participants. The State Department was invited by the VDC to send a representative, but declined. Two UC Berkeley political science professors who had agreed to speak in defense of President Johnson's handling of the war withdrew at the last minute. An empty chair was set aside on the stage with a sign taped on the back reading, *Reserved for the State Department.*

The attendees included several who would emerge as key figures in the antiwar movement over the ensuing decade, including perennial Socialist Party presidential candidate Norman Thomas, independent left-wing journalist I.F. Stone, Buddhist scholar Alan Watts, satirist and editor of the *Realist* Paul Krassner, comedian Dick Gregory, novelist Norman Mailer, Bob Moses from SNCC, Yale professor Staughton Lynd, Stanley Sheinbaum of the Center for the Study of Democratic Institutions, and folk singer Phil Ochs.

The teach-ins helped frame the antiwar side of the debate for the next several years. Separate and apart from long-running pacifist arguments against the Cold War was a critique of the dubious establishment rationale for this particular conflict. President Eisenhower had concocted the "domino theory" that suggested that if Vietnam fell under Communist control, there would be a chain reaction that could take over the entire Asian continent, including Japan, and then represent a profound threat to the United States. For many young people who were not in thrall to McCarthy-era paranoia, this simply did not pass the smell test. Moreover, the South Vietnamese government that the US was supporting often acted like a tyrannical dictatorship rather than expressing anything resembling the "democratic" values that the US claimed to support. The North Vietnamese president, Ho Chi Minh, was depicted by the Johnson administration as a puppet of the Soviet Union and Communist China, but in reality Ho was a nationalist (as well as an accomplished poet) and not a villain worthy of an American war.

Earlier in the sixties there had been tension between the South Vietnamese Buddhist community and the Catholic minority who ruled the government. Some Buddhist monks had burned themselves to death to protest discrimination by the American-backed government. A mirror of this horrible image came home on November 2, 1965, when American Quaker Norman R. Morrison immolated himself in front of the Pentagon.

By this time, Joel and I were hanging out a lot with

Peter Kinoy, a senior whose father was Arthur Kinoy, a brilliant and well-known left-wing attorney who had filed the last appeal for Julius and Ethel Rosenberg, two US citizens executed for committing espionage, and later represented Martin Luther King Jr. and many others in the civil rights and peace movements.

On November 27, 1965, SDS staged a March on Washington to protest the war. Joel, Peter, and I organized a busload of Fieldston kids to attend. The marquee speakers were Coretta Scott King and Dr. Benjamin Spock, but it was the new SDS president, Carl Oglesby, who made the speech that I remembered most clearly on the bus ride back to New York.

Speaking with mournful disappointment in the agenda of the "liberal" Democratic administration, Oglesby said: "Their aim in Vietnam . . . is to safeguard what they take to be American interests around the world against revolution or revolutionary change, which they always call communism . . . [T]here is simply no such thing, now, for us, as a just revolution . . . [We] have lost that mysterious social desire for human equity that from time to time has given us genuine moral drive. We have become a nation of young, bright-eyed, hard-hearted, slim-wasted, bullet-headed make-out artists. A nation—may I say it?—of beardless liberals . . . Some will make of it that I overdraw the matter . . . [a]nd others will make of it that I sound mighty anti-American. To these I say—don't blame *me* for *that*! Blame those who mouthed my liberal values and broke my American heart."

In August of 1966, the House Un-American Activities Committee (HUAC), which had ruined the lives of many liberals and leftists during and in the aftermath of

McCarthyism, held a hearing to investigate antiwar protesters, including Jerry Rubin, who, in defiant contrast
to intimidated witnesses in the past, appeared at the
hearing in a Revolutionary War costume, complete with
a three-cornered hat. The protesters were represented
by Arthur Kinoy, who after repeatedly trying to make
a point was physically ejected from the hearing room.
The next day, there was a photo on the front page of
the New York Times of the diminutive Kinoy (my friend's
dad was 5'2") in a choke hold while huge House security
men dragged him out of the hearing room. In 1975, when
HUAC was finally dismantled by the full House, that image was frequently cited as the beginning of the end of
the infamous committee.

Those who objected to the swagger of the new left
were not limited to old Communists or anti-Communist
Socialists. In 1966, conservative icon William F. Buckley Jr. launched the show Firing Line to give conservative
views a national television megaphone to counteract the
supposed liberal bias of the networks. (In the wake of
Goldwater's defeat, a "new right" was created parallel
to, and opposed to, the culture I was inspired by.)

Also in 1966, the National Organization for Women
was founded. Their focus was on a wide variety of areas
in which millions of women felt disadvantaged or oppressed, including the way women were often treated in
the civil rights and antiwar movements.

Art and Entertainment
On February 9, 1964, eleven weeks after the assassina-
tion of President Kennedy, the Beatles appeared on The
Ed Sullivan Show, demonstrating, among other things, that

teenage girls could be sexually attracted to guys with long hair. I was one of millions of teenage males to grow my hair as long as I could get away with while I was still in school, and longer still once there were no authorities to force a haircut. Over the next few years, the trade-off for being attractive to younger women was the hostility of older guys and authority figures who would often mock us with the question, "Are you a boy or are you a girl?"

The Beatles' massive popularity opened the door for numerous other English pop and rock bands to capture the hearts of those girls, the so-called British invasion. In July, the Beatles' witty film *A Hard Day's Night* was released. The film revealed the band's feisty antiestablishment attitude, and broadened the audience of rock and roll overnight to include older teenagers, college kids, and alienated guys. Young folkies and future rock stars such as David Crosby, Jerry Garcia, and Jorma Kaukonen hastily got electric guitars and formed rock bands. A year later, on July 25, 1965, Bob Dylan "went electric" at the Newport Folk Festival, outraging some folkie purists while inspiring countless others. Among the albums released in 1965 were the Rolling Stones' *Out of Our Heads*, Dylan's *Highway 61 Revisited*, Phil Ochs's *I Ain't Marching Anymore*, the Lovin' Spoonful's *Do You Believe in Magic*, and the Beatles' *Rubber Soul*, which had a slightly distorted, trippy photo of the band on the cover. It included the song "Norwegian Wood," which introduced Beatles fans to an Indian instrument called a sitar. Albums released in 1966 included the Beatles' *Revolver*, the Byrds' *Fifth Dimension*, and Dylan's *Blonde on Blonde*.

In the early sixties, cosmopolitan and campus cultures were impacted by European films by directors such as Sweden's Ingmar Bergman, France's Jean-Luc Godard, and Italy's Federico Fellini, who brought more psychology, impressionism, and mysticism to movies than Hollywood typically produced. British filmmakers presented the subversive comedy of Pete Sellers and Alec Guinness, as well as the angst of angry young men in films written by playwright John Osborne and others.

In America in 1966, the TV series *Star Trek* debuted and Lenny Bruce died.

LSD

From the midfifties through the midsixties there was increasing experimentation and research into mind-expanding drugs. Awareness of such herbs or chemical substances in Western civilization had been restricted to a few therapists and anthropologists until 1954, when Aldous Huxley published a description of his experiences with mescaline in the book *The Doors of Perception*. (A dozen years later the book's title would inspire the name of rock band the Doors.)

Huxley was a native of England, where he achieved fame as a writer, most notably with his visionary novel *Brave New World*. He was also a pacifist who had been close to Bertrand Russell as a young man. In the 1930s, Huxley moved to Los Angeles, where he became deeply involved with Eastern religions, in particular the Vedanta form of Hinduism. Huxley's spiritual teacher, Swami Prabhavananda, was dubious about the spiritual validity of mescaline, but Huxley, while remaining involved with the Vedanta Society, insisted that some of the experiences he got from psychedelics (a word that his friend Humphry Osmond coined in 1956) were consistent with those achieved through meditation and other spiritual practices.

Huxley befriended Los Angeles psychotherapist Oscar Janiger, who was then conducting research with another psychedelic known as LSD. The formal scientific name for the chemical was lysergic acid diethylamide and it had been accidentally discovered in Switzerland in 1943 by a chemist named Albert Hoffman. (In the sixties, we started calling it "acid.") Separate from his larger study, Janiger launched a project with artists because he believed they could contribute language and depth to an understanding of LSD that were inaccessible to traditional scientific observation. In addition to Huxley, Janiger gave LSD to actors Cary Grant, Jack Nicholson, and Rita Moreno, classical music conductor André Previn, and author Anaïs Nin, as well as several visual artists who created paintings under the influence.

Janiger concluded that he could not understand his research without some personal experience, and over the course of his lifetime he took LSD thirteen times. His preference was to stay as invisible as possible and to avoid controversy. Janiger would not publish or otherwise publicly reveal any of his research for several decades.

Huxley, although shy of conventional publicity, was nonetheless one of the Western world's most prominent public intellectuals and he believed that transmission to others was part of his purpose in life. In *The Doors of Perception* he pointed out that what made William Blake so influential was not merely the grandeur of his inner visions but his talent for rendering them through his art and poetry.

Huxley wrote of the expanded appreciation he had for music while taking mescaline. His rhapsodic perceptions about Bach's music, reproductions of famous paintings he observed on a walk to a local store in Hollywood, and the pulsing inner life of flowers were remarkably similar to the kinds of experiences that acidheads like me would rave about in the late sixties.

Huxley contextualized his mescaline experience as compatible with the Hindu notions of dharma and the Gospel of Jesus Christ. "[T]his purely aesthetic Cubist's-eye view gave place to what I can only describe as the sacramental vision of reality. I was . . . back in a world where everything shone with the Inner Light, and was infinite in its significance."

Yet Huxley was carefully calibrated in his spiritual claims. "I am not so foolish as to equate what happens under the influence of mescaline or of any other drug, prepared or in the future preparable, with the realization of the end and ultimate purpose of human life: Enlightenment, the Beatific Vision. All I am suggesting is that the mescaline experience is what Catholic theologians call a 'gratuitous grace,' not necessary to salvation but potentially helpful and to be accepted thankfully, if made available."

Huxley viewed psychedelics with a sense of discretion that would not be shared by the more flamboyant Dr. Timothy Leary—a brilliant Harvard psychology professor with a restless mind who was intrigued by the use of psilocybin mushrooms in religious rites by the indigenous Mazatec Indians of Mexico.

In 1960, Leary took psilocybin in Mexico, and immediately developed an evangelistic enthusiasm about psychedelics. Leary belatedly read *The Doors of Perception;* finding great commonality in their experiences, he befriended Huxley.

Leary soon launched a research project at Harvard centered around LSD. Although there was no scientific way of determining the exact effect of psychedelics on the brain, he speculated that the chemical temporarily removed habits of thinking created in early childhood, causing users to experience the world through the uninhibited senses of a baby. "We think that LSD temporarily suspends your imprint—instead of seeing everything like a tired old snapshot." He also believed that the chemical (or "sacrament," as he was soon to call it) permitted access to parts of the brain that were not consciously available to most people. Yet Leary also echoed Huxley's sense of proportion on the spiritual value of psychedelics: "You don't worship a sacrament, you use it as a key."

Like Janiger, Leary felt that artists were essential to a deeper understanding of LSD. He reached out to Janiger's younger cousin, Allen Ginsberg. After his first LSD trip, Ginsberg shared Leary's experience of "agape." The poet had been exploring Eastern religion in the years since he'd become a beat celebrity and the acid experience conformed to many of his spiritual concepts. He was so inspired by that first acid trip that he called the White House from Leary's home to see if he could persuade recently elected President Kennedy to take LSD with the Soviet premier, Nikita Khrushchev. (The poet was not put through to the president.)

Ginsberg agreed to help turn on other artists to LSD and soon thereafter he hosted Leary in New York. In a harbinger of the various reactions that would play out on a mass stage later in the decade, not everyone had the same experience. They gave some to jazz legends Dizzy Gillespie and Thelonious Monk. A week later Ginsberg saw Dizzy at the Five Spot (a popular club for downtown jazz fans) and asked him how he liked the drug. The trumpeter replied, "Whatever gets you high, man." Not long afterward Ginsberg encountered Monk at the same club and the pianist pointedly asked if he had anything stronger.

Poet Robert Lowell and novelist Jack Kerouac took LSD in Ginsberg's East Village apartment. Ginsberg recalled that Lowell liked Leary, but couldn't shake off his habitual gloom. At one point Leary exuberantly said, "Love conquers all," and Lowell pensively responded, "I'm not so sure about that." Kerouac was similarly ambivalent. Once the acid kicked in, he was silent for over an hour, and then, while looking out the window of Ginsberg's apartment on 2nd Street between avenues A and B, the author of *On the Road* mused, "Walking on water wasn't built in a day."

A couple of years later, Leary and his colleague Richard Alpert, who had been a precocious academic star, were fired by Harvard for doing research into LSD that included studies with undergraduates. Before his first LSD trip in 1961, Alpert considered himself "an adult in a world that was defined by the intellect. The high priests of America were scientists and intellectuals. What was valued is what *you knew you knew*. Introspection was rejected. What was respected was what could be measured from outside, not from inner experiences. Anything you couldn't measure was treated as irrelevant."

Decades later, long after he had changed his focus to Eastern spiritual traditions and been renamed Ram Dass by his guru, Alpert would still acknowledge the huge debt he owed to LSD for having liberated him from that mind-set: "I was teaching at Harvard and had a highly valued position, a promise of tenure. Then I had these chemicals and I questioned the entire social structure. A part of me that I met was more valid than the part of me that had been part of the whole social game."

After being fired by Harvard, Leary was given the use of a mansion in Millbrook, New York, by several members of the Hitchcock family, heirs to the Mellon fortune, who admired his work. He created an organization for the study of psychedelics called the Castalia Foundation, named after a fictitious intellectual colony depicted in Hermann Hesse's novel *The Glass Bead Game* *(Magister Ludi).*

When Huxley found out he was dying, he asked Leary to get him some LSD. Huxley's wife Laura injected him with the psychedelic. Huxley passed away while tripping on November 22, 1963, the same day that John F. Kennedy was assassinated. It would require the most hardened rationalist not to take note of the synchronicity of these deaths and their relationship to what we now call "the sixties."

Near the end of his life, Huxley had advised Leary on how to deal with the wave of young psychedelic seekers of my generation he foresaw materializing. "Be gentle with them, Timothy. They want to be free, but they don't know how. Teach them. Reassure them." He had once told Leary, "Do good stealthily." Wishful thinking. Leary had an insatiable appetite for the spotlight. Of course, as things turned out, Leary himself would have far less influence and control over the way the masses handled psychedelics than could be imagined at the time.

Ram Dass

Even while performing on a much larger media platform, with a kind of showmanship that Huxley never aspired to, Leary tried to uphold Huxley's values. He and Alpert continually stressed the importance of "set and setting" for LSD trips, suggesting that there should always be a guide and that the environment should be carefully selected for positive, inspiring, and nurturing qualities. Huxley had introduced Leary and Alpert to *The Tibetan Book of the Dead*, which he felt connected ancient wisdom to the psychedelic experience. They oversaw a new translation of the text that was reimagined as a guide to LSD sessions. It had suggestions on how to navigate through the kinds of personality issues that could cause a bad trip. (On the Beatles' *Revolver*, one of the best-selling albums in the world in 1966, the lyrics of the John Lennon song "Tomorrow Never Knows" were taken directly from the Leary/Alpert version of the ancient text.)

Leary and Alpert were also involved in a study of twenty theology students at Boston University. They created two groups: one took psilocybin, the other took a placebo. Both groups listened to the same sermon on Good Friday and immediately afterward taped a description of their experiences. These descriptions were sent to theologians around the United States without letting them know which group each participant was in.

Of those who took psilocybin, nine out of ten were deemed to have had a revelatory experience. Of the other group, the theologians only identified one. This did not constitute scientific "proof" but it was enough for Leary and Alpert to validate their instincts about the relationship between psychedelics and spirituality.

When mass media and rock and roll propelled LSD to the status of a household word, the criticisms from various establishments increased. Reporters had no trouble finding antipsychedelic doctors, many of whom cited the increased presence of hippies on bad trips in hospital emergency rooms. There were reports of people who while tripping thought they could fly and jumped off buildings to their deaths. In 1969, Art Linkletter, who hosted the popular TV shows *People Are Funny* and *House Party*, would become a high-profile critic of LSD in general and Timothy Leary in particular. Earlier that year, Linkletter's twenty-year-old daughter Diane had jumped to her death from a sixth-floor kitchen window. Linkletter claimed that she was on LSD and blamed Leary for having popularized the drug.

One can sympathize with the anguish of a parent in Linkletter's position and still disagree with his conclusions. The autopsy of his daughter showed that in fact there was no LSD in her system, but Linkletter speculated that she'd had an LSD flashback. Diane Linkletter's boyfriend, Edward Durston, told the cops that she was determined to kill herself and that drugs were not a factor in her death. Nonetheless, Linkletter continued to blame Leary and the counterculture for his daughter's death and became a prominent anti-LSD voice in the media.

Some biologists emerged in the media suggesting that LSD could lead to chromosome damage in a way that might cause birth defects in children. In the late sixties this assertion was given credence even by some of the underground media. The passage of time and births of millions of people to parents who took LSD proved that no such pattern existed.

Shortly before Christmas 1965, Leary was arrested in Laredo, Texas, for possession of a small amount of marijuana. The judge who gave him the exorbitant sentence of thirty years in prison referenced Leary's pro-psychedelic writing as one of the reasons. The Supreme Court overturned that decision in 1969 on Fifth Amendment grounds, but the template for legal persecution of Leary was set. Richard Nixon, before being elected president, absurdly called him "the most dangerous man in America."

In his 1967 book *Alternating Current*, Octavio Paz wrote:

We are now in a position to understand the real reason for the condemnation of hallucinogens and why their use is punished: the authorities do not behave as though they were trying to stamp out a harmful practice or a vice, but as though they were attempting to stamp out dissidence. Since this is a form of dissidence that is becoming more widespread, the prohibition takes on the proportions of a campaign against a spiritual contagion, against an opinion. *What the authorities are displaying is* ideological *zeal: they are punishing a heresy, not a crime.*

Decades later, in 1989, Ram Dass still saw the criminalization of LSD as a defense of the establishment rather than having any legitimate public health purpose. "People were raised to respect authority," he explained. "After LSD, many people saw what they felt inside as being as valid as any external institutions. So it undermined authority and was a threat to social structure. Soon, society realized people are less controllable when they have had an experience of intuitive validity."

Another public proselytizer of LSD in America in the early sixties was the celebrated author Ken Kesey, who in his early twenties had voluntarily participated in a study of psychedelics at Menlo Park Veterans Hospital in Northern California. The study, it turned out, was the CIA-funded Project MKULTRA. The government wanted to figure out if psychedelics could be used in espionage or warfare. In 1960, at the age of twenty-five, Kesey began writing the best-selling novel *One Flew Over the Cuckoo's Nest*.

After Kesey published his second novel, *Sometimes a Great Notion*, he decided to come out of the psychedelic closet and took several of his friends on a trip to New York on a brightly painted bus he called Furthur. This was the debut of a loosely knit group of psychedelic adventurers around Kesey whom he called the Merry Pranksters. He agreed to have journalist Tom Wolfe follow him around for a year. Wolfe's book *The Electric Kool-Aid Acid Test*, in which Kesey is the main character, was as influential in glamorizing LSD as Leary's media appearances were.

Kesey was into a much more anarchic, festive approach to LSD than Leary and Alpert. He didn't have much use for ancient texts; his belief was to just get as far out as you could. Yet there was still a sense of mission. Furthur was driven by Neal Cassady, who was famous for having been the basis for the character Dean Moriarty in Kerouac's *On the Road*. Comedian Hugh Romney, who had emerged in the hip Greenwich Village folk world earlier in the sixties, joined the Merry Pranksters for a time and affectionately recalls it as "a chance to sign up on a spaceship and make energetic progress toward the good."

One of Kesey's frequent sayings to the group that

clustered around him was, "Get them into your movie before they get you into theirs." Wolfe suggested that Kesey wanted "control" of the Pranksters and he inaccurately portrayed the novelist more like a cult leader than a catalyst who helped empower a diverse collection of people to do their own thing.

Ken Kesey

At a Berkeley teach-in about Vietnam prior to a march on the Oakland Induction Center, Kesey surprised radicals by insisting, "You're not gonna stop this war with this rally, by marching. That's what *they* do." Kesey then played "Home on the Range" on his harmonica and suggested that the members of the crowd *observe* the war and then "turn your backs on it and say fuck it." Wolfe cited this moment in *The Electric Kool-Aid Acid Test* as an example of Kesey's flakiness. Former SDS president Todd Gitlin also criticized Kesey's speech: "This was not what the organizers wanted to hear on the verge of a march into fearsome Oakland to confront the army base." But with the hindsight of half a century, I feel that Kesey was getting at a poetic truth.

On November 27, 1965, Kesey threw a multimedia party called "The Acid Test" at Prankster Ken Babbs's house. It featured music by a band named the Warlocks. A week later there was a second "Acid Test" and the members of the Warlocks played again, but under a new name: the Grateful Dead.

Word about LSD quickly reached the minds of teenagers like me and Joel Goodman. Joel first smoked marijuana the year before I did, when we were both in tenth grade. A younger student was interviewing Allen Ginsberg for our high school paper, the *Fieldston News*, and Joel was asked to go along to keep him company, presumably to avoid putting a teenage boy in a position where he was alone with the poet. After the interview was done, Ginsberg took out a joint and asked the kids if they wanted to get high. "It was very, very pleasant," Joel remembers, but he had no idea how to get more for himself.

Joel had long, curly brown hair similar to Bob Dylan's on the cover of *Blonde on Blonde*, and it was a time when hair length and body language magically connected hip people. One day, not long after the Ginsberg initiation, Joel was in a local hardware store when a young Puerto Rican clerk named Lucky asked him if he wanted to buy some pot. Joel and Lucky quickly grew close, and Joel became a dealer to some of his friends like me.

I still remember the music that was playing at the party at Peter Kinoy's parents' apartment when I first smoked pot: the Beatles' *Rubber Soul*, the Stones' *Out of Our Heads*, and the Lovin' Spoonful's *Daydream*. (The Kinoy parents were not there. Both Peter and his younger sister Joanne, who I had a big crush on at the time, later told me that they had been subject to, and ignored, grim lectures on the perils of drugs and the unique vulnerability of the families of political radicals.)

The next week, I was walking down a corridor in school when an older kid named Paul Mintz urgently called me over to listen to a song on one of the portable record players that had recently been introduced into the marketplace. It was Bob Dylan's "Ballad of a Thin Man," the one with the chorus that goes, "*Because something is happening here, but you don't know what it is. Do you, Mister Jones?*" Mintz and I weren't friends; his mind was just so blown by the brilliance of the song that he had to play it to anyone who looked receptive. I was definitely an apt target. *Something was happening*, and Joel, Peter, our other friends, and I were in on it, and my parents and the people who made decisions in Washington weren't. As Joel recalls, "There was the world that was in the newspapers and that our parents and teachers lived in, and then there was the real world that *we* lived in . . . Of course, I was oblivious to the fact that while I was riding the subway, straight people had actually built it and kept it running. So in retrospect, maybe *both* worlds had some reality to them."

Richard Alpert (like Leary and Kesey) had been an achiever. I, however, was a nonachiever. For years, I got mediocre grades. (Since I did well on intelligence tests, the teachers' name for kids like me was actually "*under-achiever*.") I was terrible at sports, and extremely awkward socially. Alpert had used LSD in part to opt out of the "game" he had won but felt trapped in. I was thrilled that there was an alternative to the game I was doing so poorly at.

Joel remembers, "The idea was to try to love everybody. There was a feeling that we were part of a kind of chumminess that we were excluded from otherwise. We weren't sports stars or straight smart kids. It was a perfect fit to have a place to belong to and a milieu. Add that to the general conviviality of getting high with friendly people. It was kind of idyllic."

Lucky had a connection to the pure LSD manufactured by the Sandoz company in Switzerland, where it had been discovered. Since the media had been completely wrong about marijuana leading to heroin use, and about the war in Vietnam, we had no problem rejecting the scare stories about jumping off roofs. Lucky told us solemnly, "You don't have to be scared of yourself." We were in.

We had a vague respect for Leary but didn't pay any attention to his advice about how to trip. We looked out for each other. We avoided weird scenes and mostly stayed inside listening to music, watching TV, coloring with markers, and philosophizing about the meaning of life. Sometimes we'd go to Central Park, or to an Indian restaurant on West 110th Street (we thought we were part of a very elite group who knew about curry); I liked to go to the movies on acid, and saw *2001: A Space Odyssey*, *Marat/Sade*, and *Blow-Up* while tripping. The only time I got a little freaked out was when I was watching *How*

I Won the War, starring John Lennon. I whispered worriedly to Joel, "Either this is very strong acid or this is a very weird movie." Later, when I rewatched the film, my faith in acid was reinforced: the problem *was* the movie.

One of the biggest values of LSD to me was to uncouple me from assumptions that the intellectual world I'd grown up in had made about what was considered "deep" and "serious," which I always found depressing. I loved the "permission" to be happy. We all did. That was a big part of the revolution that was not televised. After an apparent revelation on an acid trip, I wrote a column in the *Fieldston News* in which I asserted that external accomplishments such as good grades should not define us. After all, we didn't choose our friends based on their grades, but on intuitive connections. While researching this book, I came across something that Dr. Leary had written, saying virtually the same thing. I can now see that I may have been more influenced by him than I admitted at the time.

Peter Kinoy, who'd always had a gift for drawing and painting, recalls an evening when he took acid and, in an homage to Picasso's *Guernica*, stayed up all night creating a collage of images about the recent Newark race riots. His father liked it so much that he hung it in his Rutgers Law School office. "I felt it was the first time my dad understood that the culture that meant so much to me connected with what he cared about," Peter says.

On October 6, 1966, LSD became illegal in California and it was soon banned all over America. Leary had already contrived a quixotic response. On September 19, he had announced the creation of the League for Spiritual Discovery, which was incorporated as a religion in what would turn out to be a futile attempt to get psychedelics relegalized by defining them as religious sacraments.

One of the organization's stated purposes was "to help each member discover the divinity within by means of sacred teachings, self-analysis, psychedelic sacraments, and spiritual methods and then to express this revelation in an external life of harmony and beauty . . . to help each member to devote his entire consciousness and all his behavior to the glorification of God. Complete dedication to the life of worship is our aim, as exemplified in the motto, 'Turn on, tune in, drop out.'"

The big winner of the moment, however, was the aforementioned Augustus Owsley Stanley III. Owsley was thirty-two years old in 1967 and his nickname was "Bear." He was the descendant of a political family from Kentucky. His father was a government attorney. His grandfather, A. Owsley Stanley—a member of the United States Senate after serving as governor of Kentucky and in the US House of Representatives—campaigned against Prohibition in the 1920s.

By the end of 1966, Owsley, who had studied chemistry, was geared up to manufacture millions of acid tablets that became known by their colors, including Monterey Purple, White Lightning, and Blue Cheer—which became the name of a very loud Bay Area rock band.

Because Owsley's form of delivery of the psychedelic was a tablet, the purity was assured. (They couldn't be diluted or contaminated as could be done to the contents of capsules.) Soon thereafter, a group in Orange

County, California, replicated some of Owsley's ethos and called themselves the Brotherhood of Eternal Love. Their signature tablet was called Orange Sunshine.

By all accounts, Owsley and the members of the Brotherhood were sincere inner seekers and psychedelic evangelists, but because LSD was illegal, the dealers were, by definition, criminals. Despite their cosmic aspirations, they brought with them a connection to other criminals and to some of the darkness and paranoia that go with the territory.

Meanwhile, all the currents of the counterculture were being magnified a hundredfold by newspapers, magazines, radio, and television—which were collectively being referred to by the suddenly trendy term "the media."

CHAPTER 3
THE MEDIA AND THE MESSAGES

The Diggers had cautioned that the media could distort or co-opt fragile new cultures and that too much attention could create toxic ego trips and/or paranoia in newly minted, hip celebrities. SDS's Todd Gitlin worried about the media's influence as well: "The mass media not only shapes how others view the group but has tremendous influence over how the group perceives its own identity."

Even Dr. Martin Luther King Jr. was attacked by some in the civil rights movement for cherishing his visibility. In February of 1968, King responded in what turned out to be one of his final sermons at his home congregation, Ebenezer Baptist Church in Atlanta. He began by describing two apostles of Jesus who asked to sit next to him in heaven. Although it was easy to condemn such egotism, King suggested that we all have the desire for attention. He called this the "drum major instinct—a desire to be out front . . . We like to do something good. And you know, we like to be praised for it . . . And somehow this warm glow we feel when we are praised or when our name is in print is something of the vitamin A to our ego." After giving examples of how this instinct could be perverted, King maintained that the key to life was not to repress this universal desire but to harness it to serve others. Contemplating his own funeral, he said, "If you want to say that I was a drum major, say that I was a drum major for justice. Say that I was a drum major for peace. I was a drum major for righteousness."

Of course, there was only one Martin Luther King Jr., but there were many people in the counterculture and various protest movements of the sixties who shared his view that the media was an indispensable tool for social change. It was certainly what got to me as a teenager.

Marshall McLuhan

In 1967, most media were primarily driven by the desires of advertisers, and advertisers wanted the baby boomers—more than twenty million of whom turned eighteen between 1964 and 1970. One of the most influential people in the way many counterculture figures and hippies interacted with the media was a Canadian academic who had been born before World War I.

Marshall McLuhan was fifty-six in 1967, yet listening to recordings of him half a century later, the man who coined the phrase "the medium is the message" is still quite a trip. McLuhan, who taught English and led culture and communications seminars at the University of Toronto, published *The Gutenberg Galaxy* in 1962, in which he coined the phrase the "global village" to describe the effects of television on most of the world. In 1964, he published his best-known book, *Understanding Media*, which suggested that the media itself should be the focus of study, not merely the things the media covered. He articulated many theories that are now taken for granted but at the time were revelatory.

Like Andy Warhol, McLuhan perceived depth in pop culture. "Rowan and Martin say, *We don't tell jokes, we just project a mood*," he remarked approvingly of a schlocky but popular network TV show of the sixties. McLuhan's affect was that of a slightly impatient being from another planet who was dumbing down obvious ideas for us earth people. (When the TV series *Star Trek* debuted in 1966, some critics speculated that Mr. Spock's otherworldly persona was modeled in part on McLuhan.) He patiently explained, "Old medium is typically content of new medium. Novels were content of movies, movies of TV. Now we live imaginatively in old culture, horse opera, *Bonanza* land—more comfortable emotionally than modern suburbia." (*Bonanza*, set in Nevada in the 1860s, was one of the top-rated network dramas of the 1960s.) In a televised conversation for the BBC with John Lennon and Yoko Ono, McLuhan said, "What people see is a rearview mirror. The future of the future is the present. The past went thataway."

In a *Newsweek* cover story published about McLuhan in March 1967, novelist George P. Elliott said, "It is not possible to give a rational summary of McLuhan's ideas. His writing is deliberately antilogical, circular, repetitious, gnomic, outrageous." Yet McLuhan could also be clear. He attributed the generation gap to the fact that the young grew up on TV and the older people didn't, and opined, "Without television there would be no civil rights legislation."

Many in academia discounted him but the American advertising community was enthralled and political conservatives took note. In November of 1967, Ray Price, an adviser to Richard Nixon, wrote the future president a memo about McLuhan's theories, suggesting they be taken into account in the upcoming campaign.

In March 1967, McLuhan and a graphic designer, Quentin Fiore, published a best-selling book called *The Medium Is the Massage*, the title of which was a twist on his earlier work. It sold nearly a million copies. McLuhan divided media into "hot" and "cool" categories (TV was cool) and extolled the power of TV commercials, Fellini films, and other entertainment that communicated in nonlinear ways. An LP version of the book, produced by John Simon, was released on Columbia Records. (Simon went on to produce *Music from Big Pink* by the Band and *Cheap Thrills* by Big Brother and the Holding Company the following year.) For a moment, McLuhan was the Western world's most famous public intellectual.

Timothy Leary attributed "Turn on, tune in, drop out" directly to McLuhan; he said it had been cooked up at a lunch in late 1966. McLuhan also befriended Abbie Hoffman, John Lennon, and Yoko Ono, but no one's counterculture shtick owed more to McLuhan than Jerry Rubin, who used McLuhan collaborator Quentin Fiore to design his book *Do It!*, which contained many McLuhanesque observations aimed at the radical community, including:

Walter Cronkite is SDS's best organizer.

Have you ever seen a boring demonstration on TV? Just being on TV makes it exciting . . .

Television creates myths bigger than reality.

Every reporter is a dramatist, creating a theater out of life.

I never understand the radical who comes on TV in a suit and tie. Turn off the sound and he could be the mayor!

You can't be a revolutionary today without a television set— it's as important as a gun!

MASS MEDIA

Many network TV programs, popular radio shows, and mass-circulation news weeklies such as *Newsweek*, *Look*, and the *Saturday Evening Post*, along with major dailies like the *New York Times*, gave extensive coverage to various aspects of the counterculture. Although they often did so through jaundiced eyes and they distorted things, the mere exposure of certain ideas and images magnified their power enormously. The playing field also included magazines aimed at men, such as *Esquire* and *Cavalier*, that wanted to reach young guys with long hair.

The most schizophrenic was *Playboy*, which persisted in conveying a fifties fantasy view of the sexuality of women while giving significant editorial space to interviews with countercultural figures like Leary, Dr. King, and Lenny Bruce. In 1967, Ward Just of the *Washington Post* wrote, "If World War II was a war of *Stars and Stripes* and Betty Grable, the war in Vietnam is *Playboy* magazine's war." *Playboy* ran articles as early as 1965 sharply criticizing America's policies in Vietnam, but made sure to write sympathetically of the soldiers themselves. Antiwar

118 ❦ Danny Goldberg

journalist David Halberstam wrote about the troops in *Playboy* in 1971: "We admired their bravery and their idealism, their courage and dedication in the face of endless problems. We believed that they represented the best of American society." In a 2017 *New York Times* article, Amber Batura explained, "Troops in Vietnam could turn to *Playboy* for coverage of their own war without fearing criticism of themselves."

The most influential magazines by far were the newsweeklies *Time* and *Life*, both of which were part of the media empire controlled by their founder, Henry R. Luce. In his 1980 memoir *Soon to Be a Major Motion Picture*, Abbie Hoffman wrote, "I've always maintained that Henry Luce did much more to popularize acid than Timothy Leary. Years later I met Clare Boothe Luce at the Republican Convention in Miami. She did not disagree with this opinion."

On the surface, this is a bizarre contention because Luce was a political conservative who had coined the phrase "The American Century" in a 1941 essay. His wife Clare was a Republican congresswoman in the forties and the US ambassador to Italy and Brazil during the Eisenhower administration. Yet both Henry and Clare took LSD in the 1950s, and as a result, the Luce publications gave repeated mass exposure to psychedelics, most of it positive.

Miami University professor Stephen Siff wrote that Luce "was unembarrassed by his use of LSD, likely seeing himself as similar to the respectable, traditionally minded spiritual seekers depicted using the drug in his magazines." In an article for *Slate*, Jack Schafer listed half a dozen pieces in *Time* and *Life* magazines that celebrated psychedelics, including the 1957 *Life* article "Seeking the Magic Mushroom," which is what motivated Timothy Leary to go to Mexico to try the stuff.

Mrs. Luce's acid trips were recorded in her papers, now at the Library of Congress. She giddily described sorting mosaic glass by her swimming pool and looking through a kaleidoscope. When Henry first took the drug, he asked UCLA professor Sidney Cohen (who himself had taken LSD) to record notes, including the observation, "Now things are getting sharper . . . This perception is wonderful." When Cohen's book *The Beyond Within: The L.S.D. Story* was published, *Time* gave it a rave review.

There were also numerous TV talk shows that welcomed members of hip culture, but often put them in adversarial situations. This was especially common on *The Alan Burke Show* and *The Joe Pyne Show*, whose hosts were forerunners of conservative talk radio tough guys. Also broadcast on national TV were the more effete *The David Susskind Show* and the newly minted *Firing Line* hosted by William F. Buckley Jr., whose contempt for all things liberal and radical was balanced by an intellectual curiosity and commitment to making guests feel relatively comfortable.

UNDERGROUND PRESS

New York had the most media because the population of the city and its surrounding suburbs was over ten million people, much greater than any other American metropolis. New York's bohemian, intellectual, and beatnik roots gave rise to hip ideas even before the Beatles and Vietnam were household words. At several New

York City tabloids there were guys who had favorably written about the civil rights movement, the beats, and jazz and folk music, including Nat Hentoff, Pete Hamill, Jimmy Breslin, and Al Aronowitz. (Aronowitz carved a special place in history for himself when he introduced the Beatles to Bob Dylan, who proceeded to turn the Fab Four onto pot for the first time.)

However, most of the straight press always felt a step away from the "real world" of hipness. Mass media popularized but also distorted youth culture. Even the most empathetic writers felt obliged to maintain an "objective" distance that often made coverage seem more like they were trying to explain our frame of mind to our parents' generation than writing for us.

This dilemma was addressed in part by the advent of a more personal, subjective "new journalism" that started to emerge in the late sixties. Tom Wolfe and Joan Didion were among its stars, but even literary talents of that caliber maintained a critical distance.

By contrast, people in the underground media regarded themselves as *advocates* of the counterculture, not merely as reporters. Their unabashed enthusiasm was part of what made us trust them even if the quality of the writing was uneven.

In the early and midsixties, the *Village Voice* was the only publication in New York that articulated some of the criticisms of the establishment that my friends and I were developing. As the sixties culture exploded, the *Voice* kept a foot in the old left intellectual world and off-Broadway theater and downtown art galleries, while increasingly embracing the counterculture. The *Voice* was one of the first publications to review rock music with intellectual rigor, first by Richard Goldstein and later by Robert Christgau.

The *New York Review of Books* was created in 1963 during a strike of New York dailies by Robert B. Silvers, Barbara Epstein, A. Whitney Ellsworth, and Elizabeth Hardwick. They were encouraged by Epstein's husband, Jason Epstein, an editorial director at Random House, and Hardwick's husband, poet Robert Lowell, and they published an extraordinary array of literary luminaries in early issues, including Hannah Arendt, W.H. Auden, Truman Capote, Paul Goodman, Lillian Hellman, Norman Mailer, Mary McCarthy, Susan Sontag, William Styron, Gore Vidal, Robert Penn Warren, and Edmund Wilson. In addition to book reviews, they printed interviews with Soviet dissidents, such as Aleksandr Solzhenitsyn and Andrei Sakharov, but on American issues, the political and cultural attitude was staunchly left wing, particularly regarding the Vietnam War.

Other publications that sometimes displayed the opinions of the older left included the *New Yorker, Harper's*, the *New Republic* (it would not turn to the right until the eighties), the *Nation*, and *I.F. Stone's Weekly*, a favorite of my parents because of Stone's uncompromising position on McCarthy during the fifties. For the most part these publications viewed the counterculture as an unserious movement in a serious time.

To the rapidly expanding population of antiwar protesters and potheads, even these virtuous publications often felt passé. The first to fill the vacuum was the *Los Angeles Free Press*, started by Art Kunkin in 1964. At the age of thirty-four, Kunkin had managed the Social Workers Party publication the *Militant*, and he recognized that humorless Marxist rhetoric was not going to connect with the kids with long hair. The *Freep*, as it became known, covered rock and roll and dope, as well as a wide variety of protests, and it became the bulletin board for the free concerts that took place most weekends in LA following the Easter Be-In.

The following year, the *East Village Other* (known by the acronym *EVO*) was born in New York. *EVO* was less literary, but far more outrageous and profane than the *Voice*, and it found an immediate audience of young New York freaks like the kids I hung out with.

In a missive posted in 2002 on a website commemorating *EVO*'s reign from 1965–72, Ed Sanders recalled, "During the summer of 1965, [Walter] Bowart, [Allen] Katzman, and others . . . decided to found a newspaper. Poet Ted Berrigan . . . came up with the name the *East Village Other*, with 'Other' coming, of course, from Rimbaud's famous line of 1871, 'Je est un autre,' I is an Other. Another account has Ishmael Reed coining the name." Sanders continued, "*EVO* became a soapbox for The New Vision. It was part of a generation that fervently believed that important and long-lasting changes would occur in the United States which would bring free medical care to all . . . plus an end to war and the growth of personal freedom and good vibes." *EVO* was also known for innovative graphics and introduced alt-comic artists Art Spiegelman and R. Crumb to New York readers.

Like mainstream tabloids, the underground press could gravitate toward crass sensationalism to help sell papers, and was sometimes crude at a moment just before sexism and homophobia were recognized as reactionary pathologies. *EVO* had a weekly photo feature of women that referenced the Fugs song lyric, "*Slum goddess from the Lower East Side.*"

By the end of the decade, there were more than one hundred such alternative weeklies around the country aimed at freaks. Although the underground press people saw themselves as part of the countercultural movements, they still had to survive as small businesses. EVO's flyer to ad agencies read,

> *Do you want to reach the thousands who influence the tastemakers? A dynamic new media exists . . . Ours is an influential audience. It is a buying audience that is first to respond. Local advertisers have found it to be an effective selling media. Ask yourself, "Who's hip?" Then ask, "Do I want to reach them?" If you do, our media will serve your needs. Try us.*

A coordinating organization called Underground Press Syndicate (UPS) was formed in April 1967 at a meeting in San Francisco at Michael Bowen's place, not long after the Easter Be-Ins. Among those who attended were Art Kunkin of the *Los Angeles Free Press*, Katzman and Bowart of *EVO*, Max Scherr of the *Berkeley Barb*, as well as representatives from the *Fifth Estate*, Chicago's *Seed*, Austin's *The Rag*, and Mendocino's *Illustrated Paper*.

Predictably, Peter Berg of the Diggers barged in midway through, accusing them of elitism. The underground press people took the chastisement in stride, but the scrutiny of the radicals now informed the way they thought about themselves. The EVO guys said they needed to get national ads from companies based in New York, but they also felt obliged to concoct a movement rationale: they would also give coverage to certain rock records and books that would undermine the corporate state.

The one tangible result was an agreement among the papers that they could share each other's articles at no cost. The UPS issued a statement of values, which included a commitment to:

—*Warn the "civilized world" of its impending collapse, through communications among aware communities outside the establishment and by attracting the attention of the mass media*
—*Note and chronicle events leading to collapse*
—*Advise intelligently to prevent rapid collapse and make transition possible*
—*Prepare the American public for the wilderness*
—*Fight a holding action in dying cities*

Allen Cohen later wrote, "This statement indicates clearly the apocalyptic feeling of the time. Even the war seemed to us to be a symptom or symbol of the general fall of the American civilization."

My favorite underground publication was the *Realist*. When I had my ears glued to a transistor radio under my pillow during high school, listening to WBAI late-night shows, no one turned on my brain more than *Realist* editor Paul Krassner, who was a regular guest on *Radio Unnameable*. A former *Mad* magazine writer, Krassner started publishing the *Realist* in 1958 when he was twenty-six. Instead of a typical editorial title, Krassner listed himself in the satirical magazine's masthead as "Zen Bastard." Among his memorable aphorisms were,

"Irreverence is our only sacred cow," and, "No Vietcong ever called me Whitey."

Krassner did a series of "impolite interviews," the first of which was with Alan Watts, soon to be followed by Dick Gregory, Joseph Heller, and Norman Mailer, with whom Krassner had a spirited debate about masturbation (Krassner was for it, Mailer against). Mort Sahl wanted to have a mock trial of President Johnson, Dean Rusk, and Robert McNamara, and suggested Krassner as defense counsel, to which the Zen Bastard replied, "My plan is to plead insanity." Another early subject was Krassner's friend Lenny Bruce. Krassner would later edit the comedian's autobiography, *How to Talk Dirty and Influence People*.

Paul Krassner

In 1963, when anticommunism was still a centerpiece of mainstream American political ideology and censorship still a real threat to writers, the *Realist* sold a red, white, and blue bumper sticker that read, *FUCK COMMUNISM*. Novelist Kurt Vonnegut described the publication as "a miracle of compressed intelligence nearly as admirable for potent simplicity, in my opinion, as Einstein's $E=mc^2$ . . . At the beginning of the 1960s, FUCK was believed to be so full of bad magic as to be unprintable . . . By having FUCK and COMMUNISM fight it out in a single sentence, Krassner wasn't merely being funny as heck. He was demonstrating how preposterous it was for so many people to be responding to both words with such cockamamie Pavlovian fear and alarm." Krassner made thousands of dollars selling the bumper stickers and with some of the proceeds he paid for a ticket for radical journalist Robert Scheer to travel to Vietnam, one of the first nonestablishment writers to report on the war.

Until his early thirties, Krassner eschewed all drugs and alcohol, but after hearing about LSD from many friends, he took it for the first time in April 1965 at Timothy Leary's house in Millbrook. Just as Aldous Huxley has been transported by listening to Bach a decade earlier, Krassner absorbed the soundtrack to *A Hard Day's Night* and wept. For his second trip, he hung out with Richard Alpert at the Village Vanguard. Then, in early 1966, he went to San Francisco and participated in one of Ken Kesey's "Acid Tests."

Krassner had the Diggers guest-edit an issue of the *Realist* and he himself did an interview with the *Oracle* in 1967. Here's an excerpt:

Oracle: *Did your atheism change after LSD in any quantitative way?*

Krassner: *No, no! How could it change? There was a different god I didn't believe in. People were Christian before Christ ever existed. People were humanistic before Humanism was ever organized. People were very loving before LSD was ever discovered.*

Oracle: *Leary said that in ten years we'll have a psychedelic president.*

Krassner: *Just because Bobby Kennedy takes Dexedrine doesn't mean he's psychedelic.*

In San Francisco, *Ramparts* magazine had started as an insular Catholic publication earlier in the sixties with a circulation of several thousand copies, but in 1964 it became the most sophisticated of counterculture publications when Warren Hinckle took over as publisher. He immediately hired Robert Scheer, the journalist Krassner had sent to Vietnam, and soon named him as editor. *Ramparts* was the only underground publication to have a glossy cover that could be displayed along with straight magazines, and it was one of the few with original international reporting. In 1967, it ran a photo essay titled "The Children of Vietnam," one of the key catalysts that led Dr. King to criticize America's involvement in the war for the first time. *Ramparts* published Che Guevara's diaries, including an introduction by Fidel Castro. *Ramparts* was also the first to publish the diaries of future Black Panther leader Eldridge Cleaver, which were later expanded into the best-selling book *Soul on Ice*.

When Greek prime minister Andreas Papandreou was imprisoned by a military junta in 1967, his then-wife Margaret asked for help from Los Angeles activist Stanley Sheinbaum. Sheinbaum met with several of the junta's chief witnesses against Papandreou, who said their testimonies against the prime minister had been coerced; they then reiterated this on the record to Scheer. The resulting *Ramparts* article triggered Papandreou's release.

The magazine was also known for compelling covers, such as one which had a photo of four hands of the magazine's senior staff burning draft cards. By 1967, *Ramparts'* national circulation was up to a quarter of a million.

My favorite example of the way the underground/mainstream media feedback loop worked is a false story that spread like wildfire in early 1967 suggesting that people could get high by scraping the inside of banana peels, boiling the residue, drying it, rolling the resulting "bananadine" into a joint, and smoking it. As with many stories from the stoned sixties, there are various versions in print, but I am pretty sure it all started at a concert by Country Joe and the Fish.

EVO, the *Oracle*, and the *Realist* all blurred the lines between reporting, embellishing, and being taken in by a story that was too much fun to ignore. (The *EVO*'s website has a great recap of this story in a piece called "Anatomy of the Great Banana-Smoking Hoax of 1967," by Cary Abrams and Brooke Kroeger.) As Joe McDonald wrote on his website in 2008, the band was on a plane ride to a gig at the Kitsilano Theatre in Vancouver in mid-February 1967 when the band's drummer, Gary "Chicken" Hirsh, told him that he had heard that there was a chemical in banana peels that could get you high if you smoked it. Hirsh's notion that banana skins had the same hallucinogen in it as marijuana was erroneous, but Joe was happy to believe it for the moment. "We were living on peanut butter and banana sandwiches at the time and just throwing the peelings away, so this seemed like a good idea."

At the very same concert, the band's crew told them they were putting LSD into a water bottle in case anyone wanted to trip. They all had some, but because water with LSD tastes just like water without it, and because the banana thing had such an appeal to them, when the band got very high during the show, they attributed it to smoking the "bananadine" joints they'd rolled.

A week later, when they noticed that the subsequent smoking of bananas didn't have any effect on them, they realized that it had simply been the acid. However, during those few days before that occurred to them, their manager ED Denson wrote a *Berkeley Barb* column that referenced people getting high on smoked banana peels in Vancouver and even provided the "recipe" for how to do so.

At almost exactly the same time, Donovan's *Mellow Yellow* album was released. A few months earlier the title song had been a hit single so everyone in the hip world knew the lyric, "*Electrical banana is gonna be a sudden craze.*" Years later, Donovan would reveal that he was referring to a banana-shaped vibrator that had just been produced in England, but having heard about the banana-smoking rumors in America just before the album's release, he was coy about it in interviews at the time and he succeeded in making himself seem like he was ahead of the curve.

On the day the editors of *EVO* came across Denson's column in the *Barb*, Paul Krassner happened to be hanging out in their office. He had just finished reading a metaphysical book called *The Morning of the Magicians*, which said that one of LSD's primary effects was the release of serotonin in the brain. He mistakenly thought that bananas contained it too. That was enough for *EVO* to run a story about bananas. The *Oracle*, not wanting to be left behind, ran its own version of the story as well.

Within days, on March 4, the *San Francisco Chronicle* had a *front-page* story saying a Haight Street store window had a recipe for how to prepare banana peels to get high. Jerry Rubin, who in the wake of the Be-In was doing everything he could to cozy up to hippies, told the reporter that bananas "work every time." By March 14, UPI picked it up from a student newspaper in Ann Arbor and it became a national story, soon covered in the *New York Times*.

To a teenager like me, rock stars like Donovan seemed to be a vessel for wisdom. If Donovan said something was going to be the "next phase," it seemed like a good bet. And we wanted to believe it. To be able to easily get high without having to worry about being busted or feigning friendship with dope dealers? Heaven!

Thus, like many thousands of kids subject to the same echo chamber, some of my friends and I tried smoking bananas and we found out immediately that this did absolutely nothing to alter our consciousness. As far as we were concerned it was a dead issue, but the "story" would linger for a few months.

On March 30, the *Wall Street Journal* had a story with the headline, "Light Up a Banana: Students Bake Peels to Kick Up Their Heels. Exhilarating Effect Is Gained by Legal Puffing, Some Say; A Marijuana Farm Lies Idle." On April 7, *Time* ran a piece focusing on the speed with which information about the psychedelic counterculture spread.

Some on the radical left took the banana fad as an example of hedonism on the part of stoners. Todd Gitlin wrote an "Open Letter to the Hippies," reminding them that the primary importer of bananas to the United States was the United Fruit Company, which was complicit in imperialist oppression in Latin America.

On the April 10 telecast of the Academy Awards, host Bob Hope quipped, "Instead of dinner tonight I just smoked a banana." It had taken less than two months for a hippie fantasy to become a mainstream joke.

Politicians predictably jumped into the fray. On April 19, Congressman Frank Thompson, a New Jersey Democrat, introduced the Banana Labeling Act, requiring a warning sticker similar to that on cigarette packaging. Shortly thereafter, Dr. James Goddard, commissioner of the Food and Drug Administration (FDA), declared that the agency would be conducting tests to determine if smoking banana peels was intoxicating. On May 29, the FDA announced that the tests resulted in "no detectable quantities of known hallucinogens."

THE COVER OF *TIME*

Time had a long tradition of naming a "Man of the Year" (now, "Person of the Year"), and at the beginning of 1966 they had given the nod to the head of the US armed forces in Vietnam, General William Westmoreland. One year later, they named the entire generation of people "twenty-five and younger" as their "People of the Year."

On July 7, 1967, *Time*'s cover story was "The Hippies: Philosophy of a Subculture." Group Image, the New York music and art commune, designed the cover. Although there were a few obligatory sarcastic lines (a photo caption read, "Beards, beads, and bangles—conforming nonconformity"), the writer (*Time* did not have bylines with their pieces in those days) clearly had more affection for the culture than was typically found in mainstream media. The piece began: "One sociologist calls them 'the Freudian proletariat.' Another observer sees them as 'expatriates living on our shores but beyond our society.' Historian Arnold Toynbee describes them as 'a red warning light for the American way of life.' For California's Bishop James Pike, they evoke the early Christians: 'There is something about the temper and quality of these people, a gentleness, a quietness, an interest— something good.'" Only in the second paragraph was it acknowledged that to worried parents, "[hippies] seem more like dangerously deluded dropouts."

The article asserted that if there were such a thing as a hippie "code," it would include:

> —*Do your own thing, wherever you have to do it and whenever you want.*
> —*Drop out. Leave society as you have known it. Leave it utterly.*
> —*Blow the mind of every straight person you can reach. Turn them on, if not to drugs, then to beauty, love, honesty, fun.*

Time estimated that there were around three hundred thousand self-identified hippies in the US at the time, and that they were predominantly white, middle class, educated, and ranging in age from seventeen to twenty-five. "Hippies preach altruism and mysticism, honesty, joy, and nonviolence . . . Their professed aim is nothing less than the subversion of Western society by 'flower power' and the force of example."

In deference to *Time*'s Cold War politics (and consistent with the worst nightmares of political radicals), the five pages of text and six additional pages of photos mentioned neither Vietnam nor civil rights nor any other political issues intertwined with hip culture. The closest they came to acknowledging hippie engagement in the larger society were references to a New York protest of leash laws for dog owners, a $2,100 bail fund for people busted for pot, and a report from Dallas that a hundred "flower children" had protested an ordinance that would prohibit public gatherings at Stone Place Mall. (In other sections of the same issue, *Time* reported on the recent race riots in Buffalo and how troop levels in Vietnam were up to 463,000 while some generals said they needed to get the number to 600,000.)

Most of the photos showed anonymous hippies at locales such as a rural commune, a crash pad on the Lower East Side, and a geodesic dome in Drop City, Colorado. The only images of living celebrities were of Timothy Leary ("Grand shaman of psychedelia"), the Grateful Dead, and the Beatles. There were also photos of Henry David Thoreau, Mahatma Gandhi, Aldous Huxley, Gautama Buddha, and St. Francis, who were called "antecedents from the past."

The *Time* cover story printed the *Random House Dictio-*

nary of the English Language's definition of "psychedelic": "Of or noting a mental state of great calm, intensely pleasurable perception of the senses, esthetic entrancement and creative impetus; of or noting any of the group of drugs producing this effect." The magazine went on to write favorably of "an impassioned belief in the self-revealing, mind-expanding powers of potent weeds and seeds and chemical compounds known to man since prehistory but wholly alien to the rationale of Western society." University of Chicago theologian Martin E. Marty was quoted on the subject of hippies: "They reveal 'the exhaustion of a tradition: Western, production-directed, problem-solving, goal-oriented and compulsive in its way of thinking.'" An unnamed West Coast hippie defined shared counterculture values: "The standard thing is to feel in the gut that middle-class values are wrong . . . the way America recognizes that communism is all wrong."

The piece ended on as positive a note as it had begun:

Indeed, it could be argued that in their independence of material possessions and their emphasis on peacefulness and honesty, hippies lead considerably more virtuous lives than the great majority of their fellow citizens. This, despite their blatant disregard for most of society's accepted mores and many of its laws—most notably those prohibiting the use of drugs—helps explain why so many people in authority, from cops to judges to ministers, tend to treat them gently and with a measure of respect. In the end it may be that hippies have not so much dropped out of American society as given it something to think about.

Michael Simmons, who was twelve years old at the time and would later edit the *National Lampoon* and write for *Mojo* and *Rolling Stone*, recalls treasuring that issue of *Time*: "I carried it around for years."

Of course, while all of this media, above- and underground, were making connections in the "global village," there was another form of communication in 1967 that touched most baby boomers more deeply than all of the underground and mainstream papers and TV shows put together, and it usually involved a guitar.

CHAPTER 4
ELECTRIC MUSIC FOR THE MIND AND BODY

The "lost chord" of this book's title is metaphorical, but many of the actual chords of sixties music are the most evocative surviving manifestations of the spirit of the times. There are hundreds of books focused on individual artists who made memorable music in 1967, as well as countless playlists, box sets, radio programs, and PBS fundraising specials that enshrine and comment on them.

As a former rock critic, I am well aware that any attempt to curate music from the sixties is fraught with peril. I reiterate that this book is a subjective history and it is not remotely comprehensive. The intent is to give a bit of context for how some music of the period interacted with other aspects of the culture. Dozens of great artists and pieces of music go unmentioned, including many whom I love.

UNDERGROUND RADIO
Even though as a teenager in the sixties I had no idea that there was a music industry that helped connect us to the songs that reflected our version of the real world,

business did indeed affect us. The most effective way for artists to reach listeners was to get their music heard, and the most effective means was radio play. Previously, this would have excluded a lot of "underground" bands, but American radio was being reinvented in San Francisco in 1967.

Tom Donahue was a successful thirty-nine-year-old deejay on the San Francisco Top 40 station KYA; he began each show with his trademark line: "Here to blow your mind and clean up your face." He had become a fan of the local acid rock scene, even though most of these artists never got played on Top 40 radio. The Doors *did* have a Top 40 hit with "Light My Fire" on their eponymous debut album, but one night in January 1967, Donahue stayed up all night playing the album over and over again, and it occurred to him that there was an unserved audience who were drawn to entire albums and songs like "The End," which was more than eleven minutes long, nearly triple the length of anything that could get played on Top 40 radio (and way too weird).

The Pacifica radio stations' foray into hip late-night programming in LA and New York were anomalies. Hundreds of other FM stations in America primarily aired classical music and foreign-language or public-affairs programming, and they made very little money. Donahue discovered that KMPX in San Francisco was hovering near bankruptcy and he persuaded the owners to give him control over most of their programming for the new format that he would create, focusing on the music young hippies liked.

On Friday, April 7, 1967, Donahue's new format of "free-form," album-based rock music was launched

with "no jingles, no talk-overs, no time and temperature, no pop singles." It was an immediate success. By
the time I first visited the Bay Area in August, it seemed
like KMPX was being broadcast in every store and every
car in Berkeley. One could walk several blocks and never
miss a song or an intro. Advertising money quickly came
from hip stores and concert promoters. Since Donahue
insisted that commercials either be tailored for KMPX
or produced by his staff, the ads didn't interfere much
with the vibe of the station. Local artists like Janis Joplin regularly showed up at KMPX. When Joe Smith of
Warner Bros. Records wanted to offer the Grateful Dead a
record deal, it was Donahue who made the introduction.

Within months, FM stations in many other cities
were hiring freaks to replicate Donahue's format. There
was a new baby boomer market to address, and more
than half of FM receivers in the country could now
broadcast in stereo. There was also legal pressure. Effective in 1965, the FCC had ruled that in markets with
over one hundred thousand in population, FM stations
that were owned by AMs had to limit the amount of
time they simulcast the AM signal; this created a need
for cheap, original programming.

In Southern California, Donahue himself initially programmed KPPC, which was broadcast out of a church
basement in Pasadena. KPPC could be heard in the Los
Angeles market, and it was where Elliot Mintz would
soon move his show.

As Mintz recalls, "AM deejays shouted at amphet-
amine-driven speed, using virtually the same language
that jocks used in the fifties. On FM, it was as if you
would meet someone on the street who would describe

an experience with you. We heard disc jockeys talking *our* language. They didn't sound like radio announcers, they sounded like *us*. When they talked about music it was like they were explaining to a friend what a concert was like."

As much as the deejays identified with the hippie culture, they were subject to FCC-imposed limitations and a much straighter ownership culture than the underground press had. No songs with dirty words, no cursing on the air, and at some stations, no politics. On October 9, 1967, Donahue wrote to the KMPX staff: "Just a reminder that KMPX is a music station. Stay away from political comments or opinions. And since we do not broadcast the news, stay away from any news that doesn't involve music or musicians. The music is sufficient to speak for us."

The music spoke very loudly. For artists like Country Joe and the Fish and the Grateful Dead, "underground" was the only radio exposure they got and, as it turned out, all that they needed. For the first year or two of the format, there was no research on what worked with audiences, so the deejays programmed their own shows intuitively and could go from the blues to Ravi Shankar to Jimi Hendrix. They played long songs like Dylan's eleven-minute "Desolation Row," and invented creative tricks like the "segue" of one song into another. When the Beatles' *Sgt. Pepper's Lonely Hearts Club Band* was released in the summer, KMPX played it in its entirety—a notion that seems obvious in retrospect, but was a novelty at the time.

During the few years before corporate broadcasters took over the programming, Mintz recalls wistfully,

"We were beating on tom-toms and saying, *Hello in there . . . you're not crazy*. There wasn't first class and caboose. We were all in it together."

THE FILLMORE

By the end of 1965, the growing audience for psychedelic rock in San Francisco had created a new business. Bill Graham opened the Fillmore Auditorium on December 10, 1965, with Jefferson Airplane as the headliner.

Graham was born as Wulf Wolodia Grajonca to a Jewish family in Berlin, Germany. He was sent away to escape the Nazi regime, and was raised in a foster home in the Bronx from the time he was ten years old. He had moved to San Francisco in the early sixties, and initially he'd had aspirations to be an actor, but when he couldn't get that career going he took to managing the San Francisco Mime Troupe, a countercultural collective that was integral to the formation of the hippie scene (and which gave rise to the Diggers). Graham was soon involved as a promoter in several of the early psychedelic dances.

Graham was thirty-five years old when he opened the Fillmore. He had a vision of how the new iteration of rock and roll should be presented. He commissioned posters by local psychedelic artists such as Rick Griffin and Mouse, which soon became cherished expressions of the culture. Unlike conventional promoters who presented rock shows as cheaply as possible, Graham treated each show as an art form. He printed programs, and featured the kinds of light shows that Ken Kesey had experimented with.

Graham was the prototype of a kind of hippie businessman who genuinely understood a lot about the youth culture and who was personally well liked by most of the bands, but who was also unapologetic about the fact that he was running a business. He exuded a gleeful sense of entitlement when it came to making a profit.

Although assorted radical groups sometimes demonized him, Graham walked the line between a genuine understanding of hippie culture and the tough realities of the music business far better than any of his competitors. He was the very opposite of "laid back." He paced nervously backstage with a clipboard and personally introduced many of the shows onstage, raging at anyone who disrespected his concept of what made the Fillmore special.

Because he did so much business on the East Coast and would soon open a Fillmore East in New York, Graham ostentatiously wore a Movado watch that showed the time on both coasts. His earthy charisma worked as well on the local cops as it did on acidheads. Although he was capable of blowing up at an artist who refused to do an extra encore, Graham loved many of the bands who played for him. Artists may not have made the percentage of profits from Fillmore concerts that would later become the norm, but they felt appreciated and safe when they played there. There was a moment at the Trips Festival in 1966 when Jerry Garcia broke his guitar and Graham tried to repair it. Although the instrument proved to be unfixable, Garcia appreciated the intensity of his effort and a bond was formed that served Graham well. If a business guy was okay with the Dead, he was okay with most other artists as well.

142 ¥ Danny Goldberg

The San Francisco Sound

The Grateful Dead never had a hit song in the sixties, but they were one of the highest-profile embodiments of what came to be known as the "San Francisco Sound." They were one of the first rock bands to have two drummers—Mickey Hart and Bill Kreutzmann—and they had four members who could sing: Ron "Pigpen" McKernan, who also played the harmonica and organ, guitarist Bob Weir, bassist Phil Lesh, and Jerry Garcia, who played lead guitar, sang many of the lead vocals, and emerged as the first among equals in the eyes of most people in the extended Haight-Ashbury family.

Garcia was always very clear about the centrality of LSD to the creation of the Grateful Dead's sound and attitude. Describing their first performances at Kesey's "Acid Tests," he said, "The audience didn't come to see us but to experience something altogether different. We had the luxury of playing where nothing was expected of us. It gave us glimpses in the form that follows chaos. When you throw out all the rules, other stuff starts to happen. That was a clue to how we dealt with things in our interior way. I can't imagine any other context which would have allowed us to learn that." Mickey Hart adds, "We were just the soundtrack of the culture. We weren't playing singles. We'd play four or five hours. How are you going to bottle that?"

The Dead were mostly apolitical, but this was not the case with Country Joe and the Fish, whose name was inspired by a quotation from Mao Tse-tung that said that a "guerrilla" is like a fish that swims in the ocean of the people. They had an attitude that didn't pander in the slightest to the music business, and the ability to evoke the psychedelic spirits in concert. Donahue once said, "I don't trust anyone who doesn't like Country Joe and the Fish."

I got into the band earlier than most kids on the East Coast by another one of the quirks of fate that seemed routine at the time. One day in early 1967, a bunch of kids went over to Susan Solomon's house. Susan was a year behind me at Fieldston. Her father Seymour was a cofounder of Vanguard Records.

Country Joe McDonald

The Solomons had the best stereo system I had ever encountered—you could hear every nuance. Susan put on a record called *Electric Music for the Mind and Body* by Country Joe and the Fish, who Vanguard had just signed. We were into it right away. The kind of rock and roll they were playing didn't have a name yet, but it was obvious that they were even farther out than Jefferson Airplane, whose "White Rabbit" was a big hit at the time.

Some of us had taken LSD in the last few months and were convinced that we were part of a rarefied elite of teenage expeditionaries and mystics who were trying to discover the meaning of life in a far deeper way than our liberal parents had. My parents were smart and progressive, but their intellectual heroes were pessimistic intellectuals like T.S. Eliot and Eugene O'Neill. We acidheads were into joy. You didn't have to be depressed to be smart! We reveled in the fact that "White Rabbit" used images from *Alice in Wonderland* (which our parents had read to us as "literature") as an obvious metaphor for a psychedelic trip.

Country Joe's guitarist, Barry Melton, played long solos; the singer, Country Joe McDonald, had an attractive combination of fierceness and vulnerability; and the album included an overtly political song called "Superbird" that parodied President Johnson. The last song was called "Grace"; we correctly assumed it was written for the singer of "White Rabbit," Grace Slick. Country Joe also wrote a song that I loved called "Janis" about the Big Brother lead singer who he'd briefly dated. It felt as if there was very little showbiz distance between the band and the listeners. We studied the photos on the back of the album, trying to figure out what made such an intense group of people tick. I was particularly struck by the wild look in the eyes of Country Joe's drummer, Gary "Chicken" Hirsh.

A year or so later, Susan was interning as a substitute receptionist at Vanguard one day when the band visited the label. She and Hirsh instantly connected and by the next day she was staying with him at the Chelsea Hotel. (Paul McCartney and his soon-to-be wife Linda Eastman were beginning their romance at the Chelsea at the same time.)

Susan moved with Hirsh to the Bay Area, where members of the Dead and the Fish called her "Susie Sunshine." They married and soon after she gave birth to their son Adam, now the singer-songwriter and composer Tree Adams. Susan would come back to New York several years later. It had been difficult being a mother in the midst of the psychedelic rock scene and her marriage soon ended. She went to college and law school as a single mother. Years later, she married the Pulitzer Prize–winning writer Paul Goldberger and they had two more sons, Ben and Alex.

By 2016, Susan was the cofounder and CEO of the eleven-year-old New York Stem Cell Foundation Research Institute. When I reconnected with her, I wasn't sure what her feelings would be about the psychedelic sixties given the turmoil of the times and how it personally affected her. Yet her eyes lit up when recalling the era: "There was a sense of possibility then. People felt that they could change the world with love—and briefly, it worked."

In addition to Country Joe and the Fish, there were many other bands who helped form the San Francisco

Sound, including Santana, the Steve Miller Blues Band, Moby Grape, the Quicksilver Messenger Service, and Big Brother and the Holding Company, whose lead singer was Janis Joplin. But the first San Francisco band to make a truly national impact was Jefferson Airplane.

Bassist Jack Casady and guitarist Jorma Kaukonen had been part of the folk scene, and even at the peak of the Airplane's hippie power they played a psychedelic version of Fred Neil's folk song "The Other Side of This Life." The Airplane's sound was unique both because of the instrumental virtuosity of Kaukonen and Casady and the spooky harmonies of Grace Slick and Marty Balin. Slick told me, "We were sloppy and never rehearsed our harmonies the way Crosby, Stills & Nash did later. We just did what we felt like and that's how it came out. When we recorded, the people at RCA thought we were too weird to mess with so they let us do it the way we did in concert. Rock and roll is not Puccini."

Slick was the only true female rock star of the San Francisco scene other than Janis Joplin. She joined the group for their second album. (The band's first album featured vocals by Signe Anderson, who Slick replaced in early 1967.) The Airplane's first hit, "Somebody to Love," was written by Darby Slick, who had been in Grace's first band, the Great Society, along with his brother Jerry (who was married to Grace at the time). In a Facebook post in 2016, Darby explained that the lyrics were written in the wake of President Kennedy's death: "'When the truth is found to be lies, and all the joy within you dies,' was very much about assassination and loss. They took away somebody we loved."

Howie Klein, who later in life became president of

Reprise Records, was a student at the State University of New York in Stony Brook in the late sixties. He had a radio show on the college station and also booked the entertainment at the college. He would go to San Francisco a couple of times a year to buy pot. Bill Graham sent Howie an early tape of the Airplane to play on his show and Howie booked them to perform on February 18, 1967. It was their first trip east after the release of *Surrealistic Pillow*. To save money on hotels, the band crashed at Howie's place.

On June 3, 1967, the Airplane was a guest on the long-running teen rock and dance show *American Bandstand*. Host Dick Clark described the band as "a little controversial." The show clumsily tried to acknowledge the psychedelic moment by shooting their performance of "White Rabbit" on a set which included several lava lamps and a backdrop of a Victorian house shot by a camera which was occasionally turned upside down. After the performance, Clark asked the band, "Do parents have anything to worry about?" Paul Kantner replied, "I think so—their children are doing things that they didn't do and they don't understand."

The Airplane did not shy away from politics the way the Dead did. However, shortly after the release of *Surrealistic Pillow*, the band took some flack from the left because they agreed to do several commercials for Levi's blue jeans. In a letter to the *Village Voice* in May 1967, Abbie Hoffman complained about the endorsement: "It summarized for me all the doubts I have about the hippie philosophy. I realize they are just doing their 'thing,' but while the Jefferson Airplane grooves with its thing, over one hundred workers in the Levi Strauss plant on the Tennessee-Georgia border are doing their thing, which consists of being on strike to protest deplorable working conditions." The band opted out of doing anything more for Levi's; in fact, they never did another commercial for anyone.

Despite Hoffman's criticisms, no lasting damage was done. Hoffman soon became friends with Slick, and the Airplane was the only group written about favorably in Anita Hoffman's *Trashing* (published under the pseudonym Ann Fettamen). On their first trip to New York, in addition to their regular gigs, the band played a free concert for the Diggers on the roof of the Chelsea Hotel.

They were also as into psychedelia as the Dead were. The Airplane visited Leary in Millbrook, and handfuls Orange Sunshine acid were often thrown into the audience at their shows. In her memoir, Grace Slick described her first peyote trip: "Instead of viewing certain things or people as passing scenery, as something inconsequential, the peyote made everything and everyone seem equally important. Suddenly I could see no isolation, no overabundance. It was all just energy, exhibiting itself in infinite dimensions." Not all that different from Huxley's description in the fifties, nor from what my friends and I talked about—that is, when we could actually form the words.

MONTEREY

Lou Adler was thirty-three years old in 1967 and was a powerhouse in the then-small Los Angeles music business. His label Dunhill Records had Steppenwolf under contract, and Adler had produced and released "Eve of Destruction," but his biggest artist was the Mamas

& the Papas, who'd had a string of hits that resonated with hippie audiences. Even though the group did not have a guitar hero and was more pop than rock, the Mamas & the Papas' harmonies and lyrics connected with potheads (especially on the song "California Dreaming") and the photos of the band on the album cover gave them a distinctly hip aura. Adler and John Phillips, the group's leader, were approached by promoter Alan Pariser and William Morris agent Benny Shapiro, who had a contract with the fairgrounds where Monterey Jazz Festival had been taking place. They were planning the first Pop Festival, and they'd booked Ravi Shankar and some blues acts but they realized they needed a bigger name to sell tickets.

"They offered us more than the Mamas & the Papas usually got for a show," remembers Adler, "but that night at three in the morning, John called me with the idea that to do something special, all of the artists should perform for free with profits going to charity." Phillips thought that with this approach they could afford to have three days' worth of performances and thereby do justice to the cultural moment. Benny Shapiro was old-school and hated the idea. So Phillips, Adler, Johnny Rivers, Paul Simon, and Terry Melcher each put up $10,000 to buy him out. Phillips and Adler opened an office at the old Renaissance Jazz Club on Sunset Boulevard in LA to pull the festival together. They only had seven weeks before June 16, which would be the opening night of the festival.

Simon & Garfunkel immediately committed, as did Johnny Rivers and the Byrds. To broaden their reach, Adler enlisted Andrew Loog Oldham, the producer and manager of the Rolling Stones, who had temporarily moved to Los Angeles to avoid his native London. Mick Jagger and Keith Richards had been busted for drugs in Keith's Redlands home weeks earlier and Oldham didn't want to attract the attention of the London police. He recruited the Who for the festival, and also asked Paul McCartney for advice on artists. The Beatle said that Jimi Hendrix was a must. The twenty-five-year-old Hendrix had recently electrified London club audiences with his mind-blowing virtuoso fusion of blues and rock guitar, and had dazzled the Beatles by playing a psychedelic version of the title song on their newly released *Sgt. Pepper's Lonely Hearts Club Band* at London's Albert Hall.

Then the Monterey team headed north. Adler acknowledges, "We knew we needed the fresh rock and roll coming out of San Francisco, and that people there thought of us as slick and commercial." It didn't help that Phillips had just written and produced "San Francisco (Be Sure to Wear Some Flowers in Your Hair)" for Scott McKenzie. It was an instant hit on Top 40 radio, but was perceived by the Haight hippies as a simplistic exploitation of their scene. Adler, Oldham, and Phillips flew up to San Francisco for a meeting with the managers of the Dead and the Airplane. Adler remembers, "It almost came to blows and I couldn't figure out what the fight was about. I guess they thought we were somehow gonna make money from their culture."

In his memoir *Living with the Dead: Twenty Years on the Bus with Garcia and the Grateful Dead*, the band's former manager Rock Scully gives his version:

It starts with John and Michelle Phillips of the Mamas &
the Papas coming to see us, representing themselves as fel-
low musicians who have also taken acid or maybe *taken*
acid . . . Phillips is a musician whose group we respect, but
why, we wonder, is he talking like that? The hip malaprop-
isms, the music-biz clichés, the fake sincerity. We are soon
to discover that once you get beyond the fur hat and the
beads he is just like a goddamn LA slicko. We all get the
same vibe from him: he's here to exploit the San Francisco
hippie/love phenomenon by building a festival around us
and Janis and Country Joe and Big Brother and Quicksilver
and the Airplane.

Nonetheless, in deference to Oldham, Scully kept a
relatively open mind. The trio of festival guys then met
with *San Francisco Chronicle* columnist Ralph J. Gleason,
a respected figure in the Haight community. Based on
their commitment to donate all profits to charity, Gleason gave the festival his blessing. Scully was impressed
that the Beatles PR adviser Derek Taylor was brought
in to do the press. Paul Simon's enthusiasm also had
weight with some of the San Francisco musicians. Despite lingering misgivings, the Airplane, the Dead, the
Fish, Big Brother and the Holding Company, and Moby
Grape signed on to play at the festival.

The newly powerful KMPX talked up the festival and
ticket sales exceeded expectations. The press office was
overwhelmed with 1,100 requests for credentials. Derek
Taylor said yes to everybody. The international coverage
of Monterey dwarfed even the attention that the Be-In
had received. Moreover, the festival was filmed. In order to pay for the costs of putting it on, Adler had made

a deal for $400,000 with the ABC television network. They chose as the director D.A. Pennebaker, who had made the Dylan documentary *Don't Look Back.*

The crowd at the Monterey County Fairgrounds was so large that having sold twelve thousand tickets, the promoters decided to take down the fence and let another twenty thousand people in for free. Grace Slick recalls, "Even the stalls selling food and concert items were quaint and uninfected by corporate logos and pitchmen. Police cruisers had orchids on their antennas." A large banner on stage read, *LOVE, MUSIC AND FLOWERS.*

Owsley and his partner Rhoney Gissen Stanley were there of course. Mama Cass (of the Mamas & the Papas) asked Owsley to bring acid and he arrived with thousands of purple tablets. He also carried a Murine bottle filled with liquid LSD, which he made available to all of the musicians backstage. Ravi Shankar, who didn't do any drugs at all, angrily walked out of his dressing room when it was offered to him.

Jimi Hendrix, Janis Joplin, and Otis Redding all became overnight rock stars because of media excitement and word of mouth about their performances. Grace Slick wrote of it:

> *Were we, the bands, there to invoke the spirits? The gods? Were we pagan? No labeling was necessary. We were all shamans of equal power. Channeling an unknown energy, seeking fluidity. I felt like a princess in a benign court—one without thrones or crowns. I could see "royalty" in every direction. The audiences was just more of "us." The performers were just more of "us" . . . It was shades of Huxley, Leary, the surrealists, Gertrude Stein, Kafka—the inex-*

haustible list of artists who'd encouraged multiple levels of observation. It was our turn. We were ready to breathe, ready to celebrate change.

Perhaps no artist was more affected by Monterey than Eric Burdon, whose group the Animals had been one of the stars of the British Invasion a few years earlier, most notably with their cover of the old blues song "The House of the Rising Sun." Burdon had been mesmerized by seeing Hendrix take rock and roll to a whole new level in London and was enthralled by the Haight-Ashbury scene and by acid (he wrote a song called "A Girl Named Sandoz," a reference to the original Swiss manufacturer of LSD). The band was well known by the time they took the stage on the first night of the festival. Rock critic Joel Selvin wrote that "Burdon did nothing short of reinvent himself in front of the audience."

Two months later, Eric Burdon and the Animals (as the band was now called) released the single "San Franciscan Nights." The record starts with a spoken word intro by Burdon: "This following program is dedicated to the city and people of San Francisco, who may not know it, but they are beautiful and so is their city." He urged Europeans to "save up all your bread and fly Trans Love Airways to San Francisco, USA. Then maybe you'll understand the song. It will be worth it, if not for the sake of this song, but for the sake of your own peace of mind." In England the B-side was "Gratefully Dead," another gesture of respect to the San Francisco scene. In November, the band released Burdon's song "Monterey," a celebration of the festival, with shout-outs to many of the artists he saw play there.

Adler recalls, "By the end the policemen had flowers in their hair and the national guardsmen had painted flowers on their shaved heads. For one weekend the harsh realities of Vietnam, student unrest, the Cold War, racism, and urban riots were suspended and even transcended."

Brian Jones of the Rolling Stones was there, and at John Lennon's request arranged to have a photographer friend smuggle back a couple dozen of Owsley's purple tabs to London. Also present was actor Dennis Hopper, as well as Peter Tork and Micky Dolenz of the Monkees, who were so impressed with Hendrix that they asked him to open up for them on their upcoming tour. After the first couple of dates, there were so many complaints from parents of young Monkees fans about Hendrix's sexuality that he was dropped, but by then it didn't matter. As Slick says, "If any musician represented that era, it was Jimi Hendrix." His talent was so extraordinary that he immediately entered the pantheon of rock icons alongside the Beatles, the Stones, and Dylan.

Adler, Phillips, and Pennebaker all thought they had a feature film, not a mere TV program. Adler gleefully told me, "ABC was run then by Tom Moore, a Southern 'gentleman,' so we showed him Hendrix fornicating with his guitar and predictably he said, *Not on my network*. He *gave* us the film. They were fine with losing the $400,000. They just wanted to get us out of the office."

The film, *Monterey Pop*, is considered one of the best rock films ever. Yet at the time, its existence fanned flames of mistrust among the San Francisco contingent. The Dead refused to be included unless they could also approve the way they were portrayed and where the foundation made donations—two bridges that were too long for Adler to cross. Joplin initially refused to let the Big Brother set be filmed, but her performance was so explosive that her new manager, Albert Grossman (who also managed Bob Dylan), persuaded her to repeat the set so she could be in the movie. It is now one of the performances Joplin is most remembered for. She had seen Otis Redding at the Fillmore while she was on acid a few days earlier, and later said his show had inspired her to dig deeper.

After the festival, Adler became aware that the Grateful Dead had taken the backline amplifiers from the festival, so he called Scully to ask for them back. "Why don't you come and get them," Scully sneered, "and wear some flowers in your hair."

Gleason had brought a young journalist named Jann Wenner to Monterey. In November, Wenner would start publishing his new magazine, *Rolling Stone*. The first page of the inaugural issue had a piece by Michael Lydon, "The High Cost of Music and Love: Where's the Money from Monterey?" It reported that there was a net profit of $211,451 (including the money from ABC). All of that was given away to various charities by the Monterey International Pop Foundation that Adler and Phillips had set up, but the article implied that the promoters and artists had been profligate in incurring expenses, citing as an example the $345 spent on a hotel room for Johnny Rivers. In a further attempt to ingratiate the new magazine with the Monterey skeptics around the Dead, the piece concluded, "A festival which should and could have been all up front still leaves questions asked and unanswered."

Fifty years later, all income allocated for the festival

producers from licensing of film footage is still given out by the foundation to a variety of organizations in the name of the artists who performed at Monterey. Looking back, the carping seems absurd, but given the sense of dread that the hippie community was experiencing as mass media overwhelmed its subculture, a certain amount of paranoia was to be expected.

NEW YORK

The Lovin' Spoonful's lead guitarist, Zal Yanovsky, left the band in mid-1967 in the wake of a pot bust that had happened earlier in the year in San Francisco. A Canadian citizen fearful of being barred from the States, Yanovsky had been pressured into setting up the bust of a pot dealer, an act for which he was demonized in much of the hip world. There was an unsigned full-page ad in the *Los Angeles Free Press* asking fans not to buy the band's records and women "not to ball them." Ralph Gleason defended the Lovin' Spoonful in an early *Rolling Stone* piece, but the bad vibes ended Yanovsky's role in the group and that pretty much eroded their relevance, although they would not officially disband until 1969.

The Lovin' Spoonful's lead singer, John Sebastian, continued to make wonderful music as a solo artist. In the context of twenty-first-century arena-rock nostalgia, Sebastian is not a commercial giant like Bob Dylan or Eric Clapton, but in 1967, he was as incandescent in creativity and influence as anyone.

The departure of the Lovin' Spoonful from the rock culture was a huge loss and an early wake-up call about the fragility of the scene. The band's fragmentation hit particularly hard in New York City, where they had been the princes of Greenwich Village for most of my high school years. (Louie Gross, the first guy I bought pot from, boasted that he had sold to the Lovin' Spoonful and, man, was I was impressed!)

However, New York hip culture was very resourceful, no one more so than Steve Paul, whose club the Scene briefly became a powerful magnet for rock-and-roll culture. Paul was born in 1941 and at the age of seventeen decided that being a press agent was his path to becoming part of the show-business world that enthralled him. He figured out how to get items into gossip columns in New York City daily newspapers, of which there were seven at the time. "The rule was you needed either to give them three jokes or three pieces of gossip they wanted for every item you'd get for your client," he says. "I wasn't good with jokes so I was spending all my time desperately trying to get people to tell me secrets."

With the energy of obsessive youth, Paul succeeded well enough that at the age of eighteen he got the gig as press agent for the Peppermint Lounge, which became internationally famous as the launching pad of the Twist dance craze.

In 1964, a showbiz vet at the age of twenty-two, Paul hustled the money to open the Scene, which was located on 46th Street near Eighth Avenue. He attracted a unique cultural mix, including Allen Ginsberg, Richard Pryor, Tennessee Williams, Liza Minnelli, and Sammy Davis Jr. Andy Warhol and his "Superstars" were also regular customers. (There is a photo of Edie Sedgwick meeting Mick Jagger at the Scene in the book *Edie: An American Biography*.)

Paul greeted patrons at the door with insults or

cosmic witticisms. Photographer Linda Eastman, who would marry Paul McCartney a couple of years later, was a fixture. The then-unknown Tiny Tim opened most shows with a solo ukulele performance of music from decades past.

The Scene entered another realm of hipness after Paul saw the Jimi Hendrix Experience at the Monterey Pop Festival and booked their first New York dates in June of 1967. Hendrix fell in love with the place and would frequently jam there after the other artists were done with their sets. In 'Scuse Me While I Kiss the Sky, Hendrix biographer David Henderson wrote:

> Jimi soon found the Scene club irresistible . . . Fans did not hassle you there . . . you could go there and party, or play and just sit alone and drink, and no one restrained you either way . . . He could jam any time he wanted to . . . When the chairs would finally be upside down upon the tiny tables. When Steve Paul himself would finally have to pull the plug, while Jimi, alone in his universe, would be totally unaware of the hour or of the devotees and workers who patiently waited within the exhilaration of his sound. At the Scene, Jimi would completely let himself go—playing all he knew and didn't know, going beyond sharing— playing all. Trying to get it all out.

During the making of the Electric Ladyland album, Hendrix would often work out arrangements at the Scene and then walk a few blocks to the recording studio, the Record Plant, and lay down tracks.

The Doors played their first gigs in New York at the Scene, and in the next few months Jeff Beck, Traffic, and the Chambers Brothers followed suit. The Scene closed in 1970 because of some issues with mob-connected owners of the building, but this didn't end Paul's career in the music industry.

After reading a short *Rolling Stone* piece about Johnny Winter, Paul flew to Texas and became his manager. He subsequently managed Johnny's brother Edgar, roles in which Paul made far more money than he ever had at the Scene. But for many of Paul's friends, this transition reminded them of what he had said when Tiny Tim had a novelty hit and performed on *The Tonight Show*: "Tiny Tim, who was the universe, gave it up to become a mere star."

Psychedelic energy could not be contained by elites and it soon migrated to Long Island, where singer and organist Mark Stein, bassist Tim Bogert, drummer Joey Brennan—later replaced by Carmine Appice—and lead guitarist Vince Martell formed the Pigeons. The band name was changed to the Vanilla Fudge after they got signed to Atlantic Records. The Fudge were very loud and played long, trippy extended versions of songs like the Supremes hit "You Keep Me Hangin' On." Their first album came out in 1967, and although they never got attention from the early rock critics, stoner fans loved them and the band is considered one of the seminal origins of what would come to be known as "heavy metal."

The death of John Coltrane from cancer at the age of forty on July 17 was a devastating loss, but it focused even more attention on his 1965 masterpiece, *A Love Supreme*, which was informed by a deep spiritual vision. Coltrane was influenced by both Muslim and Hindu texts. A posthumous album called *Om*, released in 1967, included chants from the *Bhagavad-Gītā*. A religious congregation in San Francisco regarded Coltrane as a saint and eventually formed the Saint John Will-I-Am Coltrane African Orthodox Church, which incorporated his music and his lyrics as prayers in its liturgy.

While most of the jazz world remained fixed in the zone of virtuosity and prehippie cool, a few embraced psychedelia in the space that Coltrane had helped to create. Ornette Coleman, long an innovator, released *The Empty Foxhole* with Charlie Haden on bass and Coleman's ten-year-old son Denardo on drums. Denardo says, "The title was obviously a reference to Vietnam."

The trippiest figure to emerge from the jazz world was Sun Ra. Like Marshall McLuhan and Buckminster Fuller, Sun Ra was in his fifties in 1967. Born Herman Poole Blount, he was a highly talented pianist who got work at a young age in local Alabama bands. In his twenties, he claimed to have had a spiritual experience that transported him to the planet Saturn and back. In the early fifties, he legally changed his name to Le Sony'r Ra, which was soon shorted to Sun Ra. ("Ra" is a reference to ancient Egypt's god of the sun.) An avid reader of history and mystical texts, Sun Ra became a fixture in the Chicago music scene with his label El Saturn Records and a band with frequently changing members called the Arkestra.

Sun Ra and the Arkestra arrived in New York in the early sixties and within a few years became as ubiquitous as the Fugs at rock shows, benefits for countercultural causes, and outdoor celebrations. The Arkestra had flamboyant stage shows and costumes, and Sun Ra's mystical intensity both fit in perfectly with and broadened the psychedelic scene. Although most mainstream jazz players thought he was too weird, Dizzy Gillespie and Thelonious Monk were both vocal admirers.

PSYCHEDELIC ROCK SPREADS ITS ROOTS

The hippie idea traveled around the country seemingly overnight. The *New Yorker*'s Ellen Willis would write of "the bohemianization of rock" and insisted that "psychedelic music was not so much a sound as a spirit." That spirit was not limited to New York and California. In Philadelphia, Todd Rundgren created Nazz in 1967 and went on to have a career that still evoked psychedelia decades later. In Detroit the MC5 were formed in 1964, and by 1968 had recorded one of the seminal political rock albums with an energy that prefigured the punk movement. Believe it or not, Ted Nugent's first band, the Amboy Dukes, based in Detroit, released a psychedelic rock song, "Journey to the Center of Your Mind," in 1968; it was a period when Bob Seger was also developing his career in Michigan prior to his debut release in 1969.

There was a vibrant music scene in Boston fueled by the city's vast college population. The psychedelic bands Ill Wind and the Hallucinations were local favorites. In 1968 an assortment of record company executives and local radio programmers tried to declare the "Bosstown Sound" as the successor to the scene in San Francisco. The young community of rock critics sharply criticized the contrived gimmick but the scene would nurture many important rock bands of the early seventies, including the Cars, Aerosmith, and the J. Geils Band, which Peter Wolf, a popular underground deejay, joined as lead singer in 1967.

Duane Allman and his younger brother Gregg grew

up in Daytona Beach, Florida, where they formed their first bands, the Escorts and the Allman Joys. I saw them in another incarnation, Hour Glass, at the Fillmore in 1967, two years before they finally formed the Allman Brothers Band, which fused blues roots with psychedelic culture, and created "Southern rock."

One of the most intense psychedelic local music scenes sprouted in 1965 in Austin, Texas, home to a lot of excellent roots musicians and to the University of Texas, which, like various other colleges at the time, included many students who were enthusiastic about LSD. Singer-songwriter Steve Earle, who was precocious enough to take acid in his early teens, recalls that the players at football rival Texas A&M referred to the University of Texas team as "the hippies" instead of their traditional nickname, the Longhorns. The center of the scene was a club called the Vulcan Gas Company. Bands that emerged from Austin included the Conqueroo, Shiva's Headband, and the 13th Floor Elevators, whose first album, *The Psychedelic Sounds of the 13th Floor Elevators*, released in 1966, is, along with the Airplane's debut album, considered one of the first psychedelic rock albums ever released.

FOLK MUSIC IN PSYCHEDELIC TIMES

Even though Dylan's adaptation of rock and roll had made a lot of the folk scene seem passé, some singer-songwriters who played acoustic guitars still found a way to be a part of the 1967 zeitgeist.

It is hard to imagine Arlo Guthrie's "Alice's Restaurant" having made much impact either five years earlier or five years later, but when I first heard it live in the studio on *Radio Unnameable* on February 27, 1967, I was entranced. My Fieldston classmate Paz Cohen lived across the street from the WBAI studios on East 39th Street and volunteered there, and I could actually hear her laughing in the background. The song immediately became a huge favorite of WBAI's audience. Laura Rosenberg, another Fieldstonite, hung out at WBAI too, and it was where she fell in love with weekend late-night host Steve Post, whom she eventually married. Laura recalls, "For most of the year, WBAI had 'Alice's Restaurant' to themselves and it was a huge help in the fundraising marathons. They'd promise to play it when $10,000 in total pledges came in and the phones would light up."

By the end of 1967, Reprise Records had signed Guthrie and released his debut album, ending WBAI's monopoly on the song but mainstreaming it to underground rock stations and record stores around the country. *Alice's Restaurant* was the first album reviewed in the first issue of *Rolling Stone* in November. Written by Wenner, the review ended with a salute to Guthrie: "It's his first album and it is, without qualification, excellent." The album made such an impact that Arthur Penn, whose *Bonnie and Clyde* was one of the big countercultural film hits of 1967, agreed to direct a movie of *Alice's Restaurant* (not a music video, but a full-length feature film), starring Guthrie, which United Artists released in 1969.

Arlo, the son of Woody Guthrie, was twenty years old at the time, and the album's title song is best remembered for presenting a satiric approach to avoiding the military draft. The verses are spoken, the chorus is sung, and it's a sardonic, laid-back, shaggy-dog story that conveys the hip sensibility of the moment. To listen to Arlo describe loading garbage into a Volkswagen microbus was to think you had made a new friend who would just as soon smoke a joint with you as perform. It's not until almost eight minutes in that Guthrie reveals the song is actually political. Yet by the end, antiwar sentiment is vivid and the message is clear—do whatever you need to do to avoid the war.

Arlo Guthrie and Pete Seeger

In 1967, Phil Ochs left Elektra Records to sign with A&M Records in the hopes of greater commercial success. By all accounts, Ochs was jealous of Bob Dylan and thought a label change would help. The resulting album, *Pleasures of the Harbor*, did not achieve Ochs's commercial dreams, but it contained four of his best songs: the title song, "Flower Lady," "Outside of a Small Circle of Friends," and "Crucifixion," which was, in part, an elegy to President Kennedy. Ochs was arguably the most reliable attendee of antiwar protests and other left-wing concerts of anyone in the folk or rock worlds. "There is no way to overstate the importance of Phil Ochs to the movement," says Cora Weiss.

Judy Collins made a major contribution to musical culture in the late sixties by introducing two songwriters whose work would resonate for many decades. She was the first to record Leonard Cohen's songs "Suzanne" and "Dress Rehearsal Rag," on her 1966 album *In My Life*. On her 1967 album *Wildflowers*, Collins sang Cohen's "Sisters of Mercy" and "Hey, That's No Way to Say Goodbye." As a result of this attention, Cohen was signed by Columbia Records and released *Songs of Leonard Cohen* later in 1967. On *Wildflowers*, Collins also made the first recording of Joni Mitchell's "Both Sides Now," which became a hit and also led to Mitchell's first album, *Song to a Seagull*, in 1968.

Joan Baez released the album *Joan* in 1967, but her impact was greater that year as an activist. A pacifist since her teenage years, her ideas were influenced by Thoreau, Gandhi, and A.J. Muste. Baez had established the Institute for the Study of Nonviolence in 1965 with philosopher Ira Sandperl. The previous year at Berkeley, she had sung to support the Free Speech Movement and refused to pay the estimated 60 percent of her taxes that would go to the Defense Department, saying, "I do not believe in war."

Baez was close to Dr. King and appeared in the South whenever asked in connection with protests. Like Mahalia Jackson, she was often asked by King's aides to privately lift his spirits with a song. She performed "We Shall Overcome" at the March on Washington in 1963, and was among the few who encouraged King to oppose the Vietnam War. Baez was arrested as part of Stop the Draft week in Oakland in October 1967. While she was serving her thirty-day sentence at the Santa Rita Rehabilitation Center, King and Andrew Young visited her. So did antidraft activist David Harris, whom she would marry in March 1968. (At the Woodstock Festival in 1969, Baez performed pregnant with Harris's child while he was in jail for draft evasion.)

One day in the spring of 1967, a bunch of Fieldston heads were sitting in a circle in Central Park playing a stoned kissing game when Baez and a guy walked by, then sat down and played with us for a few minutes. She actually kissed me on the cheek. We didn't even make a big deal about it afterward.

Joan Baez

Bob Dylan's 1967 album *John Wesley Harding* featured another reinvention of his sound and a return to more acoustic instruments, albeit with a Nashville production, after having released three albums in the previous two years, *Bringing It All Back Home*, *Highway 61 Revisited*, and *Blonde on Blonde*. In May 1967, the documentary *Don't Look Back* was released, which followed Dylan on tour in England the previous year and further enhanced the singer-songwriter's mythic status. There is no way to overstate Dylan's influence on other artists or on my generation. We all quoted his lyrics: acidheads, political radicals, mainstream liberals, and fans of folk, rock, and poetry. Like millions of people, I was more affected by Dylan's work than that of any other artist. I just can't think of anything new to say about him.

LONDON

Notwithstanding the cultural power of British rock and fashion, it was an American who brought the hippie idea most fully to the London music scene in 1967. Joe Boyd was a native of Boston and a sound engineer who had worked for the Newport Folk Festival (he was in charge of the sound when Dylan went electric in 1965). Boyd moved to London, originally to work for Elektra Records, and produced the Incredible String Band's first album, *The 5000 Spirits or the Layers of the Onion*, a hippie classic.

At twenty-five years old, Boyd was tuned into London's growing psychedelic scene. One of his closest friends was John "Hoppy" Hopkins, who by the sixties was a trendy photographer. Earlier in his life, Hopkins had been a nuclear technician who quit his job because he believed in disarmament. He also loved LSD. The two of them somehow got the wherewithal to open a club called UFO. UFO became the center of a psychedelic explosion in London that compressed into nine months the arc of discovery, creativity, popularity, and implosion that took two years in Haight-Ashbury.

UFO opened its doors on Friday, December 23, 1966, at ten thirty at night, and didn't close until six the following morning. Pink Floyd was a quasi house band there, performing dozens of times. Careers launched at UFO include the Crazy World of Arthur Brown and the Soft Machine. Procol Harum played at UFO in 1967 on the night "A Whiter Shade of Pale" was released.

Emulating the Fillmore, UFO featured light shows and advertised their concerts with psychedelic silkscreened posters. After the bands played, the club showed popular movies, most frequently samurai films directed by Akira Kurosawa or black-and-white American comedies starring W.C. Fields. UFO also hosted the British premiere of New York's avant-garde director Jack Smith's *Flaming Creatures*. Yoko Ono was a frequent attendee and populated her film *Bottoms* with UFO patrons.

Nigel Grainge, who would go on to start Ensign Records and sign Sinead O'Connor and Thin Lizzy among others, was in his early twenties and went to UFO weekly. His favorite band was Tomorrow. Although they never made it to America, Tomorrow epitomized the London psychedelic scene. Their most beloved song was "My White Bicycle," an homage to the bikes that the city of Amsterdam made available for free to its citizens and visitors. Boyd says, "The sixties . . . peaked just before dawn on July 1, 1967, during a set by Tomorrow." He called his memoir of the sixties *White Bicycles*.

In the book, Boyd wrote,

> *An atmosphere of agape was pervasive in 1967; people were fundamentally quite nice to each other. Most hippies pitied rather than hated the straights. I suppose it helped that we were stoned much of the time. What London witnessed in the spring of '67 was more than an endorsement of a new musical style, it was mass immersion in the subculture that gave rise to it.*

In another parallel with San Francisco, there were tensions between those who were primarily into psychedelia, art, and music, and radicals whose emotional connection was more political. The club allowed just about any leftist group to pass out information about rallies and bail funds, but Boyd kept a strong hand on the music. The hippies never developed the rapport with local skinheads the way the Diggers had with the Hells Angels, and when some long-haired patrons were beaten up, Boyd asked Michael X, a leader of London's black nationalists, to provide "security." The sight of black men in berets and karate poses deterred the skinheads from causing any other incidents.

John Lennon played a test pressing of the soon-to-be-released *Sgt. Pepper's Lonely Hearts Club Band* at UFO, and Jimi Hendrix hung out there when he returned to London. Boyd recalls booking the band the Move, who he loved, but who attracted a different crowd of "weekend hippies." He laments, "There was no stopping the juggernaut. The underground was becoming the mainstream. Kaftans and beads were everywhere." So was the press. The reactionary tabloid *News of the World* published a front-page piece about teenage girls going topless at UFO and the landlord of the building evicting the club. Boyd tried relocating to the much bigger Roundhouse venue but the economics didn't work with the higher security and rental costs, so UFO was gone by the end of September.

The Rolling Stones' year revolved largely around their drug bust. Andrew Loog Oldham produced a tongue-in-cheek Stones single, "We Love You," which starts with the sound of jail doors clanking, and features Allen Ginsberg, John Lennon, and Paul McCartney harmonizing to indicate solidarity.

Another London band, the Moody Blues, were never a critic's favorite and never played UFO. Grainge, for example, considered them a pop band with one hit, "Go Now," to their name, and that had come out in 1965. Yet in 1967 they reinvented themselves and released one of rock's few concept albums of that era, *Days of Future Passed*, which had the hit "Nights in White Satin (The Night)." The next year, the Moody Blues released *In Search of the Lost Chord*, and lest there was any doubt that they had become acidheads, the album included the song "Legend of a Mind," the chorus of which repeats the phrase *"Timothy Leary's dead,"* referencing the death of Leary's ego while also being a tribute to his vision.

NOT NECESSARILY STONED

There were at least two major rock artists who were publicly antidrug in 1967. Donovan was one of the most popular and influential musicians with hippies in 1967, having released the aforementioned *Mellow Yellow*, and not long before that, *Sunshine Superman*, which to me stands as one of the definitive albums of the sixties. The title song was Donovan's electric departure from the folk acoustic sound, and the backup musicians included future Led Zeppelin members Jimmy Page and John Paul Jones. The album features "Season of the Witch," a prophetic classic about the impending collapse of hippie idealism—"*Beatniks are out to make it rich / Oh no, must be the season of the witch.*"

Donovan

In 1966, Donovan had been the first British rock star to be arrested for pot. By the time his double album *A Gift from a Flower to a Garden* came out at the end of 1967, Donovan, having just turned twenty-one, was into meditation and had changed his attitude toward drugs. He included these words in the liner notes:

Must you lay down your fate to the Lord High Alchemy in the hands of the Chalk and the Drug? Magic circles he will spin and dirges he will sing through the transparency of a Queen Ant's Wing. Yes, I call upon every youth to stop the use of all Drugs and heed the Quest to seek the Sun.

Frank Zappa exploded onto the Los Angeles scene in 1966 at the age of twenty-five when his group, the Mothers of Invention, released the album *Freak Out*. The liner notes explained the title as "a process whereby an individual casts off outmoded and restricted standards of thinking." Zappa elaborated: "Less perceptive individuals have referred to us who have chosen this way of thinking and FEELING as 'Freaks,' hence the term: *Freaking Out*."

Zappa's vision was a unique mind-bending amalgam of influences that ranged from doo-wop to jazz to classical music. (Zappa had originally aspired to be a classical composer in the footsteps of his idols Edgard Varèse, Igor Stravinsky, and Anton Webern.) His lyrics were fiercely critical of "plastic" America, such as, "*Mr. America, walk on by your schools that do not teach . . . all the corny tricks you've tried will not forestall the rising tide of hungry freaks, Daddy.*"

In the summer of 1967, the Mothers did an extended run in New York at the Garrick Theatre, and at one performance Zappa invited several marines who were in the audience onto the stage to help dismember some dolls, a reference to civilian deaths in Vietnam. One of Zappa's first press photos showed him sitting on a toilet.

And yet Zappa was vocally antidrug. He told Elliot Mintz, "Freaking out is not just dancing and looking freaky. It's being aware of all the forces suppressing free speech, free exchange of ideas, and doing something about it . . . Stop taking dope and get out there and do something about your environment." Zappa never took LSD and said, "Try awareness *without* acid. [You] might find that it lasts longer."

HOLLYWOOD

Of course, Los Angeles was not only the home of Lou Adler, the Doors, the Byrds, and Frank Zappa. It was also the center of the film and television industries in the United States, and in 1967 Hollywood was a little out of sync with hip culture, although young artists like Peter Fonda and Jack Nicholson would soon catch up.

The closest thing to a bridge was *The Smothers Brothers Comedy Hour*, a prime-time show on CBS. Tom and Dick Smothers had a comedy folk act in which they played acoustic guitars and sang in the style of early-sixties folk groups, interrupting themselves with offbeat humor.

Like the members of the Monkees, Tom and Dick Smothers were personally fascinated with the counterculture and wanted in—but unlike the Monkees, they controlled their own show. The Smothers Brothers invited guests such as Joan Baez, the Who, Jefferson Airplane, Buffalo Springfield, Steppenwolf, the Doors, and Pete Seeger, who performed "Waist Deep in the Big Muddy," his antiwar song that referred to President Johnson as "the big fool." The song was initially censored by CBS, but after fierce protest from Tom Smothers, it was aired on a subsequent broadcast. Given that Seeger had been blacklisted for years from all of the networks, this was a big deal.

The show was canceled in 1969 after the network received too many complaints about its antiestablishment attitudes, but the Smothers Brothers had succeeded in gaining the respect of the hip community. Jimi Hendrix dedicated the song "I Don't Live Today" to the Smothers Brothers at the Los Angeles Forum, and Tom Smothers was among the small group that John and Yoko invited to play guitar on the recording of "Give Peace a Chance" in Montreal in 1969. (The other prominent invited guest was Timothy Leary, who sang backing vocals.)

Hollywood was still producing prehippie intellectual films such as *Who's Afraid of Virginia Woolf?* and *A Man for All Seasons*, which dominated the Oscars in 1967. The closest connectivity between Hollywood and the counterculture was *Bonnie and Clyde*, which starred Warren Beatty as one of the first mass-appeal antiheroes. The film was the subject of fierce debate between the old and new American cultures. The *New York Times* gave it a terrible review, almost killing its success until Pauline Kael wrote a rave for the *New Yorker*, after which it found such a large counterculture audience that it was celebrated on the cover of *Time* in December 1967. Perhaps the biggest American movie star was Sidney Poitier, who had won the Academy Award for his performance in *Lilies of the Field* in 1964; Poitier became the first black man to be so recognized. In 1967 he played a leading role in three blockbusters: *To Sir, With Love; In the Heat of the Night;* and *Guess Who's Coming to Dinner*. The latter was the first Hollywood movie about an interracial romance. Many young people, both black and white, found it saccharine and paternalistic, but it reached the older generations in a way that rock and roll and soul music never could.

For the moment, European films were generally more in touch with the counterculture. Among those that appealed to heads were Jean-Luc Godard's *Weekend* and Michaelangelo Antonioni's *Blow-Up*, which was nominated for Oscars for directing and writing in 1967. (*Blow-Up* has a scene in which the Yardbirds, who then included future superstars Jimmy Page and Jeff Beck, imitated the destruction of an electric guitar, which in real life was a regular shtick of the Who's Peter Townshend.) British cinema produced three films with classic antiheroes: *Alfie*, starring the young Michael Caine; *Morgan*, starring David Warner and Vanessa Redgrave; and *Petulia* (directed by Richard Lester of *A Hard Day's Night* fame), which included brief appearances by both Big Brother and the Holding Company and the Grateful Dead.

THE BEATLES

In the three years since they had been introduced to most of their American fans on *The Ed Sullivan Show*, the Beatles had dominated the pop charts, released six albums and two movies, and evolved from a pop group to a global cultural force, in part by embracing hippie culture.

The Beatles' new album, *Sgt. Pepper's Lonely Heart's Club Band*, was released on June 1, 1967. *Rolling Stone*'s Langdon Winner later wrote, "The closest Western civilization has come to unity since the Congress of Vienna in 1815 was the week the *Sgt. Pepper* album was released." I have nothing to add to the thousands who have analyzed the album's music, but as the Fab Four were by far the most beloved and famous people among baby boomers, it is worth noting a few of the ways that they intersected with the culture of 1967.

The album cover of *Sgt. Pepper's* made two large statements. Firstly, the Beatles were deconstructing their own mythology, which would be an increasing focus of the members of the band (particularly John Lennon and George Harrison) over the next few years. The cover was the concept of British artist Sir Peter Blake and his wife Jann Haworth, but the band weighed in on every creative detail, including the wax versions of their younger selves wearing dark suits, juxtaposed with their 1967 personas with longer hair and colorful mock-military uniforms. The eight Beatles and the dozens of other figures stood in front of an arrangement of flowers that spelled *Beatles* and appeared to be a grave.

The other big idea was that the Beatles were depicting themselves as part of a much wider cosmic community that included members of the counterculture like Lenny Bruce, Bob Dylan, Terry Southern, and Aldous Huxley, as well as movie stars past and present such as W.C. Fields, Fred Astaire, Bette Davis, Marlon Brando, Tom Mix, Tyrone Power, Marilyn Monroe, Laurel & Hardy, Johnny Weissmuller, Tony Curtis, Shirley Temple, and Mae West (who initially refused permission but was persuaded to change her mind after receiving letters from all four Beatles). George Harrison insisted on the inclusion of the author of *Autobiography of a Yogi*, Paramahansa Yogananda, as well as his guru Sri Yukteswar, his satguru Lahiri Mahasaya, and Mahavatar Babaji, "the deathless master." The band wanted to include Mahatma Gandhi but their label refused because it was considered disrespectful in India and would adversely affect record sales there.

Other cultural luminaries portrayed were Carl Jung,

Aleister Crowley, Dylan Thomas, Edgar Allen Poe, H.G. Wells, Stephen Crane, George Bernard Shaw, Lewis Carroll, T.E. Lawrence, James Joyce, Albert Einstein, Karl Marx, and avant-garde composer Karlheinz Stockhausen.

McCartney's "She's Leaving Home" was the definitive song about hippie runaways, written from the idealistic point of view of a teenage girl looking for life's meaning. "With a Little Help from My Friends" and "Lucy in the Sky with Diamonds" were widely viewed as having psychedelic references although the Beatles coyly denied it. When *Time* did a cover story on the band in September of 1967, it addressed the last line of Lennon's closing song, "A Day in the Life": "It's been a long way from 'I want to hold your hand,' to 'I'd love to turn you on.'"

In the throes of a level of productivity that future artists would marvel at, the Beatles also released three singles in 1967 that were not included on *Sgt. Pepper's*: "Penny Lane" (backed by "Strawberry Fields Forever"), "Hello Goodbye" (backed by "I Am the Walrus"), and "All You Need Is Love" (backed by "Baby, You're a Rich Man").

"All You Need Is Love" was performed live on a worldwide TV satellite broadcast called *Our World* on June 25, 1967, less than a month after the release of *Sgt. Pepper's*. On the broadcast, which featured different segments from all around the world, the band was surrounded by friends and acquaintances seated on the floor, including Mick Jagger, Eric Clapton, Keith Moon, Graham Nash, and various girlfriends and family members, who sang along with the refrain during the fade-out. The single was released commercially the next week and was, of course, instantly number one around the world. The lyrics had an almost evangelical intensity about them, and not long afterward, the Beatles would make a global impact, especially among hippies, in another sphere altogether.

BLACK MUSIC AND THE COUNTERCULTURE

There was no black equivalent to the underground rock stations like KMPX. The radio stations with the biggest black audiences played R&B hit singles and it was a time of enormous creativity in the genre. Motown was having one of its many peaks, Aretha Franklin and James Brown were making their most memorable records, and Otis Redding was ascendant until he died tragically in a plane crash in December. Most white rock and roll fans had one or more of their records, but stations that played black music were primarily in the same business as other broadcasters—selling advertising spots. Between racist social/political patterns in America and economic inequalities, black and white radio audiences were largely segregated. The Temptations weren't played on underground rock stations and psychedelic rock was not played on black radio, not even Jimi Hendrix. The one band whose music was played on R&B, pop, *and* underground rock stations was Sly & the Family Stone.

The Beatles and Rolling Stones had been influenced enormously by R&B and had done cover versions of songs by Marvin Gaye, Solomon Burke, the Isley Brothers, Smokey Robinson and the Miracles, and Chuck Berry on their early albums. When the Stones first came to New York they immediately went to the Apollo Theater to see James Brown. The early history of rock and roll contributed to integration if for no other reason than the fact that black and white teenagers were dancing to the same music, sometimes together. This triggered a racist backlash that resulted in a lot of R&B hits by black artists like Fats Domino being "covered" by white artists like Pat Boone, a dynamic that engendered a lot of bitterness among black artists who were effectively blocked from white audiences.

By 1967, some of the best R&B labels, particularly Motown and Atlantic, had finally created the capacity to "cross over" many big R&B hits by artists like the Supremes and Aretha Franklin onto the Top 40 radio stations and *The Ed Sullivan Show*. But the very fact of their pop success made playing a lot of those songs off-putting to most underground rock deejays, who tended to focus on the popular music of the previous generation of African Americans: the blues.

The folk scene had always included a lot of blues artists. Sonny Terry, Brownie McGhee, and Josh White were fixtures at folk festivals, and Odetta was a star. The Rolling Stones took their name from a Muddy Waters lyric, and the Grateful Dead covered Sonny Boy Williamson's "Good Morning Little Schoolgirl" on their first album. In Chicago, guitarist Mike Bloomfield and pianist Barry Goldberg started showing up at blues clubs with overwhelmingly black audiences. The older blues masters—Muddy Waters, Howlin' Wolf, and others—mentored them and welcomed them onto their stages. Bloomfield and Goldberg would be in the backup band for Bob Dylan when he went electric and later formed the Electric Flag, who played the Monterey Pop Festival and got signed there to Columbia Records. The Paul Butterfield Blues Band's album *East-West*, featuring Bloomfield on guitar, was a fixture in thousands of dorm rooms. When I was a teenager, one of the best ways of determining how much substance a new acquaintance had was checking out how many blues albums were included in his or her record collection.

American blues was even more popular in England. Guitar heroes Jeff Beck, Jimmy Page, and Eric Clapton all started as blues players. When Clapton was in the Yardbirds, the band backed up Sonny Boy Williamson on a British tour; a live album of the tour was later released. Clapton's band Cream, one of the most ubiquitous in hippie living rooms, was essentially a psychedelic blues band. Of course, Jimi Hendrix could play the blues—he could play anything.

When Bill Graham opened the Fillmore, he sought advice from Jefferson Airplane members Jorma Kaukonen and Jack Casady about who to book. They turned him on to many black artists, including B.B. King, Miles Davis, Rahsaan Roland Kirk, and Muddy Waters, who Graham would package with white rock acts.

In Berkeley, one of the most popular blues bands was led by vocalist and harmonica player Junior Wells and featured guitarist Buddy Guy. Enough of their audience was white that Wells rewrote the lyrics to the old eight-bar blues song "It Hurts Me Too" and called the new version "The Hippies Are Trying." Wells earnestly sings, *"We need more flower children / And more lovers too . . ."* In the last two minutes of the song, however, he suddenly switches to a classic blues theme: *"Somebody tell me—I just gotta know, how can you be so mean?"*

Outside of the world of the relatively civilized flower power and rock and roll, that question loomed large for many African Americans in 1967.

CHAPTER 5
BLACK POWER

In his 1968 book *Look Out, Whitey! Black Power's Gon' Get Your Mama!* Julius Lester wrote, "As early as 1962 black SNCC staff members would have parties whenever they gathered in Atlanta and these parties were open only to black people . . . They had an experience, which was practically impossible for a white to have because black people exist separately in America while having to deal with America. A black knows two worlds, while the white knows only one."

No white liberal, radical, or hippie wanted to be like the guy Lenny Bruce made fun of in his bit "How to Relax Your Colored Friends at Parties," the one who'd say things like, "You know that Joe Louis was a hell of a fighter, a credit to his race," or, "Here's to Paul Robeson."

In the late sixties, in the balance between politics, culture, and consciousness, politics was an even bigger deal in most black communities than in the white world. The draft affected millions of white men, but if you had money you could drag out your college deferment or find the right psychiatrist. If you were black, regardless of your age or gender or economic status, you couldn't avoid the realities derived from hundreds of years of slavery and Jim Crow subjugation. Elections and laws had extra impact on African Americans. As Martin Luther King Jr. explained, "They say you can't legislate morality, and that's true, but you can regulate behavior. A law cannot make a man love me, but it can prevent him from lynching me and I think that's pretty important also."

1967 was four years after Dr. King's "I Have a Dream" speech, three years after the passage of the Civil Rights Act, and two years after the Voting Rights Act was signed into law. In November 1966, Edward Brooke, a moderate Republican from Massachusetts, became the first African American ever elected by popular vote to the United States Senate. Yet millions of black Americans were still treated as second-class citizens and many had run out of patience. At great cost, including the death of many civil rights workers (and four young schoolgirls), there had been integration of lunch counters and buses, and voter registration of African Americans had begun in the South, but patterns of discrimination in housing, employment, banking, and the criminal justice system persisted in both the North and the South, and the wounds of generations of racist orthodoxy festered.

These and other factors that no white person could completely understand created the context in which Gil Scott-Heron, who could have gotten a scholarship to an Ivy League school, decided to attend Lincoln University, a historically black college where Langston Hughes, one of Gil's idols, had gone. It turned out to be the perfect place for Gil to transform his musical and poetic brilliance into the contemporary culture of the time. It was there that he first heard the Last Poets, who gave him a model for how to integrate a political sensibility into jazz and R&B, and it's also where he met Brian Jackson, who would become a longtime collaborator and bandmate.

Tom Hayden and Abbie Hoffman were among many in the white counterculture who had gone south to work in the civil rights movement earlier in the decade. Several whites, including Michael Schwerner, Andrew Goodman, and Viola Liuzzo, had been murdered by racists.

The moral power of the civil rights movement reverberated in the part of white America I grew up in through writers like James Baldwin, Ralph Ellison, and Claude Brown, whose *Manchild in the Promised Land* deeply moved me as a teenager. There was a renaissance of black comedy exemplified by older, subversive "blue" comics like Redd Foxx and Moms Mabley, and civil rights pioneers Dick Gregory and Bill Cosby—who had both black and white fans.

In San Francisco, the predominantly black Fillmore district bordered the Haight, and Roy Ballard, inspired by the Diggers, created Black Man's Free Store. Peter Coyote recalls, "When we found supermarkets resistant to long-haired freaks, we could always send a white woman with a baby there to get the cast-off food we would then give away. Blacks couldn't get the same result, so we'd send our people to get food for their project as well." Efforts like these were meaningful on a micro level, but on a mass scale the consequences of generations of cultural segregation and racist oppression loomed quite large.

STOKELY CARMICHAEL

Malcolm X's influence grew even greater after his death. Not long before he was killed, he had said that blacks shouldn't let whites into their organizations because regardless of how noble the intent, eventually whites would get a disproportionate amount of control through the influence of money. In January 1966, Floyd McKissick replaced James Farmer as executive director of the Congress of Racial Equality (CORE) and the organization changed from an interracial, integrationist, nonviolent civil rights group into one embodying a secular version of Malcom's philosophy. This dynamic also took hold at the Student Nonviolent Coordinating Committee (SNCC), which had been formed in 1960 and quickly became one of the most effective grassroots organizations in the South. By 1967, whites had been expelled from most of its chapters and boards, and the charismatic twenty-five-year-old Stokely Carmichael had been elected president, replacing John Lewis—the last president of the organization who believed in nonviolence.

Carmichael had graduated from Howard University as a philosophy major, but inspired by the civil rights movement, he went south and led voter registration efforts for SNCC in Lowndes County, Alabama. He was arrested dozens of times and was horrified by the cruel brutality of the white Southern cops. (He served forty-nine days at Mississippi's notorious Parchman Farm prison.)

The first thing Carmichael did in his new role was to withdraw SNCC from an upcoming White House Conference on Civil Rights. He wanted to immediately differentiate the new iteration of SNCC from its past, and shortly thereafter he found an ideal rhetorical way to do so with the slogan "Black Power," which was also the name of a book that Carmichael would coauthor in 1967. The phrase had appeared in Richard Wright's 1954 book of the same name and had recently been adapted by SNCC's Willie Ricks. However, it was Carmichael who injected "Black Power" into the national conversation in a widely covered speech in Greenwood, Mississippi, following the March Against Fear, at which civil rights hero James Meredith had been shot. Carmichael, who had the looks of a movie star, was a mesmerizing speaker: "This is the twenty-seventh time I have been arrested and I ain't going to jail no more! The only way we gonna stop them white men from whuppin' us is to take over. What we gonna start sayin' now is Black Power!"

In the summer of 1966, Carmichael was one of the first black leaders to oppose the war in Vietnam, and in a speech at Berkeley, he popularized the chant, "*Hell no, we won't go!*" And it was Carmichael who first said, "No Viet Cong ever called me nigger."

Because of his affinity for the mass media, some in the movement mocked him as "Starmichael," but it was that media savvy that took radical views into the living rooms of Middle America. On the CBS news show *Face the Nation*, Carmichael, dressed in a conservative suit and tie, flashed a Dennis the Menace smile as he calmly refused to rule out violence if injustice to African Americans persisted. He called for black soldiers serving in Vietnam to return and instead fight for voting rights at home. ("Are you calling for desertion?" CBS's Martin Agronsky asked incredulously.)

186 ♣ Danny Goldberg

For a time, Carmichael made a point of criticizing Martin Luther King Jr. When King asked for a suspension of picketing outside the White House for the wedding of President Johnson's daughter Luci, Carmichael sent King a telegram: "You have displayed more backbone in defending Luci than you have shown for the colored people of Vietnam being napalmed by Luci's father." Carmichael proudly asserted that "LBJ could stand in front of Congress and say, *We shall overcome*, but he will never say, *We want Black Power.*" At some protests, SNCC signs read, *Save Us from Our Black Leaders*, referred to King as an *Uncle Tom*, and mocked him as *Black Jesus*.

Yet, as Dick Gregory pointed out in his memoir *Callus on My Soul*, "As militantly as the White press portrayed Stokely, he only got into one fight during the entire Movement. As much as he and Dr. King differed, the only physical altercation Stokely ever had was when somebody pushed Dr. King during a demonstration." When King gave a sermon at Ebenezer Baptist Church in Atlanta reiterating opposition to the Vietnam War, he invited Carmichael to attend and the SNCC leader applauded respectfully from a pew in the first row.

For his part, King refused to lend SCLC's name to a *New York Times* ad signed by seven other mainstream civil rights groups repudiating Black Power. He understood that Stokely Carmichael had a different constituency than he did. He explained to Andrew Young, "If Stokely is saying the same thing I am saying, he becomes like my assistant."

Carmichael saw the freedom movement of American blacks in the context of what he viewed as an international struggle for justice. In July 1967, he traveled to Cuba and was seated as a delegate at a convention held by the Organization of Latin American Solidarity. Later that year, he visited Communist China and North Vietnam. Even so, Carmichael was disappointed by the dogmatism and authoritarianism of Communist regimes. In February of 1968 he said that communism and socialism were not ideologies "suited for black people." He advocated an African ideology "which speaks to our blackness. Nothing else."

Carmichael became an immediate target of the political establishment. A week before he was elected governor of California, Ronald Reagan sent a posturing telegram to Carmichael asking him to cancel all of his speeches in California, as if the mere presence of the SNCC leader would lead to public catastrophe.

Carmichael only served as president of SNCC for one year. He was succeeded by the equally radical H. Rap Brown, who soon became known for the quote, "Violence is as American as cherry pie." In 1968, Carmichael married South African singer Miriam Makeba, and in 1969 he renamed himself Kwame Ture and moved to Guinea. Until the end of his life, Ture remained a thought leader among African Americans. He often answered the phone by asking, "Ready for the revolution?"

ADAM CLAYTON POWELL

One afternoon in late 1967, I saw Congressman Adam Clayton Powell Jr. speak on the Berkeley campus. At the time, he was being accused of corruption and wanted to rally national support. Powell had been the most powerful black congressperson in US history. In 1961, after sixteen years in Congress, he had become chairman of the House Committee on Education and Labor, where he presided over the creation of Medicaid, the expansion of the minimum wage, education and training for the deaf, nursing education, aid for elementary and secondary education and school libraries, and legislation that made lynching a federal crime.

Powell maintained a strong connection with his Harlem district as pastor of the Abyssinian Baptist Church, where he had offered the pulpit to Malcolm X and organized and supported many boycotts to empower the community. He also had a flamboyant lifestyle, which made him an easy target for his political enemies. Powell was accused of mismanaging his committee's budget, taking trips abroad at public expense, and bringing two young women with him on overseas travel at government expense. Powell's defense was, "I will always do just what every other congressman and committee chairman has done and is doing and will do." He refused to pay a slander judgment won by a constituent in his Harlem district and feelings against him reached a critical mass in the House, which voted to exclude him in March 1967. Powell would eventually be vindicated. Represented by Arthur Kinoy, he prevailed in a lawsuit that claimed the House had no right to exclude him, and he was reelected by his constituents.

Powell was a lot older than those in the Berkeley audience, but his track record spoke for itself. "You know, you white kids and your protests are very impressive," he said, "but you don't seem to have any leaders. That's okay—there are a lot of great black leaders, we have Martin Luther King Jr., Stokely Carmichael, James

Farmer," and then he jokingly pointed to himself, "and Big Daddy. Use one of ours."

The crowd of several hundred Berkeley lefties laughed, but the various white radical and hippie clusters, whatever their other differences, were all pretty phobic about empowering any particular leader. Nevertheless, Powell's point about the richness of black leaders at the time was undeniable. In addition to those he mentioned, the Black Panthers were emerging, the NAACP still mattered, and even though it wanted nothing to do with white people, so did the Nation of Islam. No one of any race was more well known than the NOI's most famous convert, Muhammad Ali.

ALI!

During the years 1965 and 1966, Muhammad Ali successfully defended his boxing title seven times, yet he was the only heavyweight champion since Jack Johnson not to be invited to the White House. (I liked to think that if JFK had not been killed, *he* would have had Ali there.) In August 1966, the champ announced that he was filing for conscientious objector status and would not fight in the Vietnam War, saying to a confrontational press corps, "I ain't got no quarrel with them Viet Cong." At the time, Ali was going against the grain of popular opinion, even in the black community. According to *Time*, only 35 percent of blacks and fewer than 20 percent of whites opposed the war.

On February 6, 1967, Ali fought Ernie Terrell, who had persisted in calling him "Clay" in prefight interviews. The champ won by a unanimous decision, taunting Terrell as he punched him, "What's my name? What's my name?" Just six weeks later, on March 22, Ali success-fully defended his title for the ninth time, knocking out Zora Folley in the seventh round.

Five weeks after that victory, Ali formally refused to step forward when his name was called at the US Army induction center in Houston, Texas. He was arrested and was immediately stripped of his title by the New York State Athletic Commission. Within the next few weeks, other states followed suit and Ali would not be able to box again in the United States until 1970. He de-fiantly told reporters, "No, I am not going ten thousand miles to help murder, kill, and burn other people to sim-ply help continue the domination of white slave masters over dark people the world over. This is the day and age when such evil injustice must come to an end."

On June 4, 1967, in his Cleveland office, recently retired Cleveland Browns superstar Jim Brown (at the time, he held the record for lifetime rushing yards in the NFL) convened a meeting of several top African Ameri-can athletes with Ali. The group included Boston Celtics center Bill Russell (already a five-time NBA MVP), Bobby Mitchell and Jim Shorter of the Washington Redskins, Willie Davis of the Green Bay Packers, Sid Williams and Walter Beach of the Browns, Curtis McClinton of the Kansas City Chiefs, and Lew Alcindor, who would soon rename himself Kareem Abdul-Jabbar and go on to become the all-time leading NBA scorer. (Alcindor was then a sophomore at UCLA, but already one of the most famous college basketball players in the country.)

"Muhammad Ali was one of my heroes," recalled Abdul-Jabbar years later. "He was in trouble and he was someone I wanted to help because he made me feel good about being an African American." Cleveland attorney Carl Stokes, who would be elected in November as the first black mayor of a major American city, also attended.

There was no precedent in American history for any sports figure having taken such an aggressive antiestablishment stand, and some of the athletes tried to get Ali to soften his position. The army offered Ali an arrangement similar to what Joe Louis had during World War II, in which he would be spared combat and could just do boxing exhibitions. Some of Ali's advisers were attracted to this option because it would have preserved the champ's ability to make big money in the short run, but Ali wouldn't consider it. Instead he spoke of the depth of his beliefs. "He was such a dazzling speaker, he damn near converted a few in that room," recalls Jim Brown.

It is likely that Ali persuaded a lot of young America as well. At this point in time, he was the most popular American to publicly oppose the war, and to many young people he validated the antiwar movement in the same way that the Beatles had validated psychedelics.

On June 20, 1967, Ali was found guilty after a jury deliberation of only twenty-one minutes. Stokely Carmichael later said, "No one risked or suffered like Muhammad Ali. I didn't risk anything. I just told people not to go." Philosopher Bertrand Russell, then ninety-five years old, had convened an International War Crimes Tribunal in Stockholm to evaluate the situation in Vietnam, and wrote a letter to Ali that said, "You have my wholehearted support."

A handful of New York writers such as Norman Mailer, George Plimpton, James Baldwin, and Pete Hamill formed a committee to reinstate the championship to Ali, but in most of the establishment world, the reaction was overwhelmingly negative. An editorial in the *New York Times* condemned Ali, as did virtually every major sports writer in the United States. Many older black celebrities rebuked Ali, including Jackie Robinson and Joe Louis. Howard Cosell, the ABC broadcaster who had previously been one of his biggest boosters, was too nervous about pressure from his network to lend his name to efforts to support Ali. The argument was almost totally generational for both blacks and whites. Most younger people got it; most older people were deeply offended. They hadn't gotten the memo about the moral horror of the war in Vietnam or its lack of any relevance to America's interests. They blindly trusted the government, just as they had during World War II.

Although Ali was idolized by pot-smoking hippies, when he spoke at colleges he often talked about his Muslim values, which included no smoking, drinking, or drugs. He was usually greeted with adulation, except on a few occasions when interracial couples walked out, offended by his disapproval of such relationships.

Ali publicly maintained the Nation of Islam's separatist principles, but in his personal life he continued to work with whites, like his trainer Angelo Dundee, and befriended many of his white supporters. He usually adhered to the NOI insistence on staying out of electoral politics, but he made an exception and publicly endorsed Dick Gregory when he ran a quixotic write-in campaign for mayor of Chicago.

By 1971, public opinion about the war would change so much that the United States Supreme Court unanimously overturned Ali's conviction. In subsequent decades, he was invited by several presidents to the White House and became one of the most popular people in America and around the world; but in 1967 he was on the cutting edge, at moments virtually alone with his conscience and beliefs.

Singer/actor Harry Belafonte said, "He was in many ways as inspiring as Dr. King, as inspiring as Malcolm. Out of the womb of oppression he was our phoenix . . . They could not break his spirit nor deny his moral imperative."

Although they had differing religious beliefs, Martin Luther King Jr. and Muhammad Ali privately had great respect for each other. When Ali first won the championship in 1964, King was the only black leader to send him a telegram of congratulations. Two days after Ali refused induction, King preached from the pulpit at Ebenezer Baptist Church: "He is giving up millions of dollars in order to stand up for what his conscience tells him is right. No matter what you think of Muhammad Ali's religion, you have to admire his courage."

King met with Ali for about two hours on March 29, 1967. Afterward, the champ affably told reporters that although he disagreed with King regarding integration, the two men could still talk civilly like Kennedy and Khrushchev did.

Riots

The worst American race riots of the century took place during the summer of 1967. For some time, the black community in Newark, New Jersey, had been objecting to "redlining" (which placed undue economic burdens

194 ♦ Danny Goldberg

on black neighborhoods), lack of opportunity in education, training, and jobs, and police brutality.

On July 12, a black cab driver, John Weerd Smith, was arrested, beaten, and taken to Newark's Fourth Precinct, where he was charged with assaulting the officers and making insulting remarks. In the eyes of the community, Smith hadn't done anything remotely wrong. He had passed a parked police car, and was then pulled over by the two white officers.

Word of the unfair treatment spread quickly and over the course of five days, riots and destruction ultimately left a total of twenty-six people dead, including a police officer and a firefighter. Hundreds more were injured, over a thousand people were arrested, and property damage exceeded ten million dollars.

On July 23 in Detroit, police raided the Blind Pig, an unlicensed after-hours bar, and things got out of control and triggered a riot which also lasted five days, resulting in forty-three deaths, over 1,100 injuries, more than 7,200 arrests, and more than two thousand buildings were looted or destroyed. (To put this into context, the widely reported 2014 riots in Ferguson, Missouri, after the police killing of Michael Brown, resulted in no additional fatalities and less than one hundred arrests.)

Riots triggered by confrontations with police also occurred that summer in Tampa, Syracuse, Milwaukee, and Buffalo. Racial conflicts of this scale had not occurred in the United States since the Civil War. Many in the black community objected to the word "riot" and preferred the words "revolt" or "rebellion."

President Johnson appointed a commission to study the underlying causes of the riots. It was chaired by Otto

Kerner, the governor of Illinois, and included New York Mayor John Lindsay, Massachusetts Senator Ed Brooke, I.W. Abel, the president of the United Steelworkers of America, and Roy Wilkins, executive director of the NAACP.

The commission's final report was released on February 29, 1968, in book form, selling an astounding two million copies. The main conclusion was that the riots resulted from black frustration at the lack of economic opportunity. The report stated, "Our nation is moving toward two societies, one black, one white—separate and unequal." It criticized the mass media as well: "The press has too long basked in a white world looking out of it, if at all, with white men's eyes and white perspective."

The commission's suggestions included more diversity on police forces, stronger employment programs, the creation of housing opportunities in the suburbs for African Americans, and for public housing to be built on "scattered sites" instead of large high-rise projects.

Martin Luther King Jr. called the report a "physician's warning of approaching death, with a prescription for life," but the Congress and president made no effort to implement any of the commission's proposals. (When Dr. King was assassinated a few months later, riots broke out again in over one hundred American cities.)

Amiri Baraka

One of the most prominent people arrested in the Newark riot was poet LeRoi Jones, who was charged with carrying an illegal weapon and resisting arrest. Jones's poetry had been influenced by the beats, and he remained close with Ginsberg until the end of his life. At

Jones's trial, as supposed evidence of his guilt, the judge read a portion of Jones's poem "Black People!" including the lines: "*All the stores will open if you will say the magic words. / The magic words are: up against the wall mother fucker / this is a stick up!*" (In 1969, Jefferson Airplane used the phrase in the chorus of "We Can Be Together," on their *Volunteers* album.)

The poet was initially convicted and sentenced to three years in prison, but an appeals court reversed the conviction on the basis that the decision had been made primarily for his writing. Jones joked that he was charged with holding two revolvers "and two poems."

In 1967, Jones visited Professor Maulana Karenga in Los Angeles. Karenga had started an organization called US after the Watts riots of 1965; he was influenced by Malcolm X's short-lived Organization of Afro-American Unity (OAAU). In 1966, Karenga created the year-end holiday Kwanzaa as a gift-giving alternative to Christmas. He said his goal was to "give blacks an opportunity to celebrate themselves and their history, rather than simply imitate the practice of the dominant society." Kwanzaa was inspired by African traditions, and the name is derived from the Bantu "First Fruit" celebration. Shortly after meeting Karenga, Jones changed his name to Amiri Baraka.

That same year, Baraka's second book of jazz criticism, *Black Music*, was released, as was a movie version of his play *Dutchman*, which portrayed a shy black man being teased and seduced by a white woman (a film I saw while on acid).

DASHIKIS AND AFROS
In an article in the Harlem paper the *Amsterdam News*,

reporting on the Newark riots, reporter George Barner referred to a new African garment called a *dashiki*, a colorful gown worn by men that was based on African clothing and was created by a black-owned company called New Breed, run by J. Benning. Within the next couple of years the dashiki was worn in public by many black celebrities, including Jim Brown, Sammy Davis Jr., Wilt Chamberlain, and Bill Russell.

Around the same time the natural Afro hairstyle became popular with many young black women. Kathleen Cleaver, who was married to Black Panther leader Eldridge Cleaver, explained in a 1968 interview, "The reason for it . . . is a new awareness among black people that their own natural physical appearance is beautiful . . . For so many, many years we were told only white people were beautiful. Only straight hair, light eyes, light skin was beautiful, and so black women would try everything they could to straighten their hair and lighten their skin to look as much like white women . . . But this has changed because black people are aware."

BLACK PANTHERS

Adapting the name from the Mississippi organization that Stokely Carmichael had supported, the Black Panther Party was created in late 1966 in Oakland, California. It was the brainchild of Bobby Seale and Huey P. Newton, both of whom had been heavily influenced by Malcolm X when they were student activists at Merrit College. In April 1967, the Black Panther Party opened its first official headquarters in an Oakland storefront and published the first issue of the *Black Panther: Black Community News Service*. Their core identity was armed citizens' patrols which monitored the behavior of police officers and challenged police brutality in Oakland.

The Panthers also instituted a variety of community initiatives, most notably the Free Breakfast for Children program. Although the Panthers were highly regarded by black nationalists, they also had strong ties to white lefties and the hippie counterculture. Their operation was initially funded from sales on the streets of Berkeley of pocket-sized books containing sayings of Chairman Mao; they were primarily bought by white college kids. The Panthers also welcomed financial support from wealthy liberals such as Bert Schneider, who was a producer on *The Monkees* TV series, *Easy Rider,* and the anti-war documentary *Hearts and Minds.* The first few issues of the Panther newspaper were printed on a Gestetner mimeograph machine borrowed from the Diggers.

At the time, only sixteen of Oakland's 661 police officers were African American. Newton had the Panthers memorize portions of California's open-carry gun laws, and the group would record incidents of police brutality by following police cars. Membership started to really grow in February 1967, when the party provided an armed escort at the San Francisco airport for Betty Shabazz, Malcolm X's widow and keynote speaker for a conference being held in his honor.

Don Mulford, a Republican assemblyman who represented Oakland, quickly responded to the Black Panther police patrols in 1967 with a bill to strip Californians of the right to openly carry firearms. The legislation, known in the press as "The Panthers Bill," passed and was signed by Governor Reagan. While the bill was being debated, the Panthers burst onto the national scene on May 2, 1967, when thirty members, led by Bobby Seale, appeared at the state capitol building in Sacramento carrying rifles, shotguns, and handguns, which evoked both fears of and aspirations for an armed insurrection. Six of them actually entered the assembly chamber. Some legislators took cover under their desks. The Panthers claimed that they were within their rights to be in the capitol building with their guns, but they exited peacefully when ordered to do so by police.

Bobby Seale told reporters afterward: "Black people have begged, prayed, petitioned, demonstrated, and everything else to get the racist power structure of America to right the wrongs which have historically been perpetuated against black people. All of these efforts have been answered by more repression, deceit, and hypocrisy. As the aggression of the racist American government escalates in Vietnam, the police agencies of America escalate the oppression of black people throughout the ghettos of America. Vicious police dogs, cattle prods, and increased patrols have become familiar sights in black communities."

Shortly after Seale finished speaking, police arrested the group on felony charges of conspiracy to disrupt a legislative session, charges which were eventually reduced to a misdemeanor.

Headlines around the country ran above evocative photos of armed black Panthers wearing berets, bomber jackets, and dark sunglasses, walking the halls of the California capitol building. In the underground press, the Panthers were front-page news. Huey Newton, Bobby Seale, and Eldridge Cleaver were overnight counterculture celebrities, and in the black community they were fierce new role models of self-empowerment.

The Black Panther Party published a ten-point program on May 15, 1967, in the second issue of the *Black Panther* newspaper. Their demands included general goals such as full employment, an end to police brutality, and better education and housing, but also called for blacks to be exempt from the military draft and for all blacks to be released from federal, state, county, and city jails.

With typical hysterical hyperbole, FBI Director J. Edgar Hoover called the party "the greatest threat to the internal security of the country," and he supervised an extensive program of surveillance, infiltration, and harassment designed to undermine Panther leadership, incriminate party members, discredit and criminalize the party, and drain the organization of resources and manpower. Many members of the Black Panthers were killed in police raids in various parts of the country.

Due to Huey P. Newton's flair for the dramatic, a poster of him sitting on a wicker throne, wearing a beret and black leather jacket, holding a rifle in one hand and a spear in the other, soon appeared widely in head shops, college dorms, and in black communities.

On October 28, 1967, Newton was celebrating the end of probation from an assault charge when he was pulled over by Oakland policeman John Frey, and Frey was killed. Newton claimed that the officer was shot accidentally by another cop, but the Black Panther leader was arrested for murder. "Free Huey" quickly became a national slogan of the counterculture. He was convicted of voluntary manslaughter in September 1968, but the conviction was later reversed on appeal. Subsequent trials resulted in hung juries, so the charges were eventually dismissed.

The passage of decades has not fully dissipated the air of controversy that surrounded the Black Panthers. It is certain that the FBI and other law enforcement agencies targeted them wildly out of proportion to any possible threat they posed to society. It was politically driven and in some cases illegal. It is equally clear that the Panthers were not a monolithic group and that some members engaged in criminal behavior that had little or nothing to do with politics. Nonetheless, in the context of 1967, the image the Panthers projected of self-empowerment was a big deal.

Martin Luther King Jr.

In retrospect, it blows my mind how little Martin Luther King Jr.'s name was present in the underground press of the time. In 1967, Dr. King's last full year of life, he remained America's most sophisticated, progressive, spiritual, and intellectual leader. A large part of the explanation must be that he was thirty-eight years old at a moment when baby boomers of all races were convinced that they, and they alone, had some ineffable kind of authenticity.

Stokely Carmichael was not the only prominent African American who derided King's commitment to nonviolence. Julius Lester wrote that King "was too Sunday school." Adam Clayton Powell Jr. called him "Martin Loser King." Many on the white new left, anxious to be au courant with black people of their generation, followed suit. In *America Divided: The Civil War of the 1960s*, Michael Kazin and Maurice Isserman, both members of the SDS, wrote: "By the summer of 1967, most white new leftists would probably have agreed that the old interracial and nonviolent civil rights movement was not only over but was proven a failure." I asked Kazin how it was that SDS paid so little attention to King at the time and he responded, "I respected Dr. King but he was older and he was a Christian preacher."

Steve Wasserman, who first supported the Panthers when he was a Berkeley High School student, speculates, "Maybe it's because he wore a suit and tie?" Although in recent decades I have come to regard King as both a saint and the preeminent American social change agent of my lifetime, I was not paying much conscious attention to him either, and yet it's clear that King's moral and political force was indispensable to the fragile balance of American political and spiritual thought in 1967.

As spring of 1967 loomed, while King was enduring contempt from some of the younger black activist world, he permanently shattered his relationship with many in the liberal and moderate worlds when he decided to publicly oppose the war in Vietnam.

King had long harbored grave doubts about the war, in part because of his ideological affinity with American pacifists, and also because he was inclined to support third world countries in conflict with European colonists. He identified with various African independence movements, particularly that of Kwame Nkrumah, who had become the first president of Ghana after the country's nonviolent assertion of independence from Great Britain in 1957. Mahatma Gandhi's successful effort to end the British colonization of India was also one of the defining examples of nonviolence that inspired King's approach to the civil rights movement.

Charles Morgan Jr., a white lawyer who was on the board of the SCLC, is quoted in Michael Ezra's *Muhammad Ali: The Making of an Icon* as saying that King was deeply affected by the boxer's courage in refusing induction. "Martin had opposed the war for a long time but his hands were tied by our Board. Then Ali spoke out publicly, he took the consequences, and I believe it had an influence on Martin. Here was somebody who had a lot to lose and was willing to risk it all to say what he believed." (When SCLC finally opposed the war, it was Morgan, by then one of Ali's lawyers, who wrote their position paper.)

King's feelings about Vietnam were also influenced by Thich Nhat Hanh, a young Vietnamese Buddhist monk who had first written to him in 1965. Hanh was an anti-Communist, but he objected to Western domination of Vietnam and to the American-backed Catholic government, which was discriminating against roughly 80 percent of the Vietnamese population who were Buddhists. At the request of A.J. Muste, whose teachings on nonviolence had so deeply influenced King and many of his colleagues, King met with Hanh in person in Chicago in the spring of 1966.

After that first meeting, King equated the Vietnamese monks' struggle with the civil rights movement. Hanh fasted with Rabbi Abraham Joshua Heschel and radical Catholic priest Father Daniel Berrigan, and meditated with Thomas Merton. He was eventually granted a three-minute private meeting with Defense Secretary Robert McNamara. Hanh published his first book, *Viet-*

nam: *Lotus in a Sea of Fire*, in 1967. On January 25 of that year, King wrote to the Nobel committee recommending the monk for the Peace Prize. Two weeks later, on February 11, 1967, Muste died at the age of eighty-two. King said that without him, "The American Negro might never have caught the meaning of true love or humanity."

Some of King's closest advisers urged him to stay out of the public debate about the war. They felt it would burden the civil rights agenda with a position unpopular with many current allies, and would certainly alienate President Johnson, who had masterfully orchestrated the passage of civil rights and antipoverty legislation. Even pacifists such as Bayard Rustin and Andrew Young were opposed to the idea of King participating in a massive peace march scheduled in New York for April 15. King's most loyal theological allies, Rabbi Heschel and John Bennett of the Union Theological Seminary, were avoiding the march, which was expected to be particularly radical in tone.

Reverend James Bevel, who was passionate in opposing the war, helped to finally persuade King to join the march. Once that decision was made, King's advisers all agreed that he should make a speech in advance to carefully lay out his thinking, rather than have his views commingled with the cacophony of voices that always resounded at peace demonstrations. (Their concerns were well founded. Much of the press coverage of the march focused on fringe activities such as the display of Communist flags and the burning of an American flag.)

Dr. King's speech on April 4 at Riverside Church in New York turned out to be one of the most thoughtful and compelling antiwar speeches of the entire movement. He began with a simple statement: "I come to this great, magnificent house of worship tonight because my conscience leaves me no other choice." He then proceeded to lay out his reasons for opposing the war.

King said that "America would never invest the necessary funds or energies in rehabilitation of its poor so long as adventures like Vietnam continued to draw men and skills and money like some demonic, destructive suction tube." He also pointed out that African Americans were disproportionately serving, and consequently being wounded and killed in the war.

King had spent hours urging frustrated young black people not to be violent—to eschew Molotov cocktails and rioting due to tactical concerns, but also as a moral issue. How, he rhetorically asked, could he urge them to be nonviolent in American slums, but to be violent in a foreign country? King also felt a special obligation as a recipient of the Nobel Peace Prize. As he had done within the civil rights movement, he questioned his fellow Christian leaders: "Have they forgotten that my ministry is in obedience to the One who loved His enemies so fully that He died for them?"

King also restated the antiwar arguments that had surfaced at the teach-ins. Vietnam was not a "domino" in the Cold War but an independent society. The US had supported Ngo Dinh Diem, a Catholic dictator who persecuted the Buddhist majority. After Diem was deposed, the US propped up a series of military leaders, none of whom exhibited any commitment to democracy. The current US ally was General Nguyen Cao Ky, who had expressed his admiration for Adolph Hitler in a recent interview. On February 25, 1967, King said, "I see our country today intervening in what is basically a civil war, destroying hundreds and thousands of Vietnamese children with napalm." King separately observed: "Increasingly, by choice or by accident, this is the role our nation has taken—the role of those who make peaceful revolution impossible by refusing to give up the privileges and the pleasures that come from the immense profits of overseas investments."

King concluded with specific proposals: end the bombing in North and South Vietnam, a universal ceasefire, curtailment of the military buildup in neighboring Thailand and Laos, inclusion of the Communist National Liberation Front in a future Vietnamese government, and a firm date for removal of all foreign troops.

This was a radical speech, considerably to the left of liberal Democrats such as Robert Kennedy, and consistent with the positions of the black and white countercultures, who were nonetheless largely ignoring him at the time. Afterward King told reporters, "Like Muhammad Ali puts it, we are all, black and brown and poor, victims of the same system of oppression."

On April 15, King joined pacifist leader Dave Dellinger, Harry Belafonte, Dr. Benjamin Spock, Stokely Carmichael, and a quarter of a million others in New York City's Central Park. More than two hundred draft cards were burned and then the vast crowd marched to the United Nations.

The next day, President Johnson ominously said in an interview that the FBI was "watching" the antiwar movement. Meanwhile, most of the American public still clung to the hope that their government was on the right track. Polls showed that 80 percent of Americans thought that bombing petroleum facilities near Hanoi would end the war.

King's decision to oppose the president drew attacks from many in both the black and white liberal communities to whom he had previously been a hero. The NAACP board voted sixty to zero to condemn him. The *New York Times* headline read, "NAACP Decries Stand of Dr. King on Vietnam: Calls It a 'Serious Tactical Mistake' to Merge Rights and Peace Drive." (King had suggested no such thing.) Some argued that the war was actually *good* for the civil rights movement because of its integrated battalions. King was also criticized by Dr. Ralph Bunche, the other black American who had won a Nobel Peace Prize, and by Carl Rowan, who as the ambassador to Finland and director of the United States Information Agency had been the highest-ranking African American in the Kennedy administration. In his masterpiece *At Canaan's Edge*, Taylor Branch wrote that Rowan "angrily told King that millions of their fellow black people would suffer for his insults against the greatest civil rights president in American history."

A highly critical *Washington Post* editorial said of King, "He has diminished his usefulness to his cause, his country, and to his people." A *New York Times'* editorial was headlined, "Dr. King's Error," and called his position "wasteful and self-defeating" and "a fusing of two public problems that are distinct and separate."

King bitterly rebuked his liberal critics. "There's something strangely inconsistent about a nation and a press that will praise you when you say, 'Be nonviolent toward [racist Alabama sheriff] Jim Clark,' but will curse and damn you when you say, 'Be nonviolent toward little brown Vietnamese children.'" He concluded, "And I don't know about you, I ain't gonna study war no more."

By the end of April, Alabama's segregationist governor George Wallace announced that he would run for president on a platform of "victory" in Vietnam and hoped to win by securing the "white backlash" vote. Wallace denied being a racist, although he chanted, "Segregation now! Segregation tomorrow! Segregation forever!" in a 1963 speech. King said, "The white backlash is merely a new name for an old phenomenon," and described Wallace in an interview as "perhaps the most dangerous racist in America today."

The riots made it obvious that de facto segregation and bias in the North were almost as corrosive as legal Jim Crow had been in the South. As the unprecedented wave of urban violence was finally dying down, on August 16, 1967, at the peak of the media focus on Black Power, King addressed over one hundred attendees in Atlanta on the occasion of the tenth anniversary of the founding of SCLC. While he proudly listed the accomplishments of the civil rights movement in the previous decade (SCLC had voter registration teams in seventy-nine Southern counties at the time), King acknowledged that in America, blacks on average still had half of the average wealth of whites, and double the unemployment and infant mortality rates.

For some time, the supposedly "moderate" King had been saying that it didn't mean all that much to get people the right to sit at a lunch counter if they didn't have the money to pay for a meal. In 1962, King had started

"Operation Breadbasket" to deploy the tactics of the civil rights movement to address racial economic imbalances. A key tactic of the organization was to foster "selective buying" (boycotts) as a means to pressure white businesses to hire African Americans and purchase goods and services from black contractors.

In 1966, King expanded Operation Breadbasket and chose twenty-five-year-old Jesse Jackson to run the Chicago chapter. Six feet three inches tall, with a prodigious Afro and a compelling oratorical talent, Jackson quickly became SCLC's most visible Northern leader.

Operation Breadbasket helped create 2,200 new black jobs in Chicago, "bringing new income to the Negro community of about $18 million," according to an October 1967 interview with King in the *Detroit Free Press*. They had pressured the mass retailer Hi-Lo into depositing enough money into local, black-owned banks to double their assets within a year, and to increase advertising in black-owned community newspapers.

And despite criticism from all sides, King continued to spread his message. In his speech at the SCLC convention in Atlanta in August 1967, he urged, "The Negro must rise up with an affirmation of his own Olympian manhood." Noting the appeal of the phrase "Black Power," King insisted that true power meant the ability to affect social and political change. "What is needed is a realization that power without love is reckless . . . and that love without power is sentimental and anemic."

In that same speech in Atlanta, King called for a guaranteed annual income for all Americans, a proposal which would still be radical fifty years later.

King remained committed to nonviolence. He

210 ☙ Danny Goldberg

mocked those who suggested that the Watts riot had been a meaningful form of activism, reminding his audience that it had produced scant results other than a few more water sprinklers. He pointed out that it was a practical impossibility for black violence to accomplish anything meaningful given the predominance of whites in political, military, and police power structures. But King's most powerful argument was the cosmic one: "Darkness cannot put out darkness; only light can do that."

Meanwhile, at the same time, in the same country, the hippies were still trying to make the world a brighter place.

CHAPTER 6
FLOWER POWER

In the wake of the Be-Ins, there was a period in 1967 when it seemed to many in the hip world that the force of agape was sufficient to overcome society's obstacles and that a utopian vision could meaningfully change mass culture for the better.

The dramatic growth in the population of acid-heads, pot smokers, meditators, activists, and others who wanted a more joyous, caring society than the one they'd grown up in, made it seem like something better was imminent. At the same time, the more thoughtful members of the hip community were well aware that new structures and ideas were necessary to deal with the explosion of interest in their culture. Many meetings focused on the possibility of building a brave new world and the avoidance of perils in attempting to do so. Not surprisingly, among the first of these took place in Northern California.

THE HOUSEBOAT SUMMIT
"We're going to discuss where it's going. The whole problem of whether to drop out or take over." So said

Alan Watts. It was February 1967, a few weeks after the Be-In, and Watts had invited Gary Snyder, Allen Ginsberg, and Timothy Leary to discuss the future on his houseboat the *Vallejo*, in Sausalito, roughly an hour outside of San Francisco.

Watts was then fifty-two years old. A native of England who had moved to California in the early fifties, he had published *The Way of Zen* in 1957; the book had introduced Zen Buddhism to thousands of American college students. As a public speaker, Watts had a humorous colloquial approach to Eastern philosophy that allowed him to bond easily with baby boomers. He also had a radio show on KPFA.

With a couple of dozen locals in attendance as a sounding board, and with Allen Cohen recording the conversation for posterity (the *Oracle* would devote an entire issue to a transcript of the "summit"), the self-styled hippie elders tried to define various aspects of the movement that they were all simultaneously leading, following, and questioning. Watts framed the conversation by observing that an elite minority (including present company) had been able to drop out in one way or another. The question at hand was whether *millions* could do it. Gary Snyder expanded on Watts's proposition: "I see it as the problem about whether or not to throw all your energies to the subculture or try to maintain some communications network within the main culture."

But before getting into a discussion of the glorious future, Ginsberg wanted to deal with the here and now: "We're accused of being leaders. We're not though, you know. What were *we* doing up on that platform?"

Leary immediately bristled: "That's a charge that doesn't bother me at all."

Watts tried to bridge the difference, siding in substance with Ginsberg, but bowing in tone to Leary, suggesting an organically designed society with no boss— parts of society work together the way cells in the body do. But Ginsberg had not finished expressing his main concern: the reaction of many young people to Leary's remarks at the Be-In a few weeks earlier: "Everybody in Berkeley, all week long, has been bugging me and Alpert about what you mean by 'Drop out, tune in, and turn on.' Finally, one young kid said, 'Drop out, turn on, and tune IN.' Meaning: get with an activity—a manifest activity, a worldly activity—that's harmonious with whatever vision he has. Everybody in Berkeley is all bugged because they think [the] 'drop out' thing really doesn't mean anything, that what you're gonna cultivate is a lot of freak-out hippies goofing around and throwing bottles through windows when they flip out on LSD."

"Berkeley" essentially meant "political radicals." Leary didn't support the war in Vietnam, but he didn't like the antiwar movement all that much either. "I want no part of mass movements," he said. "I think this is the error that leftist activists are making. I see them as young men with menopausal minds."

Like Leary, Ginsberg was a lot older than the cut-off point for the military draft, which was a day-to-day issue that younger men had to deal with. But the poet didn't see an inherent contradiction between the inner psychedelic path he shared with Leary and the antiwar movement he enthusiastically supported.

Ginsberg recalled a recent evening he'd spent with

Berkeley radical Mario Savio. Though Savio only occasionally smoked pot, the two had gotten very high. "Yesterday, he was weeping. Saying he wanted to go out and live in nature," Ginsberg said emotionally, as if this indisputably proved the soulfulness of the hero of the Free Speech Movement.

Leary was unmoved. "I respect his sincerity, but his tactics are part of the game that created the war in Vietnam: power politics. You can't do good unless you feel good. You can't do right unless you feel right."

Ginsberg responded, "You haven't dropped out, Tim. You dropped out of your job as a psychology teacher at Harvard . . . But you're not dropped out of the very highly complicated legal constitutional appeal, which you feel a sentimental regard for, as I do. You haven't dropped out of being the financial provider for Millbrook, and you haven't dropped out of planning and conducting community organization and participating in it." He went on in this vein, citing Leary's book deals and traveling theatrical tour. Leary had multiple safety nets that were not, and never would be, available to the vast majority of teenagers who were taking acid and trying to figure out how to function in the world while staying true to their new versions of themselves.

Leary then addressed the small group in a tone better suited for a lecture hall: "The first thing you have to do is completely detach yourself from anything inside the plastic robot establishment . . . Each group that drops out has two billion years of cellular equipment to answer those questions: Hey, how are we going to eat? . . . How are we going to keep warm? . . . I can envision ten MIT scientists, with their families, they've taken

LSD . . . They drop out . . . They may use their creativity to make new kinds of machines that will turn people on instead of bomb them."

Ginsberg asked, "What can I drop out of?"

Leary snapped back: "Your teaching at Cal."

The poet chuckled. "But I need the money." Then, changing to a more serious tone, he said of hippies, "I don't think they are all gonna go out on a limb. I think they'll wind up dropping back in."

Leary responded with condescension, "Allen is not ready to drop out. Don't worry, Allen, you will when the time is right."

Ginsberg defensively replied, "I'm not worried. I'm having a good time."

The meeting continued, and Leary told of the previous spring solstice when he and others at Millbrook had taken sledgehammers to break through asphalt on part of the highway to get to the real dirt. He suggested that city life would become less and less appealing to the new version of humanity he saw coming. "There will be deer grazing in Times Square in forty years," Leary predicted grandly, and woefully inaccurately. Pressed for a road map from here to there, Leary made the far more modest suggestion that there should be prayer rooms and meditation centers in every urban neighborhood so that individuals could reconnect inwardly throughout the day.

Gary Snyder spoke of times when he was able to live in a way that would later be called "off the grid." He would get rice off the San Francisco docks, day-old vegetables thrown away by supermarkets—the kinds of things the Diggers had been doing to provide free food for children in the Haight. Snyder extolled the virtues of the Plains Indians, the Sioux, and the Comanche, echoing a long-held hippie reverence for Native Americans. "[Y]ou have to be able to specifically say to somebody in Wichita, Kansas, who says, *I'm going to drop out. How do you advise me to stay living around here in this area which I like?* . . . Find out what was here before. Find out what the mythologies were."

Leary enthused: "That is a stroke of cellular revelation and genius, Gary."

Snyder had pointed out earlier that "an ecological conscience" needed to emerge. It was one of the first times that the concept of ecology entered public discourse.

Alan Watts went on to suggest that Western man had lost touch with original intelligence through centuries of relying solely on analytic thinking. Now, with psychedelics and meditation, some were reconnecting with original intelligence, "suggesting an entirely new course for the development of civilization."

Someone in the small audience asked about getting rid of the week as a measurement of time and focusing only on the month, the lunar cycle. Watts shot this down because the week system includes Sunday for Sabbath. Without the framework of a week, Watts worried, society would jettison the day off. (He did not mention that the convention of weekends without work was the result of decades of efforts by the labor movement. The lack of mutual respect between unions and the counterculture would be bad for both movements as the subsequent decades unfolded.)

There was then a long digression about the viability of group marriage. If a new society was being built, everything was up for grabs. Watts was all for it. Leary wanted nothing to do with this notion; he believed in couples.

Another attendee raised an issue that was hanging over the fragile hippie culture: "Diggers say since the Be-In, thousands of kids have come to the city and they don't know where they're at." None of the "elders" had a solution. Another audience member asked worriedly, "Don't tribes learn to mistrust *other* tribes?" In retrospect, this was an extremely important question. In the moment, on the houseboat, however, the elders seemed stumped.

Yet Leary was determined to stay positive: "If Pepsi-Cola can be marketed around the world, so can hippie ideas."

Ginsberg returned to his earlier argument: "The whole thing is too big, because it doesn't say drop out of *what*, precisely. What everybody is dealing with is people, it's not dealing with institutions. It's dealing with them but also dealing with people. Working with and including the police."

Remarkably, Leary then changed the aggressive tone he'd been using all day. He wasn't going to ruin the vibe between him and Ginsberg over this slogan and he adroitly retreated. "You know, I always say to take what I say with a grain of salt. Half of what I say is wrong. I make many blunders. Maybe we should change it to, 'Turn on, tune in, drop *in*.'" But the media die had been cast at the Be-In, and for better or worse, Leary was stuck with the McLuhanesque slogan for the rest of his life.

Around the same time, Jerry Rubin ran for mayor

of Berkeley with a platform of: peace in Vietnam/end poverty/stop police harassment/eighteen-year-old vote/ legalize marijuana/rent control/Black Power/student power/fight racism/tax the rich/plant trees and flowers. During the last month of the campaign, Rubin thought he had a chance to win and often spoke wearing a jacket and tie. But on election day, April 4, he only got around eight thousand votes, which was 22 percent of the electorate. After that, he changed course and morphed into a radical hippie.

Jerry Rubin

The Summer of Love

Joel Selvin has written, "The Summer of Love never really happened. Invented by the fevered imaginations of writers for weekly news magazines, the phrase entered the public vocabulary with the impact of a sledgeham-mer, glibly encompassing a social movement sweeping the youth of the world, hitting the target with the pin-point accuracy of a shotgun blast."

Nevertheless, the media phrase affected reality. In April 1967, in a relatively small box near the back of the *Oracle*, a notice read:

> *Haight-Ashbury has been practicing a warless way of living and loving and creating and exchanging for a new age. New forms, successes, and failures and dreams have drawn great attention to the Haight-Ashbury.*
>
> *While American nightmares its military hells of the mind, Americans loving love and hoping peace and seek-ing wisdom and seeking guidance have turned toward the Haight-Ashbury and are journeying here.*

The notice exhorted all new visitors to bring warm clothing, food, ID, sleeping bags, and camping equipment.

The *Oracle* postulated that there were "two sides of the kettle" of Haight-Ashbury, the *Oracle* itself and the Diggers. The reality was that there were dozens of sides. The Diggers were not the only people in the hip commu-nity who felt that the *Oracle* was too pompous. One sar-castic letter to the editor called it "The Hindu Science Monitor." J.M. Jamil Brownson, who had edited the first issue of the *Oracle*, left because he felt that an ethnically diverse "rainbow culture" was being jettisoned by Co-hen and Bowen in favor of the insular white psychedelic culture.

Despite the internal differences, everyone in the hip community knew that both a great opportunity and a great crisis were at hand. The hype about the Summer of Love threatened the stability of Haight-Ashbury. Hundreds of teenagers arrived on an hourly basis in a section of the city without any capacity to contain them. The Council for the Summer of Love was formed to raise money to plan for the onslaught, but San Francisco supervisors were unsympathetic. On a citywide basis, it was not politically popular to further enable the influx of hippies. (One exception among elected officials was Willie Brown, whose state assembly district included Haight-Ashbury. In a letter to the supervisors, he requested more trash cans in the neighborhood, because of the influx of visitors.)

Some local businesses that had little or no emotional connection to a utopian notion pounced. A coffee shop sold "love burgers." Tourist buses now included hippies as a highlight of San Francisco for sightseers.

In addition to teens, a parade of writers, musicians, and artists from around the world made their way to Haight-Ashbury. Seventy-eight-year-old British historian Arnold Toynbee went to a Quicksilver Messenger Service show. The internationally famous ballet dancers Dame Margot Fonteyn and Rudolf Nureyev were busted at a party in Haight-Ashbury where pot was being smoked. Nureyev performed a jeté into the back of a police van. They were released because there was no proof that they had personally indulged in smoking weed.

Paul McCartney visited San Francisco and immediately went to the Fillmore, where the Airplane was rehearsing. The band invited him back to their apartment on Oak Street, where Marty Balin, Jack Casady, and manager Bill Thompson were staying. They offered him a new psychedelic drug called DMT, which had LSD's intensity but only lasted a couple of hours. The Beatle demurred and just smoked pot. He tried to jam, but the left-handed McCartney had a hard time playing Casady's bass. Before leaving, he played them an advance copy of the soon-to-be-released *Sgt. Pepper's* album.

The Haight-Ashbury Free Medical Clinic was founded in June 1967 by Dr. David E. Smith, who immediately became a go-to source for journalists covering the Summer of Love. Smith staffed the clinic with volunteers who contributed samples of penicillin and tranquilizers from local hospitals where they also interned. Aware of police scrutiny, Smith put up a sign on the door that read, *No dealing! No holding drugs. No using drugs. No alcohol. No pets. Any of these can close the clinic. We love you.* The clinic served more than two hundred and fifty people a day. Among the most common ailments treated at the clinic were bad trips, drug overdoses, and venereal diseases. (As of the writing of this book in 2017, the clinic is still operating.)

There were ongoing tensions between hippies and local police, who periodically enforced the drug laws and were under constant pressure from local businesses to help minimize disruptions in traffic.

Censorship of the arts was still a major issue in 1967. Lenny Bruce had died of an overdose the previous year, driven to despair by relentless and unconscionable obscenity prosecutions of his stand-up performances. Statements of support for *The Beard* (a Michael McClure play that had been shut down by the cops) came in from Norman Mailer, Robert Creeley, and Allen Ginsberg, among others.

Parallel to the Haight world, the antiwar movement was surging, but combining the cultures remained elusive. On April 15, the same day that Martin Luther King Jr. led the march to the United Nations in New York, there was a march in San Francisco to Kezar Stadium. At the outset, there were 50,000 people there, but the pacifist organizers focused the program on the earnest but unhip peaceniks. Country Joe and the Fish played from the back of a truck as the march went on, yet once inside the stadium they were only given enough time for two songs. Ginsberg complained that they had foolishly ignored the hippies and the crowd dispersed early.

Nonetheless, the Vietnam War was inescapable even at the *Oracle*. Early in 1967, they published "A Curse on the Men in Washington, Pentagon," a Gary Snyder poem which addressed those at the Department of Defense with the lines: *"To trample your throat in your dreams / This magic I work, this loving I give / that my children may flourish / And yours won't thrive."* The decision to publish was controversial within the *Oracle*, and involved a vote by the entire staff. By a margin of one vote, the paper moved forward with running the poem, a decision that resulted in a photographer, whose father worked at the Pentagon, leaving the magazine. The August issue had the line "Psychedelics, Flowers, and War" on its cover, and it included two full pages dedicated to a Michael McClure poem.

In representing the sensibilities of the community that had put Haight-Ashbury on the cultural map, the *Oracle* focused much of its energy on visions of a more positive alternate society. Many of the *Oracle* writers and artists refused to sign their work, because they felt that their writing came from a higher conscious-ness. One frequent theme in the paper was getting back to nature. A writer who identified himself by the ini-tials S.B. extolled "those who seek being rather than status and who decide to return to the land often to attain an ethical relationship with nature." Other ar-ticles focused on organic gardening and astrology. There was even a piece on Aquarian tarot cards, and another headlined, "Dialogue between Astronomer and Philosopher."

Letters to the editor poured in from newly formed hip communities around the country.

Rock and roll was not the only art form integrating and influencing hippie culture. Poster artists such as Wes Wilson and Rick Griffin created a new and mind-expanding cosmology. R. Crumb helped invent radical comics that provided satire and perspective on the counterculture, unavailable elsewhere. Richard Brautigan brought commune culture into fiction.

There was an ongoing debate between the majority of hippies who were staunch advocates of psychedelics and those who had adopted antidrug spiritual practices. The *Oracle* ran a long piece on a Hindu teacher named Chinmayananda, and an article titled, "Yoga and the Psychedelic Mind," by Bob Simmons.

The *Oracle*'s brightly colored graphics enhanced the synthesis of these notes in the hippie chord. One issue featured a gorgeous full-page Rick Griffin silkscreen of a Christlike figure pouring out two cups of energy into heads of unicorns. A writer named Tom Law (later a member of Wavy Gravy's Hog Farm commune) suggested that readers "guard carefully against feeling that we are a special, new, or unique tribe. We are the ancient tribal consciousness of man in harmonious relationship with nature . . . Let's make Haight Love together, and then move to the country where love is hanging out waiting."

Indeed, the best-known San Francisco rockers quietly moved from the increasingly chaotic Haight-Ashbury streets to Marin County, including Janis Joplin, the Dead, and the Airplane. Even the Diggers increasingly occupied Morningstar Ranch in Sonoma, which had originally belonged to Lou Gottlieb of the folk group the Limelighters.

LOWER EAST SIDE

Looking over copies of the *East Village Other* from 1967, it seems as if the Fugs performed weekly in New York at a benefit show or protest rally. The obscenity trial for the Peace Eye Bookstore finally came to court, and the store was acquitted. On February 17, 1967, *Life* put Ed Sanders on its cover, proclaiming him "a leader of New York's Other Culture."

This kind of visibility gave Sanders the clout to negotiate a deal with the mayor's office to allow a series of free concerts in Tompkins Square Park. Naturally, the Fugs played at one of them. The Lower East Side had been a predominantly black and Puerto Rican neighborhood before the hippies descended to take advantage of the low rents and there were bitter disputes about what kind of music should be played in the park.

However, all the groups were cool with a performance in the park by the Grateful Dead on June 1, 1967, on the band's first visit to New York. In appreciation of their temporarily unifying influence, NYC Parks Commissioner Thomas Hoving arranged for the New York Police Department to escort the Dead to the gig, where the band was met by a welcoming parade of approximately eighty Lower East Side hippies. The band member Pigpen was given a "key to the city" made of white carnations, which he placed on his organ for the concert. The small park was packed with three thousand people. Although it was just a few days after the cops had busted forty-one people in the neighborhood, this time the police looked the other way when joints were thrown from the stage. Maybe it was in deference to the newfound celebrity of the band, or maybe there were just too many people smoking pot to bust them. During one of Garcia's solos, a framed picture of Jesus was thrown onto the stage, damaging Pigpen's organ.

Grateful Dead

The next day, the Dead visited Timothy Leary in Mill-brook and he played them the just-released *Sgt. Pepper's Lonely Heart's Club Band*. The band then returned to the city for a couple more shows. On June 9, just before an appearance at the Café Au Go Go, the Dead had dinner at an Italian restaurant called Emilio's with Tom Wolfe, who was putting the finishing touches on his book *The Electric Kool-Aid Acid Test*.

In the early spring of 1967, Emmett Grogan, Peter Berg, and other Diggers had visited the Lower East Side and were "received in the hippie community like visiting royalty," according to Don McNeill in the *Village Voice*. Within days, Berg was a guest on *The Alan Burke Show*. Burke had a populist tough-guy persona, but he liked to have countercultural people on to argue with. He was no match for the Diggers, though, and he lost control of his show when Berg shoved a pie into the face of an audience member, a woman whom he absurdly claimed was Emma Goldman, the legendary anarchist who had died in 1940. (Some accounts of the exchange say that Berg actually called her Emma Grogan, a riff on the name of his Digger colleague). The audience member was in on the stunt, and the appearance by Berg influenced at least one New Yorker—Abbie Hoffman. While still relatively unknown, Hoffman watched carefully and plotted how to adapt Digger energy to the Lower East Side scene.

For serious old peace-movement types like Cora Weiss, Abbie was too weird. "I liked him a lot person-ally, but when he'd look at me at rallies to try to get a speaking slot, I wouldn't let him on," she says. Weiss's branch of the movement aimed to convert older adults who were getting disillusioned by the increasingly implausible Cold War rhetoric coming out of Washington.

Sometime in 1967, Hoffman had published a pamphlet called *Fuck the System* under the pseudonym George Metesky (the real Metesky was known as the "mad bomber" for having planted thirty-three bombs around New York City in the forties and fifties, and had long been held in a mental institution). The pamphlet listed ways of getting things for free in New York City, and advice on how to deal with the cops.

This very irreverence that made Abbie appealing to kids like me made him problematic for the more mainstream peace movement's agenda. Although he was an old man of thirty in 1967, Abbie had a knowing twinkle in his eye that made it obvious he was one of us, not one of them.

On the other end of the antiwar continuum, Abbie was criticized by Diggers like Coyote, who considered him to be a "media junkie." Emmett Grogan was even more cutting in his criticism of Hoffman's penchant for visibility and the two became bitter enemies. Paul Krassner told me that Anita Hoffman had told *him* that during this period Grogan raped her as a way of humiliating her husband.

These internecine tensions were invisible to me when I was a teenager. Hoffman's media presence was one of the things about him that I appreciated. Kids like me had no other way of being turned on to the sort of humorous but uncompromising rebellion that he had become famous for.

Hoffman's first full-length book, *Revolution for the Hell of It*, was published under the pseudonym "Free," but everybody knew who the real author was, as the Diggers bitterly pointed out—a Richard Avedon photo of Abbie jumping for joy was featured on the cover. The book reached hundreds of thousands of kids around the country who had never seen one of the mimeographed pamphlets the Diggers handed out.

One attitude Hoffman borrowed from the Diggers was a fierce differentiation from flower children. "Personally I always held my flower in a clenched fist," he wrote in his autobiography, *Soon to Be a Major Motion Picture*. "A semi-structure-freak among the love children, I was determined to bring the hippie movement into a broader protest."

In August, during the Newark riots, Abbie trucked in food, clothing, and blankets to the embattled city, but after that, his political and cultural actions were defined by his passion for bringing radical ideas to the mass media. With the exception of Dr. King, Hoffman understood this art better than any other activist in the sixties.

On August 24, Hoffman, Jim Fouratt, and a dozen friends entered the visitors' entrance to the New York Stock Exchange. Among them was Jerry Rubin, who had just moved to New York to help plan the protest scheduled for later in the year outside of the Pentagon. Rubin, having fully morphed into hip culture, would now say that he and Abbie were Marxists, "in the revolutionary tradition of Groucho, Chico, Harpo, and Karl."

Although Hoffman would later make the dubious claim that he had not alerted the media, several TV camera crews showed up. The cameras made the security people nervous and they asked for the visitors' names, to which Fouratt replied, "George Metesky," and said they were with the "East Side Service Organization" (the acronym of which was ESSO, the name of one of the Rockefeller oil companies). A guard confronted them and said, "Hippies are not allowed in." Abbie snapped back, "Well, look, we're Jewish. You don't let Jews in the Stock Exchange?" Perhaps worried about the prospect of a headline reading, "Stock Market Bans Jews," the guard dutifully wrote, *George Metesky and friends*, on his notepad and escorted them to seats in the visitors' gallery just above the trading floor.

Immediately, the group began throwing handfuls of one-dollar bills over the railing, laughing the entire time. (The exact number of bills is a matter of dispute; Hoffman later wrote that it was three hundred, while others said no more than forty were thrown.) A number of the people on the floor scurried and pushed each other out of the way to get the bills. The chaos itself was the conceptual art that Hoffman had envisioned—the greed of people on Wall Street was so ingrained that they would act like desperate kids in a playground even for an extra dollar or two.

The bills barely had time to land on the ground before guards began removing the group from the building. The stunt had a poetry to it that implied contempt for the selfish side of capitalism, and the news coverage of the morning made Abbie Hoffman a celebrity overnight. (A few months later, the stock exchange installed bulletproof glass panels around the visitors' gallery, as well as a metal grillwork ceiling. A spokesman told the *New York Times* that this was for "reasons of security.")

Once outside, Hoffman, Fouratt, and the other activists held hands and chanted, "*Free! Free!*" Hoffman then lit the edge of a five-dollar bill on fire, but a guy in a suit grabbed it from him, stamped on it, and said: "You're disgusting." (A few months earlier, the Diggers had burned money at a demonstration outside of the *East Village Other*'s offices, but got far less attention than Hoffman and his crew did at the stock exchange.)

Hoffman was now one of the most visible figures in the theoretically leaderless hip community of New York. He was arrested and beaten at many protests, but at the same time developed a relationship with Captain Joseph Fink of the Ninth Precinct that covered the Lower East Side. (Like many of Hoffman's political adversaries, Fink was Jewish, and Hoffman tried to connect with him on that basis.)

Hoffman showed up as a speaker at New York events as diverse as a seminar at the radical *Catholic Worker* and a meeting at the Hudson Institute, the think tank run by military-industrial-complex theoretician Herman Kahn. (One of Kahn's colleagues told Hoffman, sotto voce, "We're glad you brought your girlfriends. They are a lot prettier than ours.")

Hoffman strove to synthesize the various aspects of the left and counterculture. Although his own personal dramas would interfere with his legacy, some of the "words of wisdom" he wrote in his first book stand up pretty well as a document of the attitudes of those few who tried to fuse together hippies and "revolutionary" politics.

"The first line of defense is to turn on the enemy." (I'm pretty sure Abbie meant "turn on" in the sense of offering an adversary a joint, or at least a loving insight.) And later he instructed: "When you meet a brother, never preach to him" (just exchange info), and, "Never forget that ours is the battle against a machine not against people." He also addressed his and others' commitment to nonviolence: "Although I admire the revolutionary art of the Black Panthers, I feel guns alone will never change this System. You don't use a gun on an IBM computer. You pull the plug out."

On February 22, 1967, the Off-Broadway satire *MacBird!* opened at the Village Gate. The *Realist*'s Paul Krassner invested $3,000 in it, and I found out about the play in his publication. It was written by Barbara Garson, a Berkeley playwright and activist. I was mesmerized by the savage wit with which she adapted the plot of Shakespeare's *Macbeth* to modern American politics. It starred the then-unknown Stacy Keach as the Johnson-like title character, Rue McClanahan as Lady MacBird, and William Devane as Robert Ken O'Dunc, obviously based on Robert Kennedy. In tune with the resentment (some of it irrational) that had developed for President Johnson in the counterculture, the harsh satire suggested that the Texan had been responsible for President Kennedy's murder. In real life, President Johnson's wife, Lady Bird Johnson, had made beautifying the highways her personal project. In the play, Lady MacBird had an exaggerated obsession with flowers related to her guilt, riffing on the "out, out damn spot" moment that Lady Macbeth has in Shakespeare's original work. The *New York Times* panned its "crackpot consensus," and the *New Yorker* reviewer Edith Oliver wrote, "The cruelty and vulgarity are almost beyond description." Even more remarkably, the magazine refused to run an ad for the play. Although I didn't believe that Johnson killed Kennedy, I did believe he killed a lot of the spirit that Kennedy had inspired in America. And I knew how to differentiate between docudrama and satire. Once again, the "establishment world" and our "real world" were two very different places.

In the spring of 1967, the *Realist* reached its peak connection to the American zeitgeist. In what would be both Krassner's most famous and most *infamous* piece, he wrote a cover story called "The Parts That Were Left Out of the Kennedy Book." Historian William Manchester had been asked by Jacqueline Kennedy to write a book about her husband's assassination, but when he completed the manuscript, *The Death of a President*, the first lady took legal action, successfully forcing Manchester to remove portions of his account. Krassner's satirical imagination of those portions was written in a pitch-perfect replica of Manchester's style and stated that Jackie Kennedy had seen Lyndon Johnson literally fucking the fatal wound in John Kennedy's head. Krassner, who had a keen interest in JFK assassination conspiracy theories, was on one hand creating a metaphor for the worst fears about the killing, while at the same time testing the credulity of his readers, some of whom initially took the satire literally. This was decades before "fake news" became a phenomenon.

The very same issue had a cartoon by former *Mad* magazine artist Wally Wood that depicted Disney characters having an orgy. Krassner heard that Disney executives had considered a lawsuit to protect their legendary intellectual property, but decided against it when they realized that the *Realist* had virtually no financial assets and that any lawsuit would give more publicity to what they considered to be a repulsive image.

Around the same time, Timothy Leary announced the formation of his new religion, the League for Spiritual Discovery, at a press conference at the Village Theatre. Some of the reporters in attendance were scared to drink the coffee on the buffet table because they worried it might be dosed with LSD. Leary told a reporter for *Look*, "Someday, instead of asking what book you are reading—they'll ask what level of consciousness you're at." Krassner interrupted with, "But the same way they lie about what they are reading, they'll fake levels of consciousness too."

Leary was at his most unfiltered, asserting that children as young as seven or eight could safely take LSD. He also announced that three consciousness-raising "plays" were being produced, and would soon tour: *The Death of the Mind*, *The Resurrection of Jesus Christ*, and *The Illumination of the Buddha*.

As if Leary didn't have enough pressure on him from various branches of the government and from attacks on his penchant for publicity from the Diggers, the Progressive Labor Party's weekly newspaper *Challenge* asserted that he was actually working *for* the government. As "evidence," the magazine wrote that by urging young people to detach from "games," including antiwar activities, Leary played into the hands of the establishment. They found it sinister that the prowar Henry and Clare Luce had supposedly contributed to Leary's defense fund and that *Life* had recently published a pro-LSD story.

Despite the dizzying array of left-wing antiwar factions, there was still a group of Lower East Side freaks who felt that no one represented the precise sensibilities of the neighborhood, so they formed Up Against the

234 ♀ Danny Goldberg

Wall Motherfuckers in 1967. Their name was taken from the LeRoi Jones poem, and they were described as "a street gang with an analysis," claiming to be the Lower East Side chapter of SDS. (Todd Gitlin points out that "no application for an SDS charter was ever refused.") For their first public action, the Motherfuckers carried garbage from the Lower East Side and dumped it into the fountain in front of the recently opened Metropolitan Opera House at Lincoln Center.

BOSTON AND CANADA

Notwithstanding my myopic view that focused predominantly on New York City and the Bay Area, there were compatible communities developing in dozens of other places in the Western world by 1967.

Boston had the largest college population in the country. MIT was home to lefty icon Noam Chomsky, and Harvard had a lively SDS chapter, and had been where Leary and Alpert emerged as LSD advocates. Boston University, Brandeis, Radcliffe, Tufts, and Emerson were also among the many colleges based in the Boston area.

WBCN, which would become one of the most political and influential FM stations, did not start the "underground rock" format until March 1968, but in 1967, Boston hippies were able to watch a TV show chronicling hip culture called *What's Happening Mr. Silver?* hosted by a twenty-two-year-old British transplant named David Silver, whose day job was teaching English literature at Tufts. Silver regularly covered Boston love-ins and peace protests and was host to a who's who of the counterculture, including Abbie Hoffman and Julius Lester. He also had a surprisingly civil conversation/debate with conservative William F. Buckley Jr., who was disarmed by Silver's unpretentious decency.

In Montreal, a lot of countercultural activity was centered around a geodesic dome designed by Buckminster Fuller at the USA Pavilion at Montreal's Expo 67. (In 2017 it is an environmental museum called the Montreal Biosphere.)

Like Marshall McLuhan, Fuller was a visionary intellectual from another time who was embraced by younger kindred spirits in the counterculture of the sixties. He was seventy-two years old in 1967, but was brimming with futuristic visions, which he expressed with machine-gun verbal intensity.

A Boston Be-In

Fuller, a native of Massachusetts who mostly grew up in Maine and would later be considered one of America's greatest intellectuals, was a Harvard dropout who had an epiphany in his early thirties following the failure of his business, the death of his young daughter, and a descent into alcoholism. While contemplating suicide, he had a vision in which he felt himself suspended several feet from the ground and heard a voice saying to him, "From now on you need never await temporal attestation to your thought. You think the truth. You do not have the right to eliminate yourself. You do not belong to you. You belong to Universe. Your significance will remain forever obscure to you, but you may assume that you are fulfilling your role if you apply yourself to converting your experiences to the highest advantage of others."

Not long thereafter, Fuller invented the geodesic dome structure for which he became famous. A passionate environmentalist who coined the phrase "spaceship earth," Fuller was one of the first public figures to focus attention on the perils of dependence on fossil fuels. As early as the 1960s, he believed human societies would soon rely mainly on renewable sources of energy, such as solar and wind power. He hoped for an age of "omni-successful education and sustenance of all humanity."

In February 1967, there was a counterculture conference at the University of Toronto called Perception 67 which featured appearances by the Fugs, Paul Krassner, Richard Alpert, and hip fashion designer Tiger Morse. (Leary had been invited, but the Canadian government would not allow him entry into the country.)

Alpert and Dr. Humphry Osmond, a Candian psychedelic peer of Oscar Janiger, debated with antidrug crusaders including philosopher Charles Hanly, who called LSD "an opiate for the mentally lame, intellectually halt, and morally blind." Alpert countered, "If I have to wind up psychotic to break the status quo and get to a meaningful future, I'm ready."

On another panel, Allen Ginsberg said that LSD provided the same high as having sex, solitude, or mountain climbing, but was more reliable than any of these activities.

The last night featured Paul Krassner performing a monologue, poetry by Ginsberg, a musical set by the Fugs, and ended with remarks by Marshall McLuhan, who was wearing a prismatic disc on his forehead.

LONDON

In July 1967, at the Roundhouse in London, there was a two-week conference portentously titled the Congress on the Dialectics of Liberation. Originally conceived by therapists known as "antipsychiatrists," such as R.D. Laing, to discuss issues like treatment of schizophrenia, the mission of the congress transformed into "a unique gathering to demystify violence in all its forms," and became London's major intellectual countercultural conclave of the decade.

Most of the speakers were the big radical academic brains of the Western world at the time. Among them were my friend Joel's uncle Paul Goodman, then fifty-five years old, and Herbert Marcuse, almost seventy, who was a German Socialist and political theorist who had emigrated to the US. Marcuse was the ideological idol of many radicals around the world, including Abbie Hoffman and Angela Davis. (In *Revolution for the Hell of It*, Hoffman wrote that Marcuse smoked hash at the conference, but it is possible this was wishful thinking.)

The organizers were old-school intellectual radicals. Paul Goodman had developed a disdainful attitude toward much of the youth culture, and he lamented the hippies' apparent lack of respect for expertise, criticizing what he perceived as an obsession with "inner" experiences. In his 1970 book *New Reformation*, Goodman wrote, "I knew that I could not get through to them. I had imagined that the worldwide student protest had to do with changing political and moral institutions, to which I was sympathetic, but I now saw that we had to deal with a religious crisis of the magnitude of the Reformation in the 1500s."

Other old lefties worried that a stoner departure from rational thought could make the movement susceptible to dark social forces. British playwright Arnold Wesker, one of the founders of the Roundhouse and an antinuclear activist, had referred to hippies as "pretty little fascists."

To many in the counterculture, these criticisms were akin to those of folk music purists who had freaked out when Bob Dylan went electric. *San Francisco Chronicle* critic Ralph J. Gleason, who would become one of the founders of *Rolling Stone*, mocked many in the old left as "prisoners of logic."

There would be no rock and roll, tabs of acid, or nudity at the convention, but in a nod to the burgeoning youth culture, a panel with Emmett Grogan, Stokely Carmichael, and Allen Ginsberg took place on the last day.

Grogan wore a work shirt, corduroy pants, and a necklace of wooden beads. He gave a fiery oration that ended with the statement, "History will judge the movement not according to the swine we have removed or imprisoned but according to whether the revolution has succeeded in returning the power to the people." Grogan was rewarded with a standing ovation, after which he revealed that the words had been an English translation of a speech Adolf Hitler had given to the Reichstag in 1937. The point was to sensitize the radical audience to the moral emptiness of much of what passed for revolutionary rhetoric.

Carmichael had stepped down as leader of SNCC but remained affiliated with the organization, and had recently been named honorary prime minister of the Black Panther Party. He was dressed in a gold suit and wore dark glasses. Immediately prior to the panel, Ginsberg had introduced Carmichael to Grogan, but the Digger had just shot some heroin, which was perhaps why he refused to shake the civil rights leader's hand. Carmichael was infuriated at the slight as he walked onto the stage, but he had long before learned how to channel hurt feelings into effective public speaking.

He spoke so powerfully that Ginsberg admiringly called him "a young shaman." Carmichael referred to urban riots as "rebellions or guerrilla warfare," and rhetorically aligned America's racial struggles with movements by people of color in Africa and other parts of the third world. He lamented the recent death of Che Guevara and insisted, "[R]evolutionaries of the world [must] redouble their decision to fight on to the final defeat of imperialism."

Carmichael ended his remarks by expressing contempt for the "flower power" of young white hippies. This ephemeral "tactic," he felt, had absolutely no effect on reducing violence against black people nor in stopping the war in Vietnam. The audience of intellectuals gave him a standing ovation. A lot of the old left already believed that hippies were a self-indulgent movement of "haves" who had far too little compassion for the "have-nots."

Ginsberg had just spent several weeks in Rapallo, Italy, with the eighty-two-year-old Ezra Pound, who at that point in his life was in such a state of melancholia that he often went weeks without uttering a word. Even with such an idol, Ginsberg was an evangelist for youth culture. He played the *Sgt. Pepper's* album, Donovan's *Sunshine Superman*, and Dylan's *Blonde on Blonde*, and before Ginsberg left, Pound spoke to and embraced him.

The day before the congress commenced, Ginsberg had done a Hare Krishna chant at a rally to legalize marijuana in London's Hyde Park attended by five thousand British heads. Early on during the congress, Allen sang a musical melody he had written to an English translation by Shunryu Suzuki of the *Prajnaparamita Sutra*.

Grogan, who was a withering critic of most hip celebrities, made an exception for Ginsberg, calling him "the kind of good person that is hard to find." For additional moral support, Ginsberg brought beatnik icon William Burroughs, author of the novel *Naked Lunch*. The Beatles had included Burroughs in their montage on the *Sgt. Pepper's* album cover. He didn't speak at the conference but stood in the back, rarely removing his black raincoat and hat.

The closing-day panel with Grogan and Carmichael was to be Ginsberg's last chance to communicate with this particular gathering of intellectuals, and he had promised not to chant. He began by respectfully challenging Carmichael's depiction of hippies. "The best experience I have had has been with the younger people in America, and some few of my own generation who have had to confront the mass hallucination, or style of consciousness, or mode of consciousness, into which we were born, and had some kind of mental breakthrough, which clarified not only the nature of our own identity, but also the nature of others' identities, as being the same as our own."

Younger people! That was the key energy of the moment. Beats like Allen, left-wingers, and black nationalists had stood against both racism and materialism in decades past, but things were different now because of this vast new generation. Unlike older radical intellectuals at the congress, Allen was embracing them. He seemed to be saying that the same dominant culture that oppressed black people had stifled many young whites. The room was silent. Carmichael peered at him through his dark glasses. What possible connection was there between the "inner" worlds supposedly opened up by LSD that Ginsberg was so enraptured by and the moral nightmare of racism and other forms of oppression? Ginsberg continued, "That is not, necessarily, to preclude our taking detached action within the situation."

Action! But Ginsberg was not referring to confrontations with police. "The most detached action that I have seen taken, within the situation, is the use of LSD by the younger people, for the purpose of demystifying their own consciousness and arriving at some sort of meat-universe where they are sitting with flowers, ourselves." Earlier in the year, Ginsberg had said, "Flower power is the power of the earth itself."

The poet acknowledged that attempts by the hippie culture were experimental thus far. "We have very small community groups, in San Francisco and in New York, beginning to leave the money-wheel, and also beginning to leave the hallucination-wheel of the media, beginning to form small cooperatives, tribal units, societies of their own."

He turned to Carmichael and continued, "The reason the hippies have taken on these beads, appurtenances, music, of shamanistic groups, of ecstatic trance-state types, is because they are beginning to explore, for the first time, the universe of consciousness of other cultures beside their own." Some clusters of hippies were even "beginning to move in on authority with those weapons which have been called 'flower power,' being euphemistic for a simple, calm, tranquil equilibrium, nonviolent, as far as possible, as far as the self can be controlled, so that it can relate to other selves in disguise, including the police."

Including the police! Carmichael had sarcastically said he would have more respect for flowers if they'd had any effect on the Newark police who had, in recent days, brutally quashed the riots in their city. This was exactly the sort of language that drove him crazy about the hippies.

"Mr. Ginsberg, I don't know much about the hippie movement, but I would like to beg to differ with you," said Carmichael. "I think the reason most of them are hippies today is because they are confused little kids who have run away from their home and who will return to their culture within a year or two."

Ginsberg responded: "There's no culture to return to."

To which Carmichael fired back indignantly, "Before I find *my* individual self, I must find my *group* culture."

The poet countered with a rueful smile. "We don't have a viable group culture either, so we're in the same boat, in that sense."

Carmichael nodded respectfully but had another point to make. Nothing the hippies had done had reduced white-on-black violence.

Ginsberg was quick to answer: "Nothing *anyone* has done, not hippies *nor* the Black Power movement, has reduced such violence so far." This quiet point seemed consistent with Grogan's earlier dramatic put-on. The word "revolution" had an intoxicating sound, and angry tones could temporarily be cathartic, but what did it really mean if people's day-to-day lives became worse in their wake?

The establishment was not charmed by the earnestness of the exchange. British authorities were terrified that American race riots would spread to black sections of the UK such as Brixton and Notting Hill. As things turned out, black people in Britain did not riot that summer, but when tapes of Carmichael's remarks were made public the next month, he was banned from reentering the country.

There were a couple of other significant moments that the congress is remembered for. On the last day, six British women jumped onto the stage at the Roundhouse and bitterly complained about the inherent sexism of the meetings. Out of twenty-two speakers, only two were female and even they had been placed in secondary sessions. More effective struggles by women of the left to avoid such absurd disparities were soon to come.

Ginsberg's favorite speaker was British anthropologist Gregory Bateson, who conducted a seminar called "Ecological Destruction by Technology." Bateson introduced his theory of the effect of pollution on increasing the temperature of the earth's atmosphere. Shortly thereafter, Ginsberg told an interviewer, "You keep the heat up and the fog gathers up and pretty soon you have a cloud over the sky and you have the greenhouse effect and the earth will heat up and melt the poles and the poles will melt and drown cities." This was one of the first times the concept of "global warming" was discussed outside of scientific circles.

Despite all of the brainpower assembled at the congress, it did not encompass everything that was going on in the minds of the counterculture. There was another note in the mystic chord of 1967. The very next month, the Beatles made front-page news by meeting with a man who had very different ideas about how enlightened human beings should use their minds.

CHAPTER 7
BEING THERE THEN

Postsixties pop culture has been quite dismissive about the hippies' interest in Eastern religion. Mike Myers caricatured yogis in *The Love Guru*. In the TV show *The Sopranos*, Tony's homicidal sister Janice and suicidal girlfriend Gloria Trillo are both self-professed Buddhists. In *This Is Spinal Tap*, David St. Hubbins's girlfriend Jeanine foolishly makes up itineraries with the astrological symbol of each band member on the tour book. Edina, the burned-out protagonist of the British sitcom *Absolutely Fabulous*, chants "*Om*" while inebriated. The film *Bull Durham* opens with this voice-over from Susan Sarandon's character: "I've tried all the major religions and most of the minor ones. I've worshipped Buddha, Allah, Brahma, Vishnu, Shiva, trees, mushrooms, and Isadora Duncan."

Putting aside the fact that Buddhists don't worship Buddha, the ridicule reflects the shallowness of people who adopted superficial symbols of yoga and meditation while maintaining selfish, egotistical behavior. Like every other belief system, the Eastern religions that grew more popular in America in the sixties could be used as masquerades by bullshit artists and self-deceivers, but the existence of loudmouthed fakes didn't erase the authenticity of sincere seekers.

In 1967, the growing presence of non-Western spiritual and esoteric traditions was part of the air that animated the hippie idea. On the mass media screen, no one was bigger than the Beatles, and George Harrison's fascination with Eastern spirituality was as much a part of the band's image in their last few years together as their haircuts had been when they'd first burst onto the scene. I became a vegetarian at the end of the sixties, and when people ask me why, I still sheepishly say that it's because I read that Harrison was one.

The internationally known master of the sitar, Ravi Shankar, was a key catalyst in George Harrison's interest in Hindu paths. Harrison, who took sitar lessons from Shankar, had first played the ancient instrument on "Norwegian Wood." "Ravi was one person who impressed me," wrote Harrison in the introduction to Shankar's autobiography. "I mean . . . Elvis impressed me . . . but you couldn't later on go round to him and say, *Elvis, what was happening in the universe?*" Harrison also found that several books about Hindu practices, including Paramahansa Yogananda's *Autobiography of a Yogi* and Swami Vivekananda's *Raja Yoga*, were consistent with his LSD experiences. In 1966, George and Pattie Harrison spent six weeks in India.

Harrison was only allowed one song as a writer and singer on most Beatles albums, and on *Sgt. Pepper's*, the Harrison track was "Within You Without You." It is the second longest on the album and the only recording that didn't include other Beatles. "Within You Without You" has three time changes, a tambura drone, tablas, a weird (to Western ears) melody that Shankar had taught him, and the trippiest lyrics on the Beatles' trippiest album. It fades out with the sound of the band members laughing as an antidote to the solemnity of the song.

THE MAHARISHI

Sometime in the summer of 1967, George Harrison's wife Pattie attended a lecture by the Maharishi Mahesh Yogi. She was sufficiently impressed that three of the four Beatles (Ringo's son Jason was a newborn) attended a talk he gave on August 24 at the London Hilton on Park Lane. The Maharishi was forty-nine years old, and had announced his intention to return to India at the end of this world tour, so this was supposedly his last public appearance in the West.

He was born Mahesh Prasad Varma, and had studied with several renowned spiritual teachers in his native India. The Maharishi had introduced the concept of Transcendental Meditation (TM) in 1955. By the midsixties, he had been on British TV several times and, because of his tendency to laugh, was sometimes called "the giggling guru."

The Beatles were given front-row seats and were invited to meet the Maharishi in his hotel suite after the lecture. He had a long gray beard and wore a garland of marigolds around his neck. Harrison noticed a faint scent of sandalwood.

The Maharishi gave a mantra to all students with the instruction to repeat it in sittings twice a day. The mantra for all four Beatles was "just a sound to help follow the thoughts which pass before you like a movie." The

master told them that if even 1 percent of humanity meditated, it would dissipate dark clouds of war for thousands of years. (I have no way of knowing whether or
not this is true, but it's definitely the kind of grandiose
claim that reinforces skepticism in the minds of ratio-
nalists.) McCartney's song "The Fool on the Hill" on the
Magical Mystery Tour album, released later that year, was
inspired by the Maharishi.

He invited the band to be his guests at a training
retreat in Wales, and the next day all four Beatles, their
wives (minus Cynthia Lennon, who missed the train),
Mick Jagger, Marianne Faithfull, and Donovan took the
train from London's Euston Station to Bangor, Wales.
Mobs of fans and press photographers were waiting at
both stations. This one moment literally transformed
"meditation" from a term previously limited to small zen-
dos and yoga centers into a household word overnight.

The Beatles had to leave after only a single day of the
planned ten-day course because of the shocking news
that their manager Brian Epstein had died at the age of
thirty-two from an overdose of sedatives mixed with alcohol. This tragedy triggered another wave of enormous
media attention.

George Harrison and John Lennon appeared twice
on David Frost's TV show in the fall of 1967 to talk about
their involvement with TM. On one of the shows, John
stated that, thanks to his meditation, "I'm a better person, and I wasn't bad before."

They made arrangements to spend more time with
the Maharishi at his teaching center located near Rishi-
kesh, in the foothills of the Himalayas. They, along with
their wives, girlfriends, assistants, and numerous re-

porters, arrived in February 1968 to join a group of people training to be TM instructors, including Donovan, Mike Love of the Beach Boys, and actress Mia Farrow.

While in India, the Beatles wrote most of the songs that would be recorded on *The White Album*, including Lennon's "Dear Prudence," for Mia Farrow's sister Prudence.

"The Maharishi provided us with a device to look at our own thoughts," said Donovan, whose antidrug liner notes were a direct result of the teaching.

Ringo and his wife left after a ten-day stay; McCartney left after one month, and Lennon and Harrison stayed about six weeks, and then left abruptly following rumors of inappropriate behavior toward a few young women by the Maharishi. John was outraged. In *Lennon Remembers*, John said that when the Maharishi asked why they were leaving, he replied, "Well, if you're so cosmic you'll know why."

In an interview on *The Tonight Show*, Lennon said that it had been a mistake to believe in the Maharishi. "There is no guru. You have to believe in yourself. You've got to get down to your own god in your own temple. It's all down to you, mate."

Other musicians had mixed feelings about the Maharishi as well. Joe Boyd says in his memoir *White Bicycles* that Incredible String Band members Robin Williamson and Mike Heron met the Maharishi before the Beatles did in 1967. They were eager to discuss spirituality, but according to Boyd, the Maharishi said that meditation "was only of value when the mantra had been given personally by him or one of his cohorts, and that meant joining the organization and paying the fees," which turned them off.

250 ₹ Danny Goldberg

The Maharishi met the Grateful Dead in Hollywood in November 1967 while they were recording their second album, *Anthem of the Sun*. He personally gave a mantra to members of the band, but the others in the Dead's entourage got them from assistants. (This distinction did not go down well in the egalitarian hippie subculture of the Dead.)

Harrison later apologized for the way he and Lennon had turned on the Maharishi, and in 1992 he gave a benefit concert for the Maharishi-associated Natural Law Party. In 2009, McCartney and Starr performed at a benefit concert for the David Lynch Foundation, which raises funds for the teaching of TM to at-risk students.

HARE KRISHNA

The so-called Hare Krishna movement was the other spiritual path that George Harrison would publicly associate with.

A.C. Bhaktivedanta, a sixty-nine-year-old native of Calcutta, arrived virtually penniless in New York in 1965. He believed that his destiny was to bring awareness of Krishna, an incarnation of God, to the West. Within the Hindu tradition his approach is generally referred to as "Bhakti," which means the path of love and devotion. The Maharishi's TM revolved around the use of a mantra to detach the mind from random thoughts and emotions, a practice which is also at the core of many Buddhist paths, using the mind to conquer the mind. Bhakti yoga centers on the heart. The two practices do not inherently contradict each other, but they are quite different despite both having roots in Hindu traditions.

Bhaktivedanta believed in the cosmic power of what

he called the "maha-mantra" ("maha" meaning "great"): "*Hare Krishna, Hare Krishna / Krishna Krishna, Hare Hare. / Hare Rama, Hare Rama / Rama Rama, Hare Hare.*" Krishna is the supreme God, and Rama is an aspect or incarnation of Krishna, according to Hindus. "Hare" is a call to the female energy of the universe.

Bhaktivedanta conveyed faith in the repetition of these holy names. Within a few months, and with the help of some Indian acquaintances, he was able to rent a small storefront on Second Avenue between 1st and 2nd streets. He retained the awning that read, *Matchless Gifts*, put up by the previous tenants.

Howard Smith of the *Village Voice* was the first to write about Bhaktivedanta. He initially attracted a couple dozen students to whom he gave classes on the *Bhagavad-Gītā*, the ancient Hindu text that tells the story of Krishna and his disciple Arjuna. Bhaktivedanta also led the group in chanting at Tompkins Square Park. Avant-garde jazz saxophonist Pharoah Sanders soon joined in, as did Allen Ginsberg, whose embrace of Bhaktivedanta got the attention of the *New York Times*. The newspaper quoted the beatnik poet as saying that the Hare Krishna chant "brings a state of ecstasy."

Bhaktivedanta's devotees took to calling him Prabhupada, which means "Master." A picture of him leading chants in the park graced the cover of *EVO* in November 1966 with the headline, "Save Earth Now!!" and the maha-mantra printed at the bottom. The article inside reported, "This new brand of holy man, with all due deference to Dr. Leary, has come forth with a brand of 'Consciousness Expansion' that's sweeter than acid, cheaper than pot, and non-bustable by fuzz." Bhaktivedanta was later quoted as saying, "We are not hippies, we are happies."

Not long afterward, Ginsberg sang the Hare Krishna chant when he was a guest on William F. Buckley Jr.'s *Firing Line*. The musical *Hair* included the chant in the finale of its first act. A small indie label recorded the master and devotees chanting, and the record was advertised in various underground papers using Ginsberg's ecstasy quote.

To further expand his work, Bhaktivedanta created the International Society for Krishna Consciousness (ISKCON), which opened a temple in Haight-Ashbury in January 1967. Ginsberg greeted Bhaktivedanta at the San Francisco airport and served as master of ceremonies at a benefit for ISKCON at the Avalon Ballroom. Big Brother and the Holding Company, Moby Grape, and the Grateful Dead performed at the event. The Krishna people got along well with others in the Haight community, even the Diggers, who were impressed by the free vegetarian meals ISKCON offered to visitors.

Bhaktivedanta had strict rules for formal devotees, but was tolerant of less austere supporters. ISKCON forbade meat, extramarital sex, alcohol, marijuana, psychedelics, tobacco, coffee, and tea. At the Avalon benefit, Ginsberg told the crowd that the Hare Krishna mantra was a very good way to come down from a bad acid trip. He admitted that he was sticking with cigarettes but "if it would help matters, I'll chant Hare Krishna before going to bed for the rest of my life." As Bhaktivedanta walked out of the Avalon, past undulating, braless hippie women, he quipped to a devotee, "This is no place for a *brahmacharya*" (a Hindu term for celibate).

In the summer of 1967, the Beatles went to Greece to decompress after the release of *Sgt. Pepper's*. George brought along a recording of the Hare Krishna. One day, George and John went out on a boat and played ukuleles and banjos and chanted for six hours. "We felt exalted. It was a very happy time for us," George later recalled.

By 1969, Harrison had met Bhaktivedanta and invited several devotees to live in his home. They rerecorded the Hare Krishna chant, and the combination of modern recording and the magic of the Beatles made it an actual hit in Europe. Harrison made plans to produce some new chants for the Beatles' label, Apple Records, with a chorus of devotees that included another one of my Fieldston classmates, Joshua Greene.

Greene had attended the University of Wisconsin, where he quickly joined the staff of the campus newspaper, the *Daily Cardinal*, at a time when antiwar protests on campus were growing in intensity. Although he was against the war, he told me he was turned off by the protest leaders and transferred to New York University's junior-year-abroad program at the Sorbonne in Paris.

Greene had an interest in yoga and was captivated when he heard the new version of the Hare Krishna chant in a disco. The deejay who played it invited him to meet Bhaktivedanta in London just as the new Harrison-produced sessions were scheduled to begin. He had played organ for a college band and thus was invited to the session where *The Radha Krsna Temple* album was recorded. Although it was an album of devotional chants, it got attention from young rock fans like me because it was released on Apple Records. Greene sang and played on "Govinda," and shortly thereafter dropped out of college and went to live with the devotees in a building off Oxford Street rented by Harrison for their use as London's first Krishna temple. John Lennon was impressed enough by Bhaktivedanta that he invited the teacher to stay with him and Yoko for several months.

In his book *Here Comes the Sun*, Greene described a conversation in which John and George confronted Bhaktivedanta to try to figure out how broad-minded he was. Was he saying that *his* translation of the *Bhagavad-Gītā* was the only one that was right? And why did he exclusively focus on the name and form of Krishna? What about Shiva? Ganesha? Jesus? Bhaktivedanta acknowledged the divinity of other beings but said that he believed Krishna was unique. George diffused the tension: "I believe there was a misunderstanding. We thought you were saying your translation was the authority and that others were not. But we didn't have any misunderstanding about the identity of Krishna."

Greene explained, "This was a gesture of accommodation of all concerned. The alternative was, for George, unconscionable. Throughout history, how much suffering had fanatics caused by believing they had an exclusive handle on truth? Not that he saw [Bhaktivedanta] in such terms. But claiming only one way to God could never be George's way."

Lennon would become increasingly skeptical of all spiritual organizations, but a spiritual worldview remained a part of the way he experienced reality. When asked in 1971 whether songs like "Give Peace a Chance" and "Power to the People" were propaganda songs, he replied: "Sure. So was 'All You Need Is Love.'"

Is God Dead?

Meanwhile, a large section of mainstream American culture had been going through its own spiritual angst in the context of prosperity, modernity, and the echoes of World War II. On April 8, 1966, the cover of *Time* consisted of red letters against a black background that asked the question, "Is God Dead?" The accompanying article said that recent polls had indicated that more than eighty million Americans were agnostic, atheist, or members of religions or belief systems other than Judaism or Christianity. Of those who did identify with mainstream religions, less than half attended church or synagogue every week.

Lutheran scholar Martin Marty lamented the prevalence of "weekend Christians" who acted during the week as if God didn't exist. William Alfred, the author of the prize-winning play *Hogan's Goat*, gave the religious elitist view. He compared people who don't believe in God to a "six-year-old kid who doesn't believe in passionate love. They just haven't experienced it." Billy Graham, then forty-eight years old and at the peak of his celebrity, affirmed his unwavering belief in the Gospel. This was before the era when evangelicals were playing a role in politics, although in the next few years, Graham would appear regularly in photos with Richard Nixon and did nothing to discourage the notion that he supported the war in Vietnam.

Time's un-bylined piece smugly asserted, "In search of meaning, some believers have desperately turned toward psychiatry, Zen or drugs." Martin Luther King Jr., the man who many Americans saw as the country's most prominent Christian, was not even mentioned, nor was

Islam, Buddhism (except for the snarky Zen reference), or Hinduism. With the exception of a few lines that quoted Rabbi Abraham Joshua Heschel, the question of the existence of God apparently took place exclusively among white Christians, as far as *Time* was concerned.

But *Time* did offer respectability to doubters, which is what motivated many of the 3,500 people who sent in letters in response to the article (the most in the magazine's history). Most complained of sacrilege because of skeptical passages like, "At its worst, the image that the church gave of God was that of a wonder worker who explained the world's mysteries and seemed to have somewhat more interest in punishing men than rewarding them."

Notwithstanding its narrow cultural perch, *Time* offered a Christian lifeline to counterculture mystics who valued direct experience and rejected dogma. The magazine quoted Switzerland's Karl Barth, who they described as "the century's greatest Protestant theologian," and went on to say that Barth "has consistently warned his fellow churchmen that God is a 'wholly other' being, whom man can only know by God's self-revelation in the person of Christ, as witnessed by Scripture. Any search for God that starts with human experience, Barth warns, is a vain quest that will discover only an idol, not the true God at all."

ROLLING THUNDER

As evidenced by Gary Snyder's musings at the meeting on Alan Watts's houseboat, widespread hippie interest in nature, combined with an antipathy to racist elements in America's cultural legacy, led naturally to a fascination with Native Americans who in the sixties still referred to themselves as Indians. Of course, the fact that some tribes used peyote as a sacrament didn't hurt. The *Oracle* ran an entire issue dedicated to the American Indian.

A medicine man known as Rolling Thunder was part of the Haight-Ashbury scene and became close to the Grateful Dead. He was born John Pope in 1916 in Oklahoma. Other details of his background are unclear. At different times he identified with both the Cherokee and Shoshone tribes.

Rolling Thunder lived at Peter Coyote's house in the Bay Area during the late sixties. The former Digger says, "He was half carny, half shaman. He had real juice, but he was also a self-promoting opportunist. He was unevenly developed. He came to Haight and met the Diggers. He said he had a vision that we and others in the Haight were reincarnated souls of Indians who had been killed at Little Big Horn. I thought it was bullshit, but *good* bullshit. We understood that he represented an encyclopedia of how to live on this continent. The woods had been his drugstore, his food store, etc. We wanted to learn from him."

By this time, Coyote had begun shooting heroin and had contracted hepatitis. "Rolling Thunder cured me when no American doctor had been able to help. He walked into my room when I was bedridden and said, *There is a rattlesnake in here.* He started opening closet doors. My black hat had a band made from the skin of a rattlesnake that I'd killed and eaten. He grabbed my arm and looked at the needle tracks and said, *That's where the snake bit you.* I burned the hat with prayers. He gave me bitter root tea and in a few weeks I was cured."

Coyote says that in those days, Rolling Thunder would often complain about the Grateful Dead. "These guys have no culture. They don't know that when you call a medicine man, you're supposed to pay him." Nevertheless, he stayed close to the Dead.

I met Rolling Thunder on a visit to New York City in 1979 when he and his wife, Spotted Fawn, stayed at my apartment for a few days. One night they invited me to a Dead concert at Madison Square Garden. He was greeted at the backstage door with great deference by the crew and we were immediately taken to the dressing room to see Jerry Garcia. They spoke affably for around half an hour before the band started their show. We actually left the arena before the music even got started, as Rolling Thunder had no interest in hearing it himself, but apparently had wanted to give Garcia some energy before he went onstage.

THE I CHING

The I Ching (*Book of Changes*) went from selling one thousand copies a year to fifty thousand when a new edition was published in 1961. The hardback edition that I bought had a gray cover and it immediately became a treasured possession, which I frequently consulted. (Richard Wilhelm had translated it from Chinese to German in the nineteenth century and his version was translated into English by Cary F. Baynes in the 1930s.) One would throw three coins six times. This process would designate one of sixty-four hexagrams with spiritual guidance and several hundred varieties of emphasis within those hexagrams. The idea is that the process could tune in to seemingly random forces of the universe.

Carl Jung had written a long introduction to the Wilhelm translation, and this endorsement by one of the fathers of psychoanalysis contextualized *The I Ching* as a significant sacred text for me rather than a fortune-telling gimmick. Jung acknowledged his own initial skepticism, but he was impressed that *The I Ching* was highly respected by both Lao-Tzu and Confucius, who, he felt, were beyond intellectual reproach.

Jung explained that ancient Chinese thought focused more on the concept of "chance" as distinguished from the modernist Western belief in "cause." It seemed to me that "chance" was in the same metaphysical ballpark as "grace" and many other words that support the notion that there are forces in the universe that are not decipherable by the intellect. Or as Jung put it, "The heavy-handed pedagogic approach that attempts to fit irrational phenomena into a preconceived rational pattern is anathema to me."

The I Ching was a subject of fascination for many of my high school friends as well, but I cannot identify the moment when it became cool. All of a sudden it just was. The *Oracle* frequently referred to it, and in Anita Hoffman's *Trashing* she recalls she and Abbie using it at their wedding.

In the first issue of *Rolling Stone*, an ad for radio station KRLA in Los Angeles read in its entirety, "'The beginning of all things lies still in the beyond, in the form of ideas that have yet to become real'—I Ching: the Creative." In the song "Not So Sweet Martha Lorraine," Country Joe sings sarcastically of its use as manipulative hippie shtick: *"Now she's the one who gives us all those magical things / And reads us stories out of* The I Ching."

260 ¥ Danny Goldberg

According to the Grateful Dead's former manager Rock Scully, the band threw *The I Ching* in April 1966 after recording in Los Angeles and got the hexagram Crossing the Great Water, which encouraged them to move back to San Francisco and into the house at 710 Ashbury. The following year, on the Band's debut album *Music from Big Pink*, the song "Caledonia Mission" included the line, *"You know I do believe in your hexagram / but can you tell me how they all knew the plan?"*

One of the obvious appeals of *The I Ching* in the hippie world was that there was no organization or hierarchy attached to it. Everyone who consulted it served as his or her own priest. Thus, even the anarchistic Diggers felt comfortable enough with *The I Ching* that their newsletters typically ended with a hexagram as guidance for the coming days.

Gurus and Rugus

When Swami Bhaktivedanta announced the opening of the Krishna temple in Haight-Ashbury, he said, "I think what you are calling 'hippies' are our best potential. Although they are young, they are already dissatisfied with material life. Frustrated. And not knowing what to do, they turn to drugs. So let them come, and we will show them spiritual activities."

The so-called Hare Krishna people could be seen chanting in public in the late sixties, including at many airports. Many of them had shaved heads with a single braid of hair that remained intact, wore Indian clothing, and jumped around with big smiles on their faces while they sang. I recoiled from proselytizing but many of the Krishna followers had a sweetness to them that was less pushy than people of other faiths. One day in Central Park, a Hare Krishna devotee handed me a photo of Krishna with text on it that said that if an individual spoke the name "Krishna" once with love, he or she was forever blessed. I never made any effort to join their organization but I didn't regret accepting that photo and saying Krishna's name.

Bhaktivedanta was not the only spiritual teacher who noticed this opportunity. There was a dizzying array of forces seeking to take advantage of the hippie disenchantment with both traditional religion and materialistic rationalism.

In *Revolution for the Hell of It*, Hoffman quotes an exchange from a Ravi Shankar press conference: "What do you think of all the swamis running around New York?" The sitarist answered, "Well, I hope they're not all phonies. There are a lot of phony swamis in India."

Hilda Charlton, who would become my spiritual teacher in the early seventies, used to remind her students that the word "guru" means the replacement of darkness with light, and cautioned that some teachers were actually "rugus" who accomplished the reverse.

There is no question that a lot of wolves in sheep's clothing tried to take advantage of psychologically damaged kids who had been attracted to the hippie culture. Some were simply lame, some were in it for the money, and some were on dangerous power trips. Yet many were sincere. From my point of view, red flags to avoid included:

1. Any group that believed *their* way was the one and only way to enlightenment, and lacked respect for other approaches.

262 🌱 Danny Goldberg

2. Too much focus on money or raising money. (Fine to charge for a yoga class, a book, or ask for modest donations to keep the proverbial lights on, but if it got into hundreds or thousands of dollars, something was weird.)

3. Any culture that encouraged violation of my ethical norms.

4. Any sexual pressure.

Avoiding these four areas eliminated the darkest cults, but left an extremely wide array of approaches to exploring the meaning of life. Much of the interest in mysticism came from people who, like the Beatles, had used psychedelics. Steve Earle says that after his first acid trip, "I never had any doubt that there was a God." The vast majority of hippies shared the conviction that there were other aspects of reality beyond official externality. As the nonpsychedelic Dr. King preached, "Everything that we see is a shadow cast by that which we do not see."

To be clear, there was tremendous diversity even among those baby boomers who identified with the counterculture and/or the protest movements of the time. Millions, like Paul Krassner, rejected anything mystical and identified themselves as atheists or agnostics; they viewed astrology, yoga, and meditation as fads bordering on superstitions that were not any more "real" to them than conventional religious dogma.

There were also millions who remained with the religion they were born into, and others who were drawn to variations on older religions, such as the Nation of Islam; the "Jesus Freaks" inspired by *Good News for Modern Man*, a 1966 translation of the New Testament written in modern English; and the Jewish Renewal Movement, one of whose leaders, Rabbi Zalman Schachter-Shalomi, had taken LSD in the early sixties. Such openness to psychedelics was rare within the Judeo-Christian world.

However, Richard Alpert pointed out that most established religious leaders looked at LSD as a threat. "Religions were based on history. Priests don't have revelatory experiences, they just *talked* about people who had them long ago."

Among the dozens of mystics with foreign-sounding names, only a few penetrated the counterculture. Meher Baba, who was born in India in 1894, traveled extensively and visited Hollywood in 1932. Mary Pickford and Douglas Fairbanks held a reception for him at their home, where he met Gary Cooper, Charles Laughton, Tallulah Bankhead, Ernst Lubitsch, and Boris Karloff, among others.

In 1967, Meher Baba's presence loomed large. Posters of his smiling face with a huge handlebar mustache and the saying, *Don't Worry, Be Happy*, were displayed in head shops alongside psychedelic mandalas and photos of Hendrix and Dylan. In the *Woodstock* film there is a close-up of a poster with a photo of Meher Baba as a young man. Peter Townshend of the Who became enamored of the man and dedicated *Tommy* to him. Baba passed away in 1969.

Meher Baba had taken a vow of silence in his early thirties and only communicated in hand gestures. He also publicly rejected the value of LSD as a spiritual tool and strongly discouraged its use in a pamphlet published in 1966 called *God in a Pill?*

Richard Alpert sent him a letter asking for advice on

264 Danny Goldberg

this topic. "In the United States there are literally thousands of people who have experienced through psychedelic chemicals something which led them to undertake their spiritual journey with great seriousness," he explained. Meher Baba wrote back and said it was okay for Alpert to take acid three times and then he should stop. Obviously, this didn't really answer the larger question.

Not long after this exchange, there was a psychedelic conference in Berkeley at which some Meher Baba devotees staged a protest. Fifty years later, Alpert, long known as Ram Dass, recalls the conference with a twinkle in his eye: "I had a tab of acid, and in front of the crowd, I put it in my mouth and said, *This is the fourth time.*"

The most influential Hindu book in the sixties was George Harrison's favorite, *Autobiography of a Yogi* by Paramahansa Yogananda, which had first been published in 1946. Born in India, Yogananda moved to America in 1920 and settled in Southern California five years later, becoming one of the first to bring yoga and meditation to the United States.

Yogananda would pass in 1952, but the book has been reprinted dozens of times and has sold millions of copies. For many Westerners, it is the easiest way to absorb Hindu traditions. While unambiguous in his description of his mystical experiences, Yogananda honored Jesus Christ and was in harmony with the modern world. He recounted close friendships with the American botanist Luther Burbank and with Mahatma Gandhi, some of whose ashes are interred at Yogananda's outdoor Self-Realization Fellowship Lake Shrine in Pacific

Palisades, California. The entrance to the Lake Shrine displays symbols of Judaism, Christianity, Islam, Buddhism, and Hinduism.

The *Oracle of Southern California* (inspired by but not affiliated with the *San Francisco Oracle*) included many pieces that referenced the writings of George Ivanovich Gurdjieff, a Russian mystic and writer who conceptualized a "fourth way" and a theosophy which posits that hidden knowledge or wisdom from the ancient past can offer a path to enlightenment and salvation.

The Theosophical Society was formed in New York in 1875 by a Russian mystic known as Madame Helena Blavatsky, and her book *The Secret Doctrine* could be found in many pads and communes. Theosophy presented a cosmology that acknowledges multiple spiritual traditions as well as asserting the existence of masters, whose higher consciousness can be accessed by students who spiritually connect with them. (The grandmother of *Oracle* cofounder Michael Bowen was a member of the Theosophical Society in Ojai, California, when he was growing up.)

Another movement that attracted hippie communities was the macrobiotic diet. This was popularized in America through the writing of Japanese native George Ohsawa, who had recovered from illness after following a macrobiotic diet. Major principles include eating locally grown foods that are in season, and eating in moderation. Macrobiotics also incorporates the concept of traditional Chinese medicine that balances yin and yang elements of food and cookware. (There were many stoned arguments about what was yin and what was yang.)

In 1965, Ohsawa's book *You Are All Sanpaku* was translated into English and became a fixture in many hippie
kitchens. Macrobiotic restaurants, like the Cauldron
and the Paradox on the Lower East Side, both a few
blocks away from the Fillmore East, were magnets for
countercultural types of a spiritual bent.

Swami Satchidananda was one of the most popular
teachers of yoga and meditation in New York in the sixties. He came to the city in 1966 at the invitation of pop
artist Peter Max and established the Integral Yoga Institute, one of the first places to offer yoga classes in New
York. It also included a store that sold vegetarian food.
In 1969, Satchidananda gave the blessing at the outset of
the Woodstock Festival.

In Boston, Mel Lyman established the Fort Hill Community and published the *Avatar* from 1967 to '68; like
the *Oracle*, it covered the counterculture through a metaphysical prism. Lyman was a virtuoso harmonica player
who had been with the Jim Kweskin Jug Band. He had
memorably ended the 1965 Newport Folk Festival with
a mind-expanding harp solo of the spiritual "Rock of
Ages." Lyman was viewed by some of his followers as a
divine being and rumors of cultlike obedience gave him
a confusing image, although Fort Hill was one of the few
communes started in the sixties that flourished for
decades.

Buddhism, which rejected any worship of deities,
was also growing. Alan Watts was an influential figure
in the Haight community and the early underground
press. Jack Kerouac wrote a biography of Buddha, and
Gary Snyder was a devoted Buddhist whose austere example would inspire skeptics as diverse as Tom Hayden

and Peter Coyote, who would eventually become a Zen Buddhist priest.

Notwithstanding the ubiquity of oms, ankhs, and Native American symbols in the streets of Haight-Ashbury, the Lower East Side, and thousands of college dorms, there were also millions of rebellious baby boomers who were less concerned with enlightenment than they were with the still-escalating war in Vietnam.

CHAPTER 8
YOU SAY YOU WANT A REVOLUTION

As 1967 unfolded, the tribes grew further and further apart. Hippies often felt that the antiwar "leaders" were boring and/or too angry. Radicals and liberals accused hippies of being self-indulgent. The old left claimed that the new left had no discipline. Young radicals were not all that impressed with what the old left had accomplished. Within each of these broad categories there were numerous sects, which were frequently at odds with each other.

At the same time, the American government and establishment increasingly harassed the civil rights and antiwar movements. The left pondered numerous conspiracy theories. Was the spread of LSD a plot to undermine left-wing activism? How about the proliferation of other hard drugs? Were there government provocateurs who were manipulating the movement into self-destructive actions? Were any of the deaths of Panthers, rock musicians, and countercultural figures actually murders? As Stephen Stills had written, paranoia strikes deep. Many of these notions were met with skepticism from most hippies and lefties, but there was also a prudent appreciation of the old adage: *Just because you're paranoid doesn't mean they're not out to get you.*

It is certain that the FBI used wiretaps and informants and other methods, legal and illegal, with an ideological agenda that went far beyond stopping crime. Many details remain shrouded in mystery, but anyone interested in having a sense of the dark pressure that all aspects of the left were under can Google the word "COINTELPRO," which was the FBI's code name for the program that aimed to subvert the protest movements.

At a minimum, the antiwar movement deserves a lot of the credit for the "Vietnam Syndrome," a strong aversion to another war, which the right wing thought was a disease and we knew would help keep the US out of a war in Central America in the eighties (though it did not, admittedly, keep the US out of the region altogether). This would not be the utopian result of "Last Night I Had the Strangest Dream," but it was far from meaningless.

None of this was clear in 1967. For many lefties, the need to feel that *their* tribe's strategy was superior to other antiestablishment voices created a toxic myopia that delegitimized those whose antiwar tactics were just as valuable.

One weird example of counterculture infighting took place at the 1967 SDS Convention in Michigan, when Emmett Grogan and Peter Berg disrupted one of the meetings. SDS was among the many groups that Grogan disdained. Berg had called the Port Huron Statement of five years earlier "pallid and elusive." The 1967 conference was called "Back to the Drawing Boards," and Tom Hayden gave the keynote speech.

Grogan and Berg burst into the convention unin-
vited, asking for a lawyer to help another Digger who
had supposedly been arrested for swimming nude in
the nearby Platte River. Berg ridiculed SDS as all talk
and no action, in contrast to the Diggers who were
helping individual people with free food, crash pads,
and medicine. Grogan read Gary Snyder's poem "A
Curse on the Men in Washington, Pentagon," and
they stayed for more than an hour loudly insulting
SDS members.

Todd Gitlin speculated that perhaps the reason SDS
permitted the long interruption in their convention was
that the Diggers "were our anarchist bad conscience . . .
We shared in the antileadership mood." The pressure
to prove just how radical they were led to police being
described as "pigs" for the first time in an SDS newsletter in September 1967, and to a resolution condemning
Jefferson Airplane for their Levi's commercials.

An antiwar rally in Boston

A lot of the focus was put on helping draft evaders. Stanford University student body president David Harris (who would marry Joan Baez the following year) had announced the formation of the group The Resistance in April, and at its encouragement more than five thousand men had turned in or burned their draft cards in 1967.

SDS passed a resolution to help military deserters. Its author, Jeff Shero, explained,

> First, hide the guy out for a few weeks until his GI haircut grows in. Then give him your draft card and write to the draft board for another copy, telling them that you lost yours. After that, supplied with civilian clothes, he leaves for another city and gets a job . . . I intended it to be an illegal resolution. We should stand for disruption in the armed forces and for soldiers going underground.

This was fine, but many of us felt there was a dissonance between the intensity of anger that was starting to come from some of the radicals and the lack of a coherent long-term strategy to accomplish their goals. Michael Kazin, who became cochair of the SDS chapter at Harvard in 1969, told me, "It bothered me when John Lennon sang in 'Revolution,' *'You better free your mind instead.'*" The implication was that activism was less important than inner work. I reminded Kazin that earlier in the song Lennon sang, *"You say you got a real solution / Well, you know / We'd all love to see the plan."* Kazin chuckled ruefully and admitted, "Well, there wasn't one."

During this same time period, religious antiwar communities also became increasingly radical. A delegation of Quakers went to North Vietnam with medical supplies. Radical Catholic Father Philip Berrigan and his brother Father Daniel Berrigan were involved in numerous nonviolent acts of civil disobedience aimed at ending the war. On October 27, Philip Berrigan and three others (the "Baltimore Four") poured blood on Baltimore Selective Service records. As they waited for the police to arrive and arrest them, the group passed out Bibles. Berrigan told draft board employees, "This sacrificial and constructive act is meant to protest the pitiful waste of American and Vietnamese blood in Indochina." He was sentenced to six years in prison.

JEWS AND JEWS

On June 10, 1967, the Six-Day War ended with Israel's resounding victory over several Arab invaders and with the Jewish state occupying relatively large pieces of land formerly controlled by their enemies.

This created some immediate fault lines in the American left. Certain radicals, including some vocal members of the black community, identified with the Palestinians who were now under Israeli military occupation. Many left-wing Jews looked for a formula to balance their radicalism on other issues with an inclination to support the Jewish state that had been created in the shadow of the Holocaust and which had prevailed against surrounding countries aspiring to destroy it.

The Soviet Union publicly supported the Arab countries during the Six-Day War, as did several American leftist groups who typically stuck to the party line, including the Communist Party USA, the Progressive Labor Party, and the Socialist Workers Party—all of which had few members but nonetheless represented "the left" in the minds of some American Jews.

In an interview with the *New York Times* on August 15, 1967, SNCC leader Ralph Featherstone said, "SNCC is drawn to the Arab cause because it is working toward a third world alliance of oppressed people all over the world—Africa, Asia, Latin America. The Arabs have been oppressed continually by Israelis and by Europeans as well, in such countries as Algeria." He denied that SNCC was anti-Semitic, and said that they were only interested in indicting "Jewish oppressors," a category he applied to Israel, and "to those Jews in the little Jew shops in the ghettos." The vast majority of Jews, even radical Jews, were offended by that language.

During the first week of September there was a New Politics Convention at Chicago's Palmer House, which attracted several thousand delegates. I asked Todd Gitlin how one became a delegate and he laughed and said, "That's a good question." A committee had been created a year or two earlier, and a sense that there should be a gathering of the left, possibly to nominate a third-party presidential candidate, took hold and drew funding from various labor unions and wealthy individuals, including Harvard instructor Marty Peretz.

The arcane rules of the convention gave weighted voting to representatives of various groups, and a forceful alliance of black delegates succeeded in pushing through a resolution that gave them 50 percent of the total votes. It is not clear whether the rationale for this was that African Americans represented half of the American left or as recognition of past discrimination, but the most vocal black voices were not, according to Gitlin, activists who he had previously seen at SDS or SNCC meetings or any other left-wing gatherings. To this day, he wonders if some of them were provocateurs directed by the government or reactionary private interests to foment dissension within the left.

If so, they were successful. Martin Luther King Jr. spoke at the opening of the convention, but he came and went quickly and was not a delegate, nor was he present for any of the meetings. He made it clear again that he was unwilling to run for president of the United States, and without the potential of his name, the notion of a third-party challenge to Johnson and to whomever the Republicans would nominate receded. Instead, the convention focused on a series of radical resolutions amid angry infighting.

Renata Adler acidly wrote in the *New Yorker* of radicals "who seemed to find in ceaseless local organizing—around any issue or tactic demonstrably certain of failure—a kind of personal release, which effective social action might deny them . . . [There were] revolutionaries who discussed riots as though they were folk songs or pieces of local theater."

The most controversial proclamation condemned the "imperialist Zionist war" that Israel had just won. The anti-Israel resolution was actually removed in the final hours of the conference, but there were lasting wounds that remained from some of the loud anti-Semitic rhetoric expressed by a handful of black delegates. Peretz walked out of the convention and out of the American left. He told a TV crew covering the convention that "the movement is dead." Peretz later bought the previously left-wing *New Republic* magazine and shifted its ideology to the right, especially on foreign policy.

According to Adler, Dick Gregory said, "Every Jew in America over thirty years old knows another Jew who hates niggers. Well, it's even, baby." It is impossible to know the context of Gregory's remark fifty years later, but he had long worked with Jews in the entertainment business; he remained close to them, and his subsequent activism was inclusive. It seems likely to me that he was reacting to pressure from some Jews not only to oppose anti-Semitism, but to somehow take responsibility for the remarks of all other African Americans.

Dr. King made a related point in a long letter to Dr. Maurice Eisendrath of the Union of American Hebrew Congregations. After explaining that no one from the SCLC was actually a delegate to the New Politics Convention, he pointed out that those SCLC members who attended meetings, such as Hosea Williams, fought against the anti-Israel resolution and helped to get it reversed. King summarized his support of Israel's right to exist, the legitimate concerns of impoverished and occupied Palestinians, and the unhealthy influence of the oil business in the region. King lamented any effort to divide blacks and Jews and concluded, "It would be a tragic and immoral mistake to identify the mass of Negroes with the very small number that succumb to cheap and dishonest slogans, just as it would be a serious error to identify all Jews with the few who exploit Negroes under their economic sway."

Nevertheless, the psychic wounds passed on from the dreadful legacy of the Holocaust caused painful reverberations for some Jews. As Eric Alterman wrote,

For the left, the [Six-Day War's] legacy became a point of painful contention—as many liberals and leftists increasingly viewed Israel as having traded its David status for a new role as an oppressive, occupying Goliath. For many American Jews, however, most of whom previously kept their emotional distance from Israel, the emotional commitment to Israel became so central that it came to define their ethnic, even religious, identities.

There were also American Jews and others on the left who tried to balance support for Israel's right to exist with opposition to an extended occupation of the newly conquered territory. J.J. Goldberg (no relation) started the first high school chapter of SDS in 1965 at Woodrow Wilson High School in Washington, DC. He went to George Washington University in 1966 and joined the SDS chapter there as well, but quit after a few months because the head of it "was a very nice guy but he was a Maoist and an anti-Zionist." To Goldberg, Zionism was not only an expression of solidarity with a post-Holocaust Jewish state, but also a connection to democratic socialism. In the sixties, the only government that Israel had ever known was that of the Labor Party. "Pete Seeger used to sing a song in Hebrew at every concert," Goldberg remembers. "In 1960, when Ghana became the first African country to gain independence from a European colonial power, we were taught their new national anthem at the Jewish summer camp I attended."

It came as a shock to Goldberg when segments of the American left, such as those at the New Politics Convention, opposed Israel after the Six-Day War. At the same time, many of the establishment Jewish organizations were supporting the Vietnam War, in part because of veiled threats from the Johnson administration that US support for Israel could be compromised if the "Jewish community" opposed him on Vietnam.

Former President Kennedy adviser Arthur Schlesinger Jr. said that it was intellectually inconsistent to oppose the war in Vietnam and support the Six-Day War, but Goldberg disagrees. He sees both as wars of national liberation: "To me, Ho Chi Minh was akin to Ben Gurion." When he transferred to McGill University in Montreal, Goldberg also supported the Quebecois liberation movement. Yet he debated peace activist David Dellinger, who suggested that Israel should be a nonreligious state: "I felt he was singling out Jews as the only community of its size and set of traditions that didn't have their own country."

Among older Jews, no one was under more pressure than Arthur Goldberg (no relation to either J.J. or to me), who had been a leading labor lawyer and was among those who had helped negotiate the merger between the AFL and the CIO in 1955. Goldberg was secretary of labor in Kennedy's administration until Kennedy appointed him to the United States Supreme Court. When Lyndon Johnson persuaded Arthur Goldberg to leave the Supreme Court and become US ambassador to the United Nations, he was under the impression that the president would allow him to negotiate an end to the war in Vietnam. But Johnson never permitted him to do so.

Barry Goldberg, the blues piano player who was in the Electric Flag, is Arthur Goldberg's nephew. Barry was immersed in rock and roll and didn't pay much at-

tention to politics in those days, though he saw his uncle on family occasions and says that Arthur Goldberg
forever regretted having been manipulated by Johnson
into leaving the Supreme Court.

J.J. Goldberg and other Zionist Jewish lefties were
viewed with suspicion both in radical circles and in the
mainstream Jewish community. They created new institutions such as the Radical Zionist Alliance, which
supported Israel's right to exist and defend its borders,
opposed most of the settlements in the Palestinian territory, opposed the war in Vietnam, and continued to
identify with democratic socialism on economic issues.
(The notion that all American Jews thought in political
unison was almost as untrue in the sixties as it is today.
Abbie Hoffman, Jerry Rubin, Allen Ginsberg, and countless others in the counterculture and radical left had little or no emotional connection to Israel, and at the same
time, there was always a cohort of Jewish conservatives
who had contempt for the left.)

As the New Politics Convention was winding down,
Martin Luther King Jr.'s colleague Andrew Young pro-
phetically shared his feelings about the black radical demands: "These cats don't know the country has taken a
swing to the right. I wish the violence and riots had political significance, but they don't." A friend of Young's
chimed in, "They just have political consequences," to
which Young presciently replied, "Yeah, all bad."

RESISTANCE
By 1968, Tom Hayden would claim that having tried available channels and finding them meaningless, having recognized that the establishment did not listen to public

opinion, the new left was moving toward confrontation with the American government. In reality, although the antiwar movement had enormously broadened its constituency, it did not command anything close to majority support in America in 1967. There were ballot initiatives calling for withdrawal from Vietnam in two of the most antiwar cities in America in October 1967. Only 37 percent favored the antiwar resolution in San Francisco and 39 percent in Cambridge, Massachusetts.

This strengthened the argument of older peace movement leaders who wanted to focus on getting an actual majority of Americans to oppose the war. Younger radicals felt that without greater intensity, the dry arguments of peaceniks wouldn't move the needle. There was some truth on both sides of this divide.

In Todd Gitlin's book *The Sixties*, Hayden is quoted as telling the National Commission on the Causes and Prevention of Violence that "the turning point, in my opinion, was October 1967, when resistance became the official watchword of the antiwar movement." A big part of the new thinking was that the cost of disruption would make policy makers recalculate and avoid such costs. Hayden urged the movement to focus on "what cost we can impose on the heartless, cost-calculating decision-makers." He urged the left not "to become obsessed with finding ways to make the antiwar movement respectable to the editors of the *New York Times*."

"Resistance" swept through the cadres of SDS with the swiftness of a hit song, and the government responded in kind. On October 18, 1967, there was a sit-in at the University of Wisconsin, Madison, at the recruiting office of Dow Chemical, the principle manufacturer of napalm, which was causing enormous pain and death in Vietnam. Police clubbed many of the demonstrators and used tear gas on them. About seventy students ended up in the hospital. In response, many student organizations called for a general strike of the university.

Just a couple days before the Madison sit-in, on October 16, there was a march in Oakland in which demonstrators tried to block access to the Oakland Army Induction Center, which resulted in the arrest of Joan Baez, among others.

Joel Goodman and I had arrived in Berkeley several weeks earlier—ostensibly to go to college—and we joined the protest, exuberantly pushing a small Hillman car we'd bought for $100 into an intersection near the induction center along with dozens of others. Our naive notion was that this would actually delay the war machine. In reality, it only took the cops a few hours to tow them all away. Such was the fog of the antiwar movement under siege. The crowd of thousands was more riled up and unruly than I'd seen at East Coast rallies, perhaps because of the "resistance" attitude. When we saw roughly a dozen people run past us with tears coming down their faces from the tear gas, we quickly backed away to avoid getting similarly sprayed.

Mitchell Markus, who would soon become program director of CKGM-FM, the underground radio station in Montreal—and who is now the executive director of the Love Serve Remember Foundation that oversees Ram Dass's activities—also happened to be in Oakland at that time. "A friend of mine and I were driving nearby and we were so stoned that when we smelled the tear gas we thought it might get us higher. We were against the war, but we had no idea about the details of that protest."

One of the things I was reminded of when I researched this book is that there were varying accounts of how antiwar kids interacted with Vietnam vets, some of whom were already coming back from their service by 1967. Notwithstanding the fictitious account in *Rambo* in which Sylvester Stallone's character claims he was spit on by hippies, no one I knew had anything against the vets. It was obvious to me that they had no control over the war and that the villains were the "best and the brightest" in the Kennedy and Johnson administrations. The apartment that Joel and I got in Berkeley was right next door to a couple of vets who shared our enthusiasm for drugs and rock and roll and who became some of my best friends that year.

I don't claim that our experiences were typical. There is no question that some servicemen back from Vietnam felt disrespected by the changed America they returned to. Many of them needed support that was not forthcoming. However, to the extent that vets were denied the benefits that their counterparts in World War II received, the blame lies not with the counterculture nor with radicals, but with older government officials. Later in the war, many of the most effective voices against it were disenchanted Vietnam vets such as John Kerry and Ron Kovic.

Some on the radical left, black and white, were intrigued by revolutions in third world countries, such as Cuba, that had been catalyzed by small, impassioned cadres. There was a big buzz about *Revolution in the Revolution?* which was published in 1967 by French academic

Régis Debray, who had moved to Bolivia to work with Che Guevara. Debray's theory was that small groups of committed radicals could be a trigger for mass revolution.

As Martin Luther King Jr. pointed out, however, political conditions in the United States were nothing like those in countries where large majorities had opposed the existing government. As I reflect on the delusional notions of an armed leftist revolution in the United States, I can't help but be amused that they emanated from some of the same radicals who complained about hippies getting too high!

Gitlin wrote:

> There were tensions galore between the radical idea of political strategy—with discipline, organization, commitment to results out there at a distance—and the countercultural idea of living life to the fullest, right here, for oneself, or for the part of the universe embodied in oneself, or for the community of the enlightened who were capable of loving one another—and the rest of the world be damned (which it was already).

Yet many of the counterculture's most prominent figures, including Allen Ginsberg, Wavy Gravy, and Paul Krassner, were active supporters of the antiwar movement and put their bodies on the line as much as members of SDS did. (Both Wavy and Krassner sustained serious back injuries at the hands of cops at antiwar demonstrations.)

The spirit of the Be-In had not yet entirely dissipated. Stew Albert was a Berkeley radical who, like Rubin, grew closer to heads over time. "You can't overestimate the effect of acid on the scene," Albert says. "Political people started taking acid and didn't think that it was a substitute for politics, but thought that acid had something to say *to* politics. If you combined politics with the right combination of acid and grass and doing wild stunts and getting involved in the surrealistic edge, it was a marvelous way to live!" He feels that while the acid transformed radicals and appealed to the idealistic youth, the straight civil rights and peace movements often spoke the language of guilt. "We also appealed to fucking off, decadence, taking dope, and getting laid, and doing weird drawings on your body, and the stuff that's usually identified with the decline of civilization. And yet we somehow got it all packaged into some kind of romantic, idealist, revolutionary mode."

Tom Hayden had no such romantic notions about LSD or even pot. "Tom was incredibly self-disciplined and he wanted everyone else to be as well," Gitlin told me. "One day he saw me when I was stoned and he gave me a look as if to say, *What's happened to you?*"

One of the political failures of the new left was a lack of connectivity to the labor movement. In part this was a result of a generational smugness among radicals in their twenties who naively thought that the labor battles won by the previous generation were permanent. At the same time, organized labor had grown reactionary about the Cold War because of the purge of Communist-leaning leaders during the McCarthy period and because of the union jobs produced by the military-industrial complex. (Phil Ochs's song "I Ain't Marching Anymore" included the lyric, "*Now the labor leader's screamin' / When they close the missile plants.*") The AFL-CIO, for example, was led by George Meany, who was a fierce anti-Communist and unreservedly supported the war in Vietnam, exhibiting angry contempt toward the antiwar movement. (One notable exception was the United Automobile Workers union, whose president Walter Reuther was a staunch ally of Dr. King.)

EXORCISING THE PENTAGON

Although the labor movement was mostly missing, the antiwar March on Washington on October 21, 1967, was arguably the last time that liberals, political radicals, and countercultural hippies effectively combined energies.

One of my first feelings when I read Norman Mailer's *The Armies of the Night* was a wave of relief that one of the preeminent fifties literary lefties had treated sixties radicals with affection and respect in his highly personal description of the protest. Unlike Tom Wolfe's relationship with the Merry Pranksters, Mailer was both observer *and* participant. A large part of the book concerns his day in jail for civil disobedience in protest of the war. He was forty-four years old, a generation and a half older than teenage hippies, but he had always occupied a unique space among post–World War II intellectuals. In 1955, Mailer had been one of the founders of the *Village Voice*, and that same year he published a long, seminal essay called "The White Negro." Subtitled "Superficial Reflections on the Hipster," the piece presciently identified many of the sentiments that would form the hippie movement a decade later.

In *The Armies of the Night* he wrote of himself in the third person, as if "Mailer" was a fictitious character. "Mailer had a diatribe against LSD, hippies, and the generation of love but he was keeping it to himself." Yet over the course of the rest of the book, he wrote approvingly of the SDS, Jerry Rubin, Owsley, and the Fugs. Of the Fugs' lead singer, he opined,

> [I]t would be delightful to whack a barricade in the company of Ed Sanders with the red-gold beard who had brought grope-freak talk to the Village and always seemed to Mailer a little over-liberated, but now suitable . . . [N]ot for nothing had Lenin pointed out that there were ten years which passed like an uneventful day, but there was also the revolutionary day which was like ten years.

(Mailer's cultural distance did result in a couple of errors. He thought that the "V" sign flashed by hippies with their second and third fingers stood for "Victory," because that is what it had meant when Winston Churchill made the same hand signal during World War II. In the Vietnam era, we gave it a very different meaning—it was the peace sign. Mailer also incorrectly refers to A.J. Muste as an anarchist, when in fact the pacifist Muste had been at odds with anarchists since World War I.)

At the other end of the spectrum of protest from the Fugs was the earnest sixty-four-year-old Dr. Benjamin Spock, expressing pacifist indignation in his three-piece suit. Spock occupied a unique space in the movement. In the minds of those who wanted Dr. King to run for president, it was assumed that Spock would be the candidate for vice president. He also had credibility with millions of people who did not usually identify with the left. Spock's book *The Common Sense Book of Baby and Child Care*, first published in 1946, was so successful that the *New York Times* reported that in the fifties and sixties, it was outsold only by the Bible. Spock became concerned about the nuclear arms race, and from 1962 to 1967 he cochaired the National Committee for a Sane Nuclear Policy. By the middle of the decade, he was one of the most persistent voices against the war. Cora Weiss, who had been a member of Women Strike for Peace, says, "We all raised our children on Dr. Spock's book. I had one in every room in the house. He gave a legitimacy to the antiwar movement that no one else except Martin Luther King Jr. did."

Dr. Benjamin Spock

Spock felt that Timothy Leary and others had co-opted the civil rights and peace movements and turned young people away from activism in favor of turning on, tuning in, and dropping out. This needlessly distanced him from many young people who had been raised with the help of his famous book. One could make the opposite argument that the criminalization of LSD and pot had created more suspicion of government and added to, rather than subtracted from, the antiwar movement. Yet there was no denying Spock's moral authority, nor his commitment to peace. In January 1968, he, William Sloane Coffin, and others were indicted for "counseling, aiding, and abetting draft resistance."

There were tense negotiations between the more culturally moderate organizers of the 1967 March on Washington and the large number of younger radicals. Cora Weiss and Spock did not want to see Viet Cong flags or leaflets filled with profanity. Even the buttons differentiated some pacifists from their radical counterparts: *Stop the War* vs. *Support the National Liberation Front*. Jerry Rubin found wonkish speeches by earnest pacifists like A.J. Muste to be "boring." His friend Super Joel Tornabene found pacifist David Dellinger's speech "too slow for us speed freaks."

At this time, the focus in the underground press that people like me read was on Ed Sanders, who performed an elaborate "exorcism" with the quixotic goal of removing evil spirits from the Pentagon. Thousands of radicals broke away from the main demonstration to march on the gigantic five-sided building at the heart of America's military defense establishment. Some young people placed flowers in the gun barrels of the soldiers who were "guarding" the massive building from the protesters, resulting in one of the most iconic photos from the sixties. The flowers were provided by Michael Bowen, who in January of that year had been so central to the organization of the Be-In. He had since left the *Oracle* and moved to Mexico, but he returned to the States to bring two hundred pounds of daisies to the march. (Bowen's *Oracle* colleague Allen Cohen later claimed that the idea of exorcising the pentagon was first floated at the Be-In planning meeting at the end of 1966.)

The text of the incantation for the "exorcism" was read by Sanders and accompanied by the banging of cymbals, triangles, and drums. It was in a very different headspace than the reasoned antiwar speeches on the main stage of the demonstration. Here's an excerpt:

> In the name of the amulets of touching, seeing, groping, hearing and loving, we call upon the powers of the cosmos to protect our ceremonies in the name of Zeus, in the name of Anubis, god of the dead, in the name of all those killed because they do not comprehend, in the name of the lives of the soldiers in Vietnam who were killed because of a bad karma, in the name of seaborn Aphrodite, in the name of Magna Mater, in the name of Dionysus, Zagreus, Jesus, Yahweh, the unnameable, the quintessent finality of the Zoroastrian fire, in the name of Hermes, in the name of the Beak of Sok, in the name of scarab, in the name, in the name, in the name of the Tyrone Power Pound Cake Society in the Sky, in the name of Ra, Osiris, Horus, Nepta, Isis, in the name of the flowing living universe, in the name of the mouth of the river, we call upon the spirit . . . to raise the Pentagon from its destiny and preserve it . . .

The war did not end.

DUMP JOHNSON

In recent decades, Lyndon Johnson has correctly been recognized for his political brilliance in actualizing the Civil Rights Act and Voting Rights Act and the surviving elements of the War on Poverty. But in 1967, to millions of Americans, President Johnson was on the wrong side of history, morally culpable for deaths that were not related to American security, and was in thrall to outdated Cold War fundamentalism. His administration's claims of military success in Vietnam were discredited on such a regular basis that he became known for a "credibility gap."

Everyone I admired—radical, hippie, liberal, old or young—had contempt for Johnson in those days. The horror of the war gave his political enemies license to make fun of his awkward public persona. After an appendectomy, President Johnson lifted up his shirt to show his scar to the White House photographers. His televised speeches were read from a teleprompter in a singsong cadence that presented a stark contrast to the eloquent, witty, and debonair style of the martyred Kennedy.

A Tom Paxton song lyric went, *"Lyndon Johnson told the nation / Have no fear of escalation. / I am trying everyone to please. / Though it isn't really war / We're sending fifty thousand more / To help save Vietnam from the Vietnamese."*

In 1967, Woody Allen had enough success as a stand-up comedian that he was given a short-lived talk show of his own before he started directing movies. When William F. Buckley appeared with him, the conservative icon was asked who he wanted to be elected president in

1968. Buckley answered, "Anyone who could beat Johnson." Allen, an antiwar advocate, sadly chimed in, "That could be anyone including the Boston Strangler."

The war was not only anathema to hippies and radicals in 1967, but also to some older anti–Cold War Democrats who had been inspired by Eleanor Roosevelt and Adlai Stevenson. Foreign Relations Committee chairman William Fulbright of Arkansas, no one's idea of a lefty, held nationally televised hearings on the war in 1966 that eviscerated the administration's rationale for the escalation. Wayne Morse of Oregon was one of two senators who had voted against giving President Johnson war authorization after the Gulf of Tonkin incident in 1964, and he regularly reminded Americans that there had never been an actual declaration of war. In New York City, Congressman William Fitts Ryan uncompromisingly articulated the liberal antiwar argument. However, the effort that would eventually persuade President Johnson not to seek reelection was organized outside of Congress.

Allard Lowenstein was thirty-eight years old in 1967. He was the first white board member of Dr. King's SCLC, and he had unsuccessfully tried to recruit King to run for president against Johnson. Lowenstein was the main writer of Bobby Kennedy's celebrated 1966 speech in Cape Town, South Africa, during the heart of apartheid, in which the senator said:

> It is from numberless diverse acts of courage and belief that human history is shaped. Each time a man stands up for an ideal, or acts to improve the lot of others, or strikes out against injustice, he sends forth a tiny ripple of hope, and

crossing each other from a million different centers of energy and daring, those ripples build a current which can sweep down the mightiest walls of oppression and resistance.

By the end of 1966, Lowenstein was adamantly against the war. He had insider political skills that none of the radicals and hippies possessed, and he also understood that his older antiwar peers were out of touch with most young people. He told journalist David Halberstam, "These kids. No one really knows how alienated they really are. Trying to keep them in the system is very, very hard. They're bitter and they're angry. They really resent this society. Of course, there are a lot of things in this society that are very resentable."

In addition to his age, Lowenstein had other baggage with radicals. At a 1966 conference of the National Students Association (NSA), he had debated David Harris. Lowenstein, a former president of the NSA, stressed the need for organization and tactics. Harris cautioned against Americans becoming like "good Germans" during the Nazi era, and called for resistance to the military draft by civil disobedience if necessary. Lowenstein urged students to do everything possible to get a deferment, but if that failed, to serve.

In March 1967, *Ramparts* published a front-page article that revealed that the CIA had been funneling money through the NSA for a decade, hoping to influence its policies and spokespeople. In August 1967, the NSA cut ties with all groups associated with the CIA.

Nonetheless, Lowenstein was unrelenting in his support for antiwar candidates for public office. Realizing the limits of his personal appeal to young radicals, he focused on organizing elites and intellectuals. He orchestrated a letter from fifty Rhodes scholars questioning Vietnam policy, and shortly thereafter escorted forty-one antiwar student body presidents (including Harris) to a meeting with Secretary of State Dean Rusk. One of the students asked Rusk what would happen if both sides kept escalating to the point of the US dropping a nuclear bomb. Rusk took a drag on his cigarette and said: "Well, somebody's going to get hurt." Word of the callous remark spread, and within weeks there were more than two hundred student body presidents signed on to the petition against the war. They thought Rusk had lost it and it seemed like no one from the administration could rationally defend the war. To Lowenstein, this was when the antiwar movement went mainstream.

Lowenstein worked with Yale chaplain and prominent antiwar activist William Sloane Coffin to get more than four hundred members of the Yale faculty to urge an end of American bombing of Vietnam. Coffin called Lowenstein "a prophet who stands clearly within the tradition and says, *The tradition is being corrupted, let's restore the tradition.*"

Lowenstein also focused on religious leaders, persuading theologian Reinhold Niebuhr to make an antiwar declaration, and he helped Stanford theologian Robert McAfee Brown write a statement of conscience for more than two thousand religious leaders for a gathering in January 1967. A committee from that conference expressed their concerns to Defense Secretary Robert McNamara, who was known to be harboring his own doubts about the war.

Lowenstein privately met with Vice President Hubert Humphrey and Johnson's national security adviser, Walt Rostow, and found their closed-mindedness deeply depressing. He concluded that President Johnson was not going to end the war, regardless of elite pressures. In the summer of 1967, Lowenstein and writer Curtis Gans formed the "Dump Johnson" movement to recruit an antiwar Democratic nominee. One of their first allies from the liberal establishment was John Kenneth Galbraith, who had been the ambassador to India under President Kennedy and had recently become president of the Americans for Democratic Action (ADA). Galbraith said, "This is a year when the people are right and the politicians are wrong."

Having failed to get Dr. King to run, Lowenstein and his allies vainly approached Senator Robert Kennedy, followed by Senator George McGovern. In October, just before the March on Washington, Lowenstein finally found a plausible politician willing to oppose a sitting president of his own party—Minnesota senator Eugene McCarthy, who announced his campaign on January 3, 1968. McCarthy's campaign organizers felt that to have the widest possible political reach, volunteers should not look like hippies; men shaved off their mustaches and beards and cut their hair to be "clean for Gene." But it would not be McCarthy who ultimately had the potential to preside over an antiwar majority.

ROBERT KENNEDY
Like Dr. King, Robert Kennedy was peripheral to the hippie world, yet a presence. Many of us wrongly took them both for granted and assumed that they represented the center against which the left and counterculture could

rebel, rather than a bulwark against reactionary political forces which would arrive when Richard Nixon assumed the presidency in 1969.

Tom Hayden and Staughton Lynd, an antiwar Yale history professor who was a fixture at rallies, met with Kennedy in February 1967 to urge him to support withdrawal of American troops from Vietnam. At that time Kennedy expressed worry about a "bloodbath." (Not long thereafter, Hayden and Lynd visited North Vietnam and Lynd was fired from Yale as a result.)

Congressman Jonathan Bingham and Senator Robert F. Kennedy

Kennedy met with other radicals, including Phil Ochs, who he was introduced to by *Village Voice* writer Jack Newfield. Ochs played him the song "Crucifixion," and when Kennedy realized that it was about his slain brother, he silently wept. In February 1968, Kennedy asked Jefferson Airplane to play at the Junior Village Telethon for a family charity that aided differently abled young people. Airplane manager Bill Thompson recalled going to a touch football game the next day at Kennedy's house, which was also attended by Tommy Smothers. There was a jukebox in the house and Thompson noticed that it included "White Rabbit." "We knew they were using our image to get credibility with young voters," Grace Slick told me, "but we were happy to be used in that way."

Lowenstein and Jack Newfield were asked by Senator Kennedy to debate with Arthur Schlesinger, who had been a trusted adviser to President Kennedy. Schlesinger suggested that instead of RFK opposing a sitting president, he and the antiwar students could focus on a "peace plank" in the 1968 Democratic Party platform. Kennedy sarcastically asked, "When was the last time millions of people rallied behind a plank?"

Kennedy was even "straighter" than Lowenstein and had no appetite for civil disobedience. Many in the antiwar movement initially had mixed feelings about him. He had briefly worked for Joseph McCarthy's Senate Committee on Government Operations in the 1950s. As attorney general, Kennedy had been a steely advocate for his brother's interests but came up against serious issues from the left. In May 1963, he'd met with a group of black intellectuals, including James Baldwin and Lorraine Hansberry, and it had not gone well. However, in the years following his brother's assassination, Robert Kennedy had expanded his circle of friends and advisers to include many in the movement. Kennedy visited the Mississippi Delta in 1967; after witnessing the extreme poverty, he returned home and lectured his children on their obligation to help alleviate the plight of the poor.

A speech RFK made at the University of Kansas in early 1968 suggests that some of the values of the counterculture had gotten into his head. In fact, the speech seemed to imply a philosophy of life that was remarkably consistent with the values of Haight-Ashbury:

> [E]ven if we act to erase material poverty, there is another greater task; it is to confront the poverty of satisfaction—purpose and dignity—that afflicts us all. Too much and for too long, we seemed to have surrendered personal excellence and community values in the mere accumulation of material things. Our Gross National Product, now, is over $800 billion dollars a year, but that Gross National Product—if we judge the United States by that—that Gross National Product counts air pollution and cigarette advertising, and ambulances to clear our highways of carnage. It counts special locks for our doors and the jails for the people who break them. It counts the destruction of the redwood and the loss of our natural wonder in chaotic sprawl. It counts napalm and counts nuclear warheads and armored cars for the police to fight the riots in our cities. It counts . . . television programs which glorify violence in order to sell toys to our children. Yet the Gross National Product does not allow for the health of our children, the quality of their education, or the joy of their play. It does not include the beauty of our poetry or the strength of our marriages, the intelligence of our public debate or the integrity of our public officials. It measures neither our wit nor our courage, neither our wisdom nor our learning, neither our compassion nor our devotion to our country. It measures everything, in short,

except that which makes life worthwhile. And it can tell us everything about America except why we are proud that we are Americans.

A well-written speech is not the same as action. Politicians are adept at making one group feel respected while serving the interests of others. RFK had a complicated past, but there is a lot of evidence to suggest he had grown, and he came to have a spectral presence in corners of the counterculture where "politicians" were usually either ignored or reviled.

In early 1968, as Johnson looked more vulnerable, Kennedy reversed course and ran for president, greatly irritating McCarthy and his supporters, but broadening the antiwar campaign as no one else could. His assassination in June was a devastating blow, even to a radical like Hayden, who spoke of the loss for years. At the request of the Kennedy family, Hayden served as a member of the honor guard that accompanied the slain senator's body on the train from Los Angeles to Washington. When the Airplane's *Crown of Creation* album was released in the fall of 1968, a few months after Kennedy's assassination, it included an insert with an image of Robert Kennedy's dog Brumus.

Feminism Rising

The Democratic Party, the left, and the counterculture were not much more respectful to women than the rest of American society in 1967. Out of a total of 435 members of the 90th Congress in 1967, only twelve were women. An Emmett Grogan piece for the Diggers' newsletter, "The Post-Competitive, Comparative Game of a Free Society," referred to free stores for "chicks to sew dresses, make pants to order, recut garments to fit." Abbie Hoffman suggested that "revolutionaries" metaphorically "kill your mothers," and one of Timothy Leary's favorite put-downs was "menopausal mind." Rock and roll and the business around it were overwhelmingly male.

Even so, it was in the realm of political activism where the hypocrisy of left-wing sexism was most directly confronted. In 1965, two civil rights veterans, Mary King and Casey Hayden, presented a paper called "Sex and Caste" at an SDS convention in Illinois. They said that women at SDS were often treated as secondary citizens and were rarely permitted to speak publicly. To some men on the left, women's roles were limited to child-rearing and sex. This cluster of issues was referred to as the "women question."

Margery Tabankin, who had helped lead the University of Wisconsin protests and who became the first female president of the National Students Association, explained the complicated psychology: "Part of being a woman was this psychology of proving I was such a good radical, 'better than the men.' We felt we were motivated by something higher because we didn't have to go to war ourselves. Most guys didn't take women seriously, however. They were things to fuck."

Heather Booth had grown up in the New York area and became an activist in her teens, inspired by the American Friends Service Committee's work against the death penalty. She later participated in SNCC's actions against segregation at Woolworth's in 1960. In 1964, by then nineteen years old, she was part of SNCC's "Mississippi Summer" that focused on voting rights. Booth laughingly recalls the SDS discussions: "A woman would say, *I'm not listened to*, and a man would answer, *Yes you are*. Someone else complained that women were only people asked to make coffee or take notes, and a guy would say, *That's not the* only *thing you do*."

In June 1967, a resolution for "liberation of women" was brought to the SDS convention in Ann Arbor. It protested women's "colonial relation to men," and called for communal childcare centers, distribution of birth control information and devices, legalized abortion, defense against rape and domestic violence, gay rights, women's health care, and equal pay for equal work, all no-brainers in retrospect, but apparently too edgy for SDS at the time.

The leftist paper the *National Guardian* reported that some men objected to the phrase "help relieve our brothers of the burden of male chauvinism." A watered-down resolution to "study the problem" passed and was published in SDS's *New Left Notes*, but it appeared alongside a cartoon of a woman wearing earrings, a polka-dot minidress, and matching visible panties, holding a sign that said, *We want our rights and we want them now*. For many women on the left, this was the final straw. Booth recalls that at the SDS convention, "Jimmy Garrett, who was with SNCC, walked out and said to a group of us, *You're not going to get your act together unless you decide to meet by yourselves*. At first I thought he was wrong and that we should all stay together, but after an hour I realized he was right, and afterward, several of us talked among ourselves."

Booth also notes, "In the women's movement, women's liberation was the vehicle for students." By 1967, she was attending the University of Chicago, and was helping women get safe abortions (still illegal in 1967; the *Roe v. Wade* decision that legalized it nationally would not come until 1973). She was also a cofounder of the Chicago Women's Liberation Union in 1969.

The Democratic Party was not completely oblivious to the women's movement. President Johnson signed an executive order that broadened affirmative action to include discrimination based on gender, which resulted in federal agencies and contractors taking proactive measures to increase the number of women employed on federal projects.

Although I supported the policy goals, I was never a part of the women's movement. Speaking to women who were involved in the sixties, it is clear that one of the movement's many virtues was providing a euphoric sense of community, similar to the feeling many of us had about hippie culture. I got a flash of this when I spoke to Booth in 2016 while she was immersed in get-out-the-vote work to help Hillary Clinton in Florida, a few weeks before the US presidential election. The sixties were fresh in her mind half a century later and she conflated an explosion in the arts, dancing, rock and roll, and poetry, along with consciousness movements, with the hard-core activism she embraced.

Many histories of the period cite Stokely Carmichael's statement, "The position of women in the movement is prone," as the prime example of leftist male chauvinism. Booth emotionally defends him: "We all knew he meant it as a *joke*, as a sarcastic depiction about the way some of the less enlightened males in the movement felt. Stokely was personally always respectful of women."

When I ask if she had bitterness about the way SDS had acted, Booth responds, "In a way, there was a continuum and SDS was not all bad. It allowed us to find our voice. It allowed us to convene a meeting on the women's question." She continues, "There always have been people working in particular areas like women's rights, gay rights, the environment, the peace movement, and civil rights, but in my heart, I always felt like it was *one* movement and I still do."

In hippie circles there were also those who felt a metaphysical unity among the many subcultures that emerged in the sixties, though it was becoming increasingly obvious that after 1967 this unity would have to occur without relying on most of the symbols that had served to connect the tribes.

CHAPTER 9
DEATH OF HIPPIE

THE SUMMER OF LOVE CURDLES

Most of the symbols of hippie life—long hair, bright colors, psychedelic posters, hip language (*far out, crib, bummer, uptight, groovy, balling*)—would all be drained of meaning over the next couple of years.

On the summer solstice, June 21, there was a free concert on Speedway Meadow in Golden Gate Park with the Big Brother, Quicksilver, the Charlatans, and the Grateful Dead (using the sound equipment "borrowed" from the Monterey Festival). The idea was to welcome the Summer of Love, but to many in the community it was an elegy.

"The Haight-Ashbury was a gigantic media magnet, and now we would drown in the media flood. It would never be the same," lamented Allen Cohen. It could take an hour for a car to go the six blocks on Haight Street between Masonic and Stanyan. Rock Scully complained of rising prices: "We've been driven out of our community. Starting in July, it became all drug dealers. Coffee shops charging fifty cents for a cup of coffee!"

It was not only the sheer quantity of wide-eyed teenagers that strained the infrastructure of the neighborhood, it was also the juxtaposition of the most naive and vulnerable kids with the lowest types of predators.

The open sexuality in hippie culture was exploited by a predictable number of macho jerks. Some guys crudely expected hippie chicks to immediately have sex with them. Other guys creepily deployed cosmic language as a tool of seduction.

A widely quoted mimeographed circular handed out by the Diggers' Communications Company described a darker trend:

> *Pretty little sixteen-year-old middle-class chick comes to the Haight to see what it's all about and gets picked up by a seventeen-year-old street dealer who spends all day shooting her full of speed again and again, then feeds her 3,000 mikes and raffles off her temporarily unemployed body for the biggest Haight Street gangbang since the night before last. The politics of ethics and ecstasy. Rape is as common as bullshit on Haight Street.*

George and Pattie Harrison flew to San Francisco in August 1967 to check out Haight-Ashbury. He was dressed in psychedelic pants and moccasins, and wore heart-shaped sunglasses. The neighborhood had changed enormously in the few months since McCartney had visited. Garbage littered the streets. Harrison was depressed by "horrible spotty dropout kids on drugs." A couple of longhairs came up to him in his car and said, "You're our leader." Harrison was appalled: "No, you're wrong." He held up a picture of Paramahansa Yogananada as he drove off. Paul McCartney came to the same conclusion on his second visit to Haight-Ashbury, quipping, "I can't see this lasting because the media are going to get here and pretty soon [Haight Street] will turn into Rip-Off Street."

On August 3, John Kent "Shob" Carter, a twenty-five-year-old flute player and dope dealer, was found after having been stabbed to death by a twenty-three-year-old client named Eric Frank Dahlstrom, described by a Communications Company flyer as a "longhaired Marin Country daredevil bike freak with symptoms of what an untrained man might call a psychopathic personality." In his confession, Dahlstrom said it was because Shob had sold him inferior-quality acid.

On August 15, the Recreation and Park Commission banned amplified music from San Francisco parks, which ended one of the primary ways in which the community had gathered over the last few years.

As most of the early idealistic hippies left the neighborhood, the ultimate villain arrived. Charles Manson's mother was in and out of jail for robbery when he was a child. He was sent to foster homes, and was frequently arrested, eventually serving several years in McNeil Island Federal Penitentiary for forging checks. In jail, Manson read a handbook on Scientology and Dale Carnegie's *How to Win Friends and Influence People*. He was released at the age thirty-two, in March 1967.

Manson gravitated to Haight-Ashbury, saw the Dead at the Avalon Ballroom, and took LSD. He established himself as a self-styled guru, mixing a hodgepodge of occult doctrines with his own apocalyptic notions. He soon attracted a handful of followers, most of them female, who called themselves the Manson Family. The next year they would move to Southern California, and in October 1969, Manson and several followers were arrested and later convicted for the murders of actress Sharon Tate and six others.

Near the end of September, an "invitation" was given out in Haight-Ashbury:

FUNERAL NOTICE
HIPPIE
In the Haight-Ashbury District of this city, Hippie, devoted son of Mass Media
Friends are invited to attend services beginning at sunrise, October 6, 1967 at Buena Vista Park

A Communications Company handout elaborated:

Once upon a time, a man put on beads and became a hippie—Today the hippie takes off his beads and becomes a man—a freeman! Leaving behind the final remains of "Hippie"—the devoted son of mass media and the boundaries are down.
San Francisco is free! Now free
The truth is OUT, OUT, OUT!

The date of the ceremony was October 6, 1967, exactly one year after LSD had been made illegal in California. Organized by the Diggers, a couple hundred people marched through San Francisco with a mock coffin filled with beads, incense, and flowers. At the end it was burned while the "mourners" did "Indian" dances. The Psychedelic Store stayed open all night, giving everything away while *Sgt. Pepper's* played over and over again in the background.

Another Digger communiqué read:

*Media created the hippie with your hungry consent. Be
somebody. Careers are to be had for the enterprising hippie.
The media cast nets, create bags for the identity-hungry to
climb in. Your face on TV, your style immortalized without soul in the captions of the Chronicle. NBC says you
exist, ergo I am. Narcissism, plebian vanity . . . Exorcize
Haight-Ashbury . . . You are free, we are free. Believe only
your own incarnate spirit . . . Do not be bought by a picture,
a phrase. Do not be captured in words.*

Some of the marchers explained that the idea was to
bury the "term" hippie and suggested that those imbued
with the vibe would now call themselves "free men,"
a suggestion that quickly disappeared without a trace.
However, they were right about the word "hippie." It
was toast. If we had to call ourselves something, it was
"freaks," which was a lot harder for Madison Avenue to
co-opt.

On October 2, eleven people were busted for smoking pot at the Dead's house at 710 Ashbury, including
Pigpen, Bob Weir, Scully, and Danny Rifkin. They pleaded
guilty to misdemeanors and paid fines, but after that the
members of the band soon left the city for Marin County.
Soon the Psychedelic Shop closed and put a sign in its
window saying, *Nebraska Needs You More.*

The *Oracle* printed a letter suggesting that the original Haight dwellers move to Louisville: "The scene there
began to grow . . . but we need more turned-on real people." The missive added that Louisville had Victorian
houses with low rents.

On December 21, Owsley was arrested for conspiracy to illegally manufacture controlled drugs. Although he was released on bail, he was out of business. The *Oracle* published its last issue in February 1968.

NEW YORK AND LONDON

The Lower East Side also struggled under the burdens of a greater population of inexperienced kids, an influx of criminals, and an increase in police hostility. In the summer there was a "Community Breast" concert at the Village Theatre featuring Judy Collins, Richie Havens, Tiny Tim, Paul Krassner, and Hugh Romney, intended to raise money to gather content for a Digger-style free store. It soon opened at 264 East 10th Street, and in a brief burst of optimism, Paul Goodman volunteered to stack clothes.

The concept failed almost immediately. Local hippie stores that *did* charge money plundered free stuff and then sold it. Meth heads started hanging out and there were numerous fights and muggings. When it first opened, the free store had a sign out front that said, Love. By the fall, it had been replaced by one that said, Hate.

Meanwhile, Ed Sanders had asked a charismatic neighborhood hippie named Groovy to live in the back of the Peace Eye Bookstore. Groovy gave advice to young newcomers to the Lower East Side in need of help, and he offered karate lessons in the garden behind the store. At some point over the summer, they halted the lessons when the landlord, alarmed by weird-looking visitors learning martial arts, threatened to call the cops. Groovy and his girlfriend Linda moved out and found a pad a few blocks away. On October 7, both were murdered—someone had smashed their heads with a brick. A neighbor named Donald Ramsey, a self-described Yoruba priest, was arrested.

In his memoir *Fug You*, Sanders mourned, "In a better world, Groovy Hutchinson, spreader of goodwill, warder off of burns and bad acid, and finder of sleeping space for the partisans of love, might have gotten a Great Society job to help locate housing or temporary communes in the tenements."

The degradation of hippie symbols happened in Europe at the same time. Music producer Joe Boyd wrote, "The *agape* spirit of '67 evaporated in the heat of ugly drugs, violence, commercialism, and police pressure. In Amsterdam, people began stealing and repainting the white bicycles."

RATIONALIST BACKLASH

The decline of Haight-Ashbury and respect for hippies could not come quickly enough for those who had been appalled by the whole thing. It was no surprise to many of us that political and cultural conservatives like Ronald Reagan and Billy Graham demonized the hippie idea, but many liberal grown-ups were similarly contemptuous. They were not in the same moral sinkhole as the Blue Meanies, who cynically pursued the war in Vietnam, and for the most part were people of goodwill. Some were brilliant. Some were genuine altruists. They just didn't get it.

One was Nicholas von Hoffman, a political progressive who wrote for the *Washington Post* and had worked for radical organizer Saul Alinsky. Von Hoffman visited Haight-Ashbury in 1967 and published the book *We Are the People Our Parents Warned Us Against*, which seethed with indignation and contempt for the counterculture as he saw it. In the book, von Hoffman quoted a hippie girl: "I've decided that from now on I'm not going to sleep with any boy unless I know his name." And he referenced a "guy at a commune with a religious smile on his face all the time, but he would never do the dishes."

Von Hoffman did not merely cherry-pick hippie airheads—he was repelled by the whole idea:

> At a time when Negroes are fighting to get off dope and forcing their way out of the ghetto to get the good things that hips dismiss as so much plastic, it's hard for them to empathize with white kids who have all that Negroes want. It's incomprehensible that these whites should build a new ghetto and lock themselves up in it to take dope. They are an affronting put-down to the blacks, making a virtue of every sin the black man has been accused of—dirt, shiftlessness, sexual promiscuity, improvidence, and irresponsibility.

Putting aside the intellectual dishonesty of conflating marijuana and heroin, von Hoffman (who is white) seemed to be suggesting that a critique of materialism was invalid if it came from people born into relative privilege. A determination to escape from poverty and prejudice did not necessarily translate into a value system that prized superficial material success above all else. Von Hoffman also implied that focus on an inner life somehow precluded liberal reform. It did not seem to occur to him that while the liberal policies that he (and many hippies) believed in might be necessary to help transform the darkest aspects of America, they were not sufficient.

Contempt for the Haight scene also permeated "Slouching Towards Bethlehem," an essay by Joan Didion, who was thirty-two years old in 1967 when it was first published in the *Saturday Evening Post*. (The piece was later included as the title chapter in an anthology of Didion's brilliant short nonfiction.)

Like von Hoffman, Didion spent some time in Haight-Ashbury and interviewed anguished parents of runaways. "We were seeing the desperate attempt of a handful of pathetically unequipped children to create a community in a social vacuum." She reported on some grotesque extremes, such as young mothers who gave their five-year-olds LSD. There were a few young women who were indeed that irresponsible. My former classmate Susan Solomon says she witnessed such behavior in some of the people who hung around with the Grateful Dead and Country Joe and the Fish, whose drummer she married. Sara Davidson, author of the sixties novel *Loose Change*, saw it at the Wheeler's Ranch Commune. And yet there is no reason to believe that such irresponsibility was either typical or widely sanctioned in the counterculture. It is not fair to judge any community by a few of its most disgraceful members.

Didion concluded that the hippie movement was "quintessentially romantic, the kind that recurs in times of real social crisis . . . [which] lends itself to authoritarianism." This proved to be as inaccurate a prediction as Timothy Leary's suggestion that Times Square would be covered over by grass in fifty years.

One of the reasons that a number of older intellectuals were so put off by the hippie idea was that the secular religion for many in the 1950s was old-school Freudian psychoanalysis, the very worldview that Leary, Alpert, Janiger, and Kesey had all rebelled against.

LSD advocates were not the only people who were questioning the Freudian fundamentalism of the time. Gary Greenberg, a historian of psychiatry, says, "What became clear by the sixties was that analysis had become a force for conformity and adaptation." This orthodoxy was rejected by younger therapists who defined themselves as humanists. Ground zero for the humanist movement was the Esalen Institute, which was started in 1962 in Central California by two Stanford graduates— Dick Price, who had been influenced by an Aldous Huxley lecture on "human potentialities," and Michael Murphy, who had spent time at an ashram in India. By 1967, Esalen's most well-known figure was Fritz Perls, who, along with Paul Goodman, created "gestalt therapy," a post-Freudian approach to psychology that incorporated theories from Eastern traditions and had a much broader concept of what constituted mental health.

In the wake of these non-Freudian newcomers, and the spread of LSD, some conventional analysts became defensively hostile to the counterculture and formed theories that would be used by cultural conservatives in years to come. One such therapist was Dr. Ernest A. Dernberg, who was the psychiatric director of the Haight-Ashbury Free Medical Clinic, in addition to his duties at two San Francisco hospitals.

Free Clinic director David E. Smith published *Love Needs Care* in 1971. In the chapter "The Hippie Modality," Smith described Dernberg's conviction that the hippie lifestyle was a pathology. Appalled that Episcopal bishop James Pike compared hippies to early Christians, Dernberg complained to Smith that "hippies invested 'love' with a great many meanings but it signified less an intimacy and mutual respect between two people than an all-embracing feeling for man and nature. The feeling was probably an extension of the oceanic oneness associated with LSD and the toxic afterglow of hallucinogenic experience, a toxicity so strong that the young people sought to dispense with ego and see themselves as part of a psychologically undifferentiated organism, a group mind."

This disdain for agape could apply to *any* form of mystical or spiritual experience, not solely the "afterglow" of LSD, and it is really a theological attack cloaked in the language of science. Dernberg may have been influenced by Freud's book *Civilization and Its Discontents*, which views "oceanic consciousness" as inherently psychotic.

For some reason Dernberg had a particular animus toward Marshall McLuhan, as if the Canadian professor was personally responsible for the whole thing. Smith wrote, "Instead of thinking sequentially, some of them focused only on lights, color, and sound. This condition may have seemed promising to McLuhan and others who considered it an inner trip, but for most of Dr. Dernberg's patients the circus never seemed to end."

According to Smith, Dernberg detested hippie slang and rock concerts, and he also mocked interest in Eastern spirituality. As with many rationalist hippie critiques, it is hard to tell if Dernberg was dismissing all mystical philosophies (as Freud did) or merely those without kosher Western credentials. Even health food was suspect.

Smith and Dernberg did provide desperately needed medical services to people in Haight-Ashbury who had nowhere else to go. However, they had a concept of mental health that was suffocatingly narrow. As Gary Greenberg explained to me: "Like most psychiatrists in 1967, Dernberg would have been trained in the psychoanalytic theory that if you don't resolve your Oedipal conflicts, your psychosexual life will be a disaster. Homosexuality, promiscuity, fetishes, plus the symbolic versions, rebellion, fecklessness, underachieving, overachieving, all could be traced to this supposed 'failure.' The paradigm case is Bruno Bettelheim's denunciation of Vietnam War protesters as just so many neurotics who still wanted to kill their fathers and fuck their mothers."

Even if the word "hippie" was dead, there was no way that millions of people who had briefly identified with it were going back to blindly obeying such "authority."

BIRTH OF YIPPIE

Indifferent to such reactionary currents, Abbie Hoffman, his wife Anita, and Paul Krassner took a vacation in Ramrod Key, Florida, where they rented a small house the week before Christmas. It was the same week that Stokely Carmichael came back to the United States. "We would have been there cheering for him had we been in New York," Krassner wrote in the *Realist*. "For Stokely had said in Paris that 'we don't want peace in Vietnam. We want a Vietnamese victory over the US.'" (There was not a consensus about this attitude in the antiwar movement. Many of us *did* want peace.)

One night they planned to see Hoffman's favorite movie, *The Professionals*, but it was playing too far away, and a storm was brewing, so instead they watched the Dino De Laurentiis version of the *Bible*. In a 2007 essay in the *Los Angeles Times*, Krassner wrote, "Driving home in the rain and wind, we debated the implications of Abraham being prepared to slay his son because God told him to. I dismissed this as blind obedience. Abbie praised it as revolutionary trust."

Abbie Hoffman

After the film they all took LSD and got back to the house just as the storm reached full force and the acid was coming on. According to Krassner, "We watched Lyndon Johnson on a black-and-white TV set, although seen through psychedelicized eyes, Johnson's face was purple and orange. His huge head was sculpted into Mount Rushmore. Johnson said something like, *I am not going to be so pudding-headed as to stop our half of the war*, and I told Abbie we *had* to protest against the war at Johnson's convention the next summer in Chicago."

Back in New York a week later, Krassner and the Hoffmans were joined by Jerry Rubin. They stayed up all night smoking Colombian weed on New Year's Eve, talking about what to do at the convention. Krassner recalls, "I came up with 'Yippie' as a label for a phenomenon that already existed, an organic coalition of psychedelic hippies and political activists. In the process of cross-fertilization at antiwar demonstrations, we had come to share an awareness that there was a linear connection between putting kids in prison for smoking pot in this country and burning them to death with napalm on the other side of the planet."

Jim Fouratt soon joined as a Yippie organizer. In a 2013 *AlterNet* essay, Krassner wrote:

> *Our fantasy was to counter the convention of death with a festival of life. While the Democrats would present politicians giving speeches at the convention center, we would present rock bands playing in the park. There would be booths with information about drugs and alternatives to the draft. Our mere presence would be our statement.*

Hoffman and Rubin would continue to switch back and forth between being counterculture types and being radicals. In Black Panther leader Bobby Seale's book *Seize the Time*, he quotes Jerry Rubin as saying that he and others had formed the Yippies because hippies had not "necessarily become political yet. 'They mostly prefer to be stoned.'"

Given what happened the next summer in Chicago,

perhaps being too stoned to go would not have been such a bad idea. By then the notes in the culture had changed enough that the chord of 1967 was indeed lost.

EPILOGUE
REFLECTIONS IN THE CRYSTAL WIND

1968–1970

Although elements of the countercultural and antiwar movements would flicker for several years, the balance of energies changed, and changed quickly. On January 30, 1968, the North Vietnamese launched the Tet Offensive, which proved the futility of the war to many in the media and in some sectors of the establishment.

It was not the Yippies who wrought the biggest changes in American political culture in 1968. That awful distinction belonged to the assassins of Martin Luther King Jr. and Robert Kennedy. There is no way to overstate the impact of losing them.

In future decades, some Democratic pundits would blame the 1968 election of Richard Nixon on the demonstrations outside of the Democratic Convention in Chicago, but it was the party's establishment, not the peace movement, who created the space for the Republican victory. The protest was against the support for the Vietnam War by Vice President Hubert Humphrey, who had been nominated for president even though the antiwar candidates, Senator Eugene McCarthy and the slain Senator Kennedy, had fared better with primary voters. The war itself was the problem, not the opposition to it.

If I could have voted in the general election in 1968, I would have held my nose and voted for Humphrey, but to the extent that antiwar people were not inspired to do so, the blame lies not with traumatized peaceniks but with the candidate himself. Humphrey was apparently so intimidated by President Johnson that he didn't address the concerns of the antiwar movement until the last minute, and even then in an oblique manner, too little too late.

There had not been a consensus in the counterculture about the actions in Chicago. The Yippies and Tom Hayden promoted them. Allen Ginsberg and the Diggers had counseled against them. (Despite the fact that his worries about violence were ignored, Ginsberg decided to show up and chant to try to mitigate the bad vibes.)

Fragmentation of the left got worse as the months went by. Martin Luther King Jr. delivered a sermon in which he quoted from the Book of Romans. *"Be not conformed to this world: but be ye transformed by the renewing of your mind."* He warned that in the movement there were too many "non-transformed nonconformists, people who do the right thing for the wrong reasons." In 1968, much of the radical community was damaged by infighting and intense pressure from the government, which included the use of provocateurs to further splinter the movement. SNCC soon ceased to exist. The Black Panthers were heavily persecuted by the FBI. Although SDS would not formally disband until 1974, it was tearing itself apart.

The Weather Underground was created around a militant strategy that included bombing government buildings. They drew a disproportionate amount of attention in the underground press, and over the next several decades, the perverse glamour of their outlaw life attracted many novelists and filmmakers. In reality, the Weather Underground never had more than a few hundred members, and in my opinion they contributed nothing of value to the antiwar movement.

However, neither the Weather Underground nor other radicals can be blamed for the continued darkness of the war and the domestic costs of pursuing it. The Nixon administration continued the government's opposition to the antiwar movement. Their rigid determination to equate patriotism with support of the war contributed to the climate in May 1970 when nonviolent protesters were killed at Kent State and Jackson State universities by National Guard troops.

Peter Coyote believes that the greater impact of the sixties are cultural: gay rights, legal pot, the proliferation of mindfulness, yoga, nontraditional medicine, health foods, and most currents of the environmental movement. There is no question that many of the digital geniuses who created a lot of the architecture of the Internet were influenced by the psychedelic culture of the sixties. But it's important to recognize that the political forces protecting the status quo of the military-industrial complex and other massive economic interests were and are far more powerful that those which resist change on social issues.

The antiwar movement was fragmented and sometimes incoherent, but it was right. The premise that justified the Vietnam War was false. There was not a viable opposition to Ho Chi Minh, and the puppets supported by the United States had little or nothing in common with democratic values. Nor was a Communist North Vietnam ever any kind of real threat to the United States, and its ultimate victory didn't have any effect on the Cold War balance between the United States and the Soviet Union or China. Vietnam is now a popular (and safe) vacation spot for Americans.

More than any other antiwar leader, Tom Hayden remained a significant voice in political conversations on the left for decades. He was married to Jane Fonda from 1973–1990 and together they were influential thought leaders in "liberal Hollywood." In 1982, Hayden began an eighteen-year run as a member of the California legislature, departing only when term limits forced him to. He was a powerful voice on dozens of issues, including the environment, Mexican-American rights, and economic justice, and wrote twenty-two books on a wide range of issues.

I spoke to Hayden in the spring of 2016, a few months before his death, and he still had very mixed feelings about the effect of hippies on the antiwar movement. In *Hell No*, his posthumous book about the protest movement against the Vietnam War, he was still suggesting that CIA was complicit in flooding Haight-Ashbury with LSD.

Any idea that the struggle against racism had been solved by the passage of the Civil Rights Act and Voting Rights Act was contradicted by the millions of votes that Alabama governor George Wallace received in his third-party bid in 1968. The rationale of Wallace's campaign was the so-called white backlash. Lyndon Johnson had predicted that the passage of the Civil Rights Act would lose the South for Democrats for a generation. As things turned out, he underestimated how long racism would be a political force in America.

Drugs changed in 1968 as well. Heroin and methedrine (smack and speed) suddenly showed up in the rock-and-roll scene and throughout the hippie world, where just a few months earlier pot and psychedelics were all that was considered cool. At seventeen, I was no exception, mindlessly shooting hard drugs for months in 1968. There is no question that criminals could make a lot more money selling junk, and there are some on the left who harbor suspicions that the government encouraged hard drugs as well. Jim Fouratt tells of a pound of heroin mysteriously showing up at the *Oracle*. But the fact that bad guys had an agenda does not explain why so many hippies made such a destructive turn.

Peter Coyote would become a junkie for over a decade before turning to Buddhist meditation, with guidance from Gary Snyder. How, I asked him, did so many of us go from taking sacraments to reach for universal love to grasping for short bursts of euphoria or warm numbness that soon led to degradation? Coyote suggests that authority figures had lost so much credibility with their insane advocacy of the Vietnam War, demonization of marijuana, and repression of sexual energy that *all* authority became discounted, including those offering good advice about the perils of hard drugs. For Coyote and Grogan, the fact that jazz geniuses like Charlie Parker had shot heroin gave the drug an exotic allure.

"When you're inventing a new world, you're not looking at yourself objectively."

Even LSD was no longer the same. Owsley and the Orange County acid dealers, the Brotherhood of Eternal Love, were missionaries who were obsessed with the purity of their LSD. Their messianic belief in acid transcended conventional business logic. This attitude was not shared by old-school criminal drug dealers who got into the game once the money was big enough. Some acid was mixed with speed and strychnine, causing a lot of bad trips. One such tainted batch was the "brown acid" that attendees at the Woodstock Festival in 1969 were cautioned to avoid.

Michael Lang, a Woodstock promoter, had the foresight to ask Hugh Romney and his commune, the Hog Farm, to oversee the festival tent where kids having bad trips could get help. The clan had taken a lot of psychedelics over the years and exuded joyous empathy. They were an extraordinarily positive force at the festival, transmuting bad trips into good ones, and they taught those recently in distress to similarly help others.

I went to Woodstock at the beginning of my career in the music business, at a time when I wasn't even smoking pot—but I recognized the beauty and camaraderie of the crowd as an inspiring afterglow of the hippie idea that had so captivated me a couple of years earlier.

That magic was absent at the infamous Altamont Festival later in 1969, where more of the acid was bad and there was no Hog Farm. A member of the Hells Angels stabbed an unruly fan to death. The films *Woodstock* and *Gimme Shelter* are excellent documents of the two events.

1969 was also the year of the Atlanta Pop Festival. At

one point, Romney was lying on the stage tripping when blues master B.B. King stepped over him and asked with a big smile, "Are you wavy, gravy?" (King was probably referring to a track by jazz guitarist Kenny Burrell called "Wavy Gravy" on his 1963 *Midnight Blue* album.) In any case, from then on the Hog Farm leader's name *was* Wavy Gravy.

Wavy Gravy

1969 was also the year that Mario Puzo's novel *The Godfather* was published. It was a huge best seller and the basis for the 1972 movie that is perennially listed among the best American films in history. *The Godfather* and its sequel are among my favorite movies as well, but the view of human nature and the meaning of life is as close to the opposite of "All You Need Is Love" and the hippie idea as Ayn Rand's novels are.

Timothy Leary had several stressful years. After the

San Francisco Be-In in January he was the opening act to a Grateful Dead show and said, "Fuck authorities. To hell with your parents." His tone even made Owsley nervous: "Everybody was saying, *Look, Tim, you're out of control. You've got to cool it. You're bringing too much heat.*" At the end of the year, Leary moved to Orange County to live with the Brotherhood of Eternal Love. He was soon arrested again for possession of pot.

Leary was convicted and given a ten-year sentence early in 1970. As a young therapist he had helped design the psychological tests used by penal authorities to evaluate inmates. Perhaps that is why he was able to get an assignment as a gardener in a lower-security prison, from which he later escaped with the help of the Weather Underground. He spent a few years in hiding outside of the United States, was extradited and reimprisoned in 1973, and was then pardoned in 1976 by California Governor Jerry Brown.

There are some in the counterculture, including Peter Coyote, who believe that Leary was released early because he informed on others. Leary's friends maintain that he never gave authorities any information they did not already have.

Although Leary liked the spotlight, he couldn't have imagined what the intensity of the late-sixties media would be like for him, nor the ferocity of the government's reaction. I got to know Leary during the last decade of his life and found him to be brilliant, loving, and self-effacing, with a perpetual smile on his face and gleam in his eye. He cared little about money and was a mentor to dozens of young people during the years when personal computers and virtual reality emerged;

he was also an inspiration and friend to many rock musicians. Allen Ginsberg, William S. Burroughs, and Ram Dass all warmly reconnected with Leary, and he raised a son named Zach who adored him. When he died at the age of seventy-five in 1996, his last word was "Beautiful."

I believe that the operatic intensity of Leary's life in the sixties and early seventies obscures the depth of his contributions to society. He and Richard Alpert always maintained that LSD should be regulated and studied. In 2016, when "microdosing" of psychedelics was growing in use by therapists and there were Department of Defense–sanctioned experiments with the use of LSD to help veterans with post-traumatic stress disorder, the "establishment" attitude was very different than it had been decades earlier.

In an *Oracle* interview in 1967, Alpert was asked whether he thought the United States needed a revolution, and he answered that it was unnecessary because there would be a psychedelic majority in eight years. In 2016, I asked him about this inaccurate prognostication and he said with a laugh, "What we were doing wrong was predicting the future when we were *on* acid. What I was wrong about was saying *eight years*. Because if you look now and you see universities all over the country getting government permission to sponsor studies for all kinds of ways that psychedelics can help humans, this is another step forward."

Alpert traveled to India at the end of 1967. "I went because after years of experimentation with psychedelics, I kept seeing that I kept coming down, and I was looking for a map of consciousness which psychedelics did not provide me—so I realized that because of Huxley introducing Tim and me to *The Tibetan Book of Dead* that I had to go to the East to get that map of consciousness." There he met his guru Neem Karoli Baba, who was often called Maharajji. Alpert was given the name Ram Dass, which means "Servant of God." He came back to America in 1969 and created a linkage between hippie culture and ancient spiritual cosmology, first in lectures broadcast on underground radio stations like WBAI and eventually in the book *Be Here Now*, which has sold over two million copies since its first publication in 1971. It inspired me then and it still does today.

In June 1970 there was an Alternative Media Conference at Goddard College in Vermont where hundreds of underground radio and press people met each other. A chartered airplane brought the Grateful Dead and their extended family there, most of them tripping. The recently formed J. Geils Band was introduced to radio deejays. Jim Fouratt hectored the crowd for being insufficiently political. Ram Dass spoke about the spirit. Harvey Kurtzman explained the thinking behind the early years of *Mad* magazine. WBAI's Bob Fass ladled soup to attendees in the cafeteria. I wrote a piece in *Crawdaddy* that suggested it was the beginning of a new era, but I was wrong. It turned out that Blue Meanie forces were even more effective in diluting hippie values in the media than they had been in the LSD business. Within a year, alternative papers and stations were being directed by their owners to deliver information pleasing to advertising agencies. Any hip aspirations by underground radio folks needed to be justified by ratings.

There were also self-inflicted wounds in the counterculture, some of which were identified by Chögyam

Trungpa Rinpoche, a Tibetan Buddhist meditation master whose teachings were embraced by Ram Dass and Allen Ginsberg. Trungpa had escaped from Tibet with the Dalai Lama a decade earlier and had served as the spiritual adviser for the Young Lamas Home School in Dalhousie, India. He arrived in the United States in 1970 and soon coined the phrase "spiritual materialism" as a critique of attachment to external symbols of spirituality at the expense of inner work. Trungpa counseled against turning the pursuit of spirituality into ego trips, such as flaunting supposed spiritual credentials.

On a broader scale, insularity had developed in many hip circles, which undermined the spirit of agape. One of the most popular posters in head shops was *Humbead's Revised Map of the World*, which depicted a hip world revolving solely around centers in New York, San Francisco/Berkeley, Cambridge/Boston, London, and Los Angeles. This kind of smug snobbery turned off many good people, both at the time and in subsequent generations.

FLASH FORWARD

Decades later, many younger people viewed the late sixties as a time of superficial trends like the Roaring Twenties, worth remembering primarily for the interesting music and colorful fashions. To be called "stuck in the sixties" became the ultimate insult from "serious" people, who rolled their eyes at what they perceived as stoner nostalgia. I like to think that this trivialization of the era is primarily due to the effectiveness of cartoon versions of the sixties in obscuring the deeper realities of the hippie idea.

Although the mass media no longer followed the

glow of Allen Ginsberg's "bohemian torch of enlightenment," in the global village writ large, there were several
positive reverberations from 1967.

After its success on Broadway, *Hair* was produced
in dozens of cities around the world. June Christopher,
a younger Fieldston classmate who hung out with the
heads, joined the Munich production in 1969. "They
needed people of color for the rainbow tribe in the
play," she explains, "and there weren't many blacks who
also spoke German." (June's father was African American and her mother was a German Jew whose family had
left Berlin in the 1930s as Hitler was coming to power.)

There is a scene in the musical in which the entire
cast is nude, which June recalls as "truly amazing. It was
not sexual, it was an affirmation that we were all babies
of God. The feeling on the stage was, *Here I am like I came
into the world.*" June was always moved by the plight of
the character in the play who gets drafted to fight in
Vietnam and is killed there. "The idea that you would
take these beings of love and make some of them kill or
be killed was so horrible." One of the other cast members in the Munich production was Donna Summer,
who hired June as a backup singer a couple of years later
when she had her run of giant disco hits.

Just as *Hair* had virtues that were not apparent to me
in 1967, the Diggers had shortcomings that loom larger
in retrospect than they did at the time. They were indeed integral to the soul of Haight-Ashbury at its best,
and their creativity and aspirations of moral purity had
an influence on the sixties underground scene far out
of proportion to their numbers. But the extent to which
they undermined other counterculture groups gives

them a mixed legacy. There is a thin line between righteousness and self-righteousness, and between idealism and tribalism.

Peter Coyote is appropriately proud of the Diggers' legacy of performance art, free food, clothing, and concerts, and determination to expose hypocrisy in the hip culture, but he also sees some things differently with the distance of fifty years: "Sometimes when I see those blurry old videos of Emmett [Grogan], I am embarrassed by how bullied many of us were by him, the way he would wink at you like there was some deeper meaning to everything he was saying. He's my brother. I memorialize his death every year [with] full Buddha ceremonies, but he did not look at his own problems. He always thought he could act out and he got caught short when [the] zeitgeist shifted. It wasn't enough to be a streetwise gangster with refined sensibilities."

Michael Lerner, one of the radicals who met with the Haight-Ashbury hippies to plan the Be-In, had been a leader in the Free Speech Movement and was chairman of the SDS chapter at the University of California, Berkeley, from 1966–68. Lerner continued to advocate progressive ideas while deepening his connection to Judaism. In 1986 he created *Tikkun* magazine, which combines many countercultural attitudes with a progressive critique of "mainstream" Jewish politics. He coauthored a book called *Jews and Blacks* with Cornel West, and joined coalitions opposing Israel's activities in the occupied territories. He was ordained as a rabbi in 1995, and in 2016, at Muhammad Ali's multifaith memorial service at which former President Clinton appeared, Lerner was the sole rabbi to speak. Ali himself had long before planned the memorial and appreciated Lerner's support for him during his darkest times and his inclusive notion of spirituality.

The Vietnam War was also a defining event for Bill Zimmerman, who was completing a PhD from the University of Chicago in 1967. He had met Ken Kesey and Richard Alpert in California earlier in the decade and spent time in Haight-Ashbury. "Everybody sharing everything," he says. "There was naive optimism being expressed on streets everywhere. People you just met offering you places to spend the night." A couple of years later, Zimmerman immersed himself in the antiwar movement after he was fired by Brooklyn College for refusing to conduct sleep research that would be made available for military uses. He helped to organize demonstrations in Washington and worked with the Vietnam Veterans Against the War.

Zimmerman did not participate in the protests in Chicago outside the Democratic Convention in 1968. "I failed to see what could be accomplished by a bloodbath," he says. He regarded the Weather Underground with contempt: "In October 1969, they sponsored 'Days of Rage' in Chicago. The action consisted of nothing more than a few hundred 'revolutionaries' running through the streets, breaking car and house windows, taunting pedestrians, and throwing rocks at the police. Weathermen leaders assumed that such actions would inspire 'revolutionary youth' to join them. Instead they just looked ridiculous."

Zimmerman came to believe that the antiwar movement "had to make it easy for people to join us, not require them to carry foreign flags, risk arrest, or adopt a militant posture toward a government many still considered their own."

He visited North Vietnam in 1972, filmed the devastation visited on the civilian population by a Nixon bombing campaign, and sold some of the footage to *60 Minutes*, which ran eight minutes of it in prime time. He also made his own film, *Village By Village*, which was screened for Congress and also during an antiwar show organized by Jane Fonda that toured US military bases.

Along with Cora Weiss and a group of concerned physicians, Zimmerman founded Medical Aid for Indochina, which raised money for medical supplies for North Vietnam. In addition to its humanitarian virtues, he explains, "We avoided the disagreements over ideology and tactics that limited the larger antiwar movement. No one had an ideological problem with medical assistance."

Having visited Bach Mai Hospital in Hanoi not long before American bombs destroyed it, Zimmerman helped raise money to rebuild the institution, as did Wavy Gravy, who organized a benefit concert by the Grateful Dead. (The Dead were still generally avoiding politics, but they found it impossible to say no to Wavy, who reciprocated by avoiding radical rhetoric onstage. He called the band "rainbow makers.")

A different kind of reverberation came from the mind of Stewart Brand, who had taken LSD in the early sixties as part of a legal study in Menlo Park, California. Over the next few years he became part of the Merry Pranksters and helped produce the Trips Festival in San Francisco in early 1966, which was the biggest psychedelic gathering prior to the Be-In. Brand developed an obsession with the rumor that America's space agency

NASA had photos of the earth taken from outer space. He thought it would enhance brotherhood if human beings could actually see that we all lived on the same planet. A campaign launched by Brand and Buckminster Fuller made buttons that read, *Why haven't we seen a photograph of the whole earth yet?* In 1967, the government finally released a satellite photo of the earth.

In the fall of 1968, Brand used that photo on the cover of the first edition of the book-length *Whole Earth Catalog* that was subtitled, *Access to Tools*. It was a guide to books, maps, garden implements, specialized clothing, carpenters' and masons' tools, forestry gear, tents, welding equipment, and early versions of personal computers. Among the more than one million people who bought the *Whole Earth Catalog* was future Apple founder Steve Jobs. In a commencement speech at Stanford in 2005, Jobs said, "When I was young, there was an amazing publication called the *Whole Earth Catalog*, which was one of the bibles of my generation . . . It was sort of like Google in paperback form, thirty-five years before Google came along. It was idealistic, and overflowing with neat tools and great notions." He quoted the farewell message placed on the back cover of the 1974 edition: "Stay hungry. Stay foolish."

Although American environmentalism dates back at least as far as Henry David Thoreau, it entered a new phase in the wake of the sixties. Denis Hayes graduated from Stanford in 1969; he was an antiwar activist who, like David Harris, had been the student body president. Hayes came up with the idea of a national demonstration for environmental action. The first celebration of Earth Day took place in April 1970 at two thousand colleges and universities, roughly ten thousand primary and secondary schools, and in hundreds of communities across the United States. These days, Earth Day is observed in 192 countries, and coordinated by the nonprofit Earth Day Network, still chaired by Hayes.

Contrary to the perception that acidheads ignored suffering in the world, Dr. Larry Brilliant, a colleague of Wavy Gravy and a disciple of Ram Dass's guru Neem Karoli Baba, got a job with the World Health Organization and was part of the medical team that eliminated smallpox from India.

In 1978, Brilliant, Wavy Gravy, and Ram Dass started the Seva Foundation to provide health services in impoverished parts of the world. It was initially funded by a donation from Steve Jobs and a benefit performance by the Grateful Dead. Over the years, more than four million people have been cured of blindness by Seva workers in Nepal and other third world countries.

IT WAS FIFTY YEARS AGO TODAY

Some Hindus believe that this era of humanity is the "Kali Yuga," a time of spiritual darkness. Some believe there is a golden age coming. Some of us thought that it was coming in the late sixties, which definitely turned out to be wishful thinking. Some astrologers say that there is an Age of Aquarius, but even Wikipedia tells us, "Astrologers do not agree on when the Aquarian age will start or even if it has already started." Of course, many smart folks feel that such ideas are superstition or akin to fairy tales. As far as I can tell, Paul Krassner is among that latter group, although one can never be sure with the self-described "Zen Bastard."

Perhaps there was an emanation from another plane that created the counterculture that peaked in 1967, or perhaps it was just the temporary product of various historical forces. All I know is that despite the folly and the disappointments of the time, I continue to be inspired by Allen Ginsberg and Martin Luther King Jr., by dozens of those I've written about, and by hundreds who made sure their names were never known but who collectively created something beautiful, something that continues to reverberate in times both good and bad.

One of Tom Hayden's last speeches was at a 2015 conference called Vietnam: The Power of Protest, intended to counteract government attempts to marginalize the antiwar movement fifty years later. "[T]he struggle for memory and for history is a living thing. It's ongoing. It does not end . . . We challenge the Pentagon now on the battlefield of memory." Referring to a recent speech by President Obama, Hayden pointedly noted, "[He] has reminded us to remember . . . Selma, Seneca Falls, and Stonewall. But not Saigon, not Chicago, not Vietnam. We have to ask ourselves collectively why that omission exists . . . [V]ery powerful forces in our country . . . stand for denial, not just climate denial but generational denial, Vietnam denial."

Hayden knew better than anyone the foibles of the movement: "We lived like small boats floating on the sea with raging tides under us, raging crosscurrents that we could not control, only had the illusion of control. Did we think we could swing a majority of Americans to a Marxist analysis or a revolution because of the draft? Come on!" Hayden's biggest regret was, "We said we would not be like the old left, but we became like the old left. We fell into the same sectarian divisions."

On the other hand, he said, "I think we can take credit for constituencies that brought about Ron Dellums, George McGovern, Bella Abzug, and Bernie Sanders. Radicals initiate a process of social change and finally enter the mainstream . . . We took it as our mission to live fulfilling lives instead of making money."

A month after Hayden died, Donald Trump was elected president of the United States. I asked Ram Dass if he felt that more light than darkness had been generated by the counterculture. His response: "I think that it added light, but I think that what's happening now is a direct reaction from the sixties. We were very naive to think that there would be instant world peace. In the sixties there was a reaction of the right that we did not predict that is still reverberating today in this situation."

It is worth remembering that the heroes of 1967 were themselves dealing with extremely dark forces, forces that would soon assassinate the most inspiring mainstream progressive leaders, that animated a profoundly destructive FBI, that supported a racist campaign by George Wallace and then a "Southern strategy" by Richard Nixon to peel off enough Wallace voters to win the presidency. The atmosphere of 1967 included a military draft and an American war which killed thousands per week. It included a political and cultural environment in which feminists and gay activists were far more vulnerable and powerless than they would be fifty years later.

When my parents were in their early twenties, they lived in an America permeated by McCarthyism and ideological purges from government jobs, academia, and mainstream entertainment. Propaganda tools to manipulate millions of Americans date back at least as far as the early twentieth century and the PR efforts by George Creel and Sigmund Freud's nephew Edward Bernays to manufacture American support for World War I. Thus, as Billy Joel wrote, "We didn't start the fire," but it is well worth looking at mistakes that radicals and hippies made in the sixties to try to avoid them again.

One misperception was a distorted sense of time. Lenin said that a revolutionary day can seem like ten years, and there were relatively brief moments, such as the Montgomery bus boycott, the quick spread of hippie fashions and drugs, the instant ubiquity of "All You Need Is Love," and the virtual end of artistic censorship, that may have raised expectations among young people that peace and love could permeate the world in their lifetime. Patience is not unhip.

It is a grave mistake for human beings to think that they can understand everything about the meaning of life. The Greek myth of Icarus tells of how he fell to his death by flying too close to the sun. We are supposed to do the very best we can and avoid assuming that we have figured everything out.

If we are going to embrace the idea of agape, universal love, it cannot apply only to our tribe or group of tribes. It has to apply, literally, to everybody. A piece in the *Oracle* called for "love and compassion for all hate-carrying men and women." Today this seems a wee bit condescending. Calling those outside of the hippie life "hapless robot receptors" was, I can now see, not the best way to connect with strangers.

Loving everybody is very hard to do, even for saints, but that's the gig. I can see now that even the word "counterculture" was inherently polarizing. As Dr. King said, "Darkness cannot put out darkness; only light can do that."

While recognizing the fact that life's forces sometimes move backward and that darkness sometimes temporarily prevails, it is important to appreciate the good things that have happened. It could be worse, and it has been. Millions of people feel empowered today who would have felt like isolated freaks before the sixties.

Mel Brooks's character the 2,000 Year Old Man said, "There's something bigger than Phil." The hippie idea of prioritizing peace and love above all else was bigger than money, bigger than fear, bigger than sex, bigger than drugs, bigger than war, and bigger than the Beatles, but it wasn't a gateway into a new age, just a flash to indicate that something different was possible.

One of the aspects of LSD I liked best was the way that time sometimes slowed down and a single minute could seem to last for years. Conversely, the passage of fifty years sometimes feels like a few minutes. Perhaps the best way to look at the "lost chord" of 1967 is a trip that millions of people took together.

Maharaji told Ram Dass that LSD could allow you to spend a couple of hours with Christ, but then you'd have to come back down and do the spiritual work to actually live in that consciousness. Similarly, Peter Coyote says, "Acid showed you what was there but it did not deliver it. It was like having a helicopter take you to the top of a mountain and then bring you back without providing a guide to get you back up there." Moral and spiritual progress usually takes decades or even lifetimes. Hippie skeptic Kerouac said, "Walking on water wasn't built in a day," but he didn't say it could never happen.

AFTERWORD 2018
THE HIPPIE IDEA IN THE TRUMP ERA

Mark Twain supposedly said, "History doesn't repeat itself, but it often rhymes." As I was writing this afterword, the media was reflecting a reality that would have been unthinkable in the sixties: Republicans were defending Russia while Democratic liberals were defending the FBI. Yet despite the topsy-turvy developments, essential moral issues remained the same.

One night on MSNBC, Lawrence O'Donnell went on a rant because a Melania Trump speech had been introduced by a version of the song "Aquarius/Let the Sunshine In" from the musical *Hair*. The song enshrines "sympathy and trust abounding, no more falsehoods or derisions." O'Donnell acidly pointed out that Donald Trump was a baby boomer whose public and private lives were literally the antithesis of those lyrics which had been inspired by the San Francisco Be-In in 1967.

One of the greatest joys of publishing this book was meeting and reconnecting with people of my own generation who had their own memories of music (often Jimi Hendrix), psychedelics, and antiwar protests, and the sense of community that revolved around agape. However, there was also a lot of melancholy about the election of November 2016. It felt to a lot of former hippies that Trump's election and that of a Republican Congress was a repudiation of the progress with inclusivity, the environment, and egalitarianism that had been made in the preceding decades. At a memorial service for Tom Hayden shortly after the election, a friend who has been a progressive activist since the sixties mournfully told me that his seventeen-year-old son had just interviewed him for his high school newspaper about "why we failed." At a moment when many of us were hoping to complete several progressive agendas, there was a dreadful feeling of undertow toward the bad old days.

Without diminishing the seriousness of the current state of the American political system, a wider perspective than the twenty-four-hour news cycle is helpful. As dire as things seem to many of us in 2018, it is worth remembering the dark side of the late sixties when J. Edgar Hoover was running the FBI, and when our best leaders were murdered. The presidents who reigned during the second half of the sixties were profoundly flawed.

Trump and his allies have yet to conjure up anything as dangerous as the Gulf of Tonkin incident, a nonexistent attack on an American warship that President Lyndon B. Johnson used as the pretext for escalating the Vietnam War from twenty thousand American troops at the time of John F. Kennedy's assassination to over half a million when LBJ left office five years later. Johnson administration boasts about the war were so unrealistic that the phrase "credibility gap" was coined to describe what is now called "fake news."

Trump is not the first president to invite speculation about his mental health. In his memoir *Remembering America*, Richard N. Goodwin, a speechwriter for LBJ, writes that he was worried about "certain episodes of what I believe to have been paranoid behavior" displayed by the president. Both Goodwin and fellow LBJ staffer Bill Moyers consulted psychiatrists because of their worry that the president was becoming unhinged.

Like Trump, President Johnson demonized the media, telling Goodwin (without offering any evidence), "The Communists already control the three major networks and the forty major outlets of communication." LBJ's White House taping system captured him bad-mouthing the *New York Times* to Georgia senator Herman Talmadge: "You have two or three little Jewish boys up there that are—according to our phone taps and other sources of information—on the Communist side of this operation."

Nor was 2016 the first time that a foreign power influenced an American election. As John A. Farrell points out in his book *Richard Nixon: The Life*, released shortly after Trump was elected, previously unpublished notes of Richard Nixon's chief of staff H.R. Haldeman prove that Nixon directed his campaign's efforts to interfere with a Vietnam peace deal that President Johnson was negotiating shortly before the 1968 election. In return for a halt of American bombing of North Vietnam, the Communists agreed to engage in constructive talks to end the war. The deal was contingent on the agreement of South Vietnamese president Nguyễn Văn Thiệu. Nixon conveyed a message via his friend Anna Chennault that if Thiệu turned *down* the deal, Nixon would give him better terms when he took office the following year.

Hubert Humphrey had been rising in the polls as talk of the possible peace deal was made public, but his momentum stopped when those talks were thwarted the week before the election. Nixon's winning margin over Humphrey was less than 1 percent in the popular vote. Not only did Nixon's interference most likely gain him the presidency illegitimately, it gave the South Vietnamese government leverage over him since they knew his awful secret. The war then lasted five more years, during which more than twenty-five thousand additional Americans were killed. The peace agreement that was finally negotiated in 1973 was virtually identical to what Nixon had covertly sabotaged in 1968.

Just as President Obama ultimately chose not to go public with intelligence findings of pro-Trump interference by the Russians in 2016, Johnson declined to expose Nixon's perfidy in 1968 because he lacked the "absolute proof," as Defense Secretary Clark Clifford put it, of Nixon's direct involvement.

Today's alt-right has its antecedents in slave owners, plutocratic haters of Franklin Delano Roosevelt, and the John Birch Society. Paul Ryan's idol Ayn Rand and Trump's mentor Roy Cohn were both alive and spewing poison in 1967.

There is also connectivity between resistance in the Trump era and the spirit of the sixties, which has informed many progressive efforts, including women's marches, Black Lives Matter, the "Never Again" movement to restrict assault weapons, and public opposition to the Muslim immigration ban. It is also worth recalling that the word *resistance* was a preferred term for radicals in the sixties. According to my Kindle, Todd Gitlin's

The Sixties: Years of Hope, Days of Rage uses the word *resistance* eighty-eight times. It is not clear, in retrospect, how much some of the most confrontational tactics helped the cause. Gitlin acknowledges that as the Vietnam War became increasingly unpopular with the American public, so did the antiwar movement. This should be a cautionary reminder to anyone who thinks that street demonstrations are the one and only valid way to express protest against injustice.

Moreover, to avoid a rerun of some of the disappointments of the late sixties and to actually diminish the power of oligarchs, there must be a reduction in schisms among those of us not held in thrall by the right-wing media that billionaires fund. The tribal divide between the "counterculture" that focused more on inner changes and the "revolutionaries" who focused more on political protest helped neither progressive political goals nor the development of a healthier moral/spiritual balance.

One of the primary tactics of the FBI's COINTELPRO program aimed at weakening the antiwar and civil rights movements was to foment internal discord. Similarly, most of the Russian electoral interference in 2016 was intended to turn Bernie Sanders and Hillary Clinton supporters against each other.

Another lesson from the sixties is that liberal elites need to respect the energy and insights of young people if they want to win. In 1967 as now, the younger generation was both the most progressive and the largest in history. The teenagers who emerged in 2018 as spokespeople on gun issues in the wake of school shootings will not be the last members of their generation who have the capacity to change the definition of what is politically possible.

In 2016 as in 1968, some progressive young people did not vote for the Democrat. Struggling with college debt, stressed out by disappearing job opportunities, and terrified of global warming, they were not motivated by charts showing statistical economic growth during the Obama years or by Tim Kaine's harmonica playing. (To be clear—I wish this had not been the case!)

Some mainstream Democrats blame young people for low turnout or for having been seduced by the Libertarian or Green parties. Smug lectures aimed at young people do not work in the twenty-first century any more than they did in the sixties. They are like a rock band blaming the audience for not applauding instead of figuring out how to improve the show. It is equally absurd when some on the left refuse to admit that the United States and the world would be in a lot better shape today if imperfect Hillary Clinton had won, as would have been the case if Humphrey had prevailed over Nixon.

Nixon's attorney general, John N. Mitchell, promised a reporter, "This country is going so far to the right you won't recognize it." In order to have any chance of reversing the right-wing trends that began in the late sixties, mainstream Democrats and progressives need to find ways to disagree without destroying their ability to accomplish shared goals.

By early 2018, the most powerful progressive energy in America was coming from women in the "Me Too" movement. More than one male who had the sixties counterculture in his background was caught up in the wave of revulsion at sexual harassment in the workplace.

344 ♥ Danny Goldberg

The fact that many Hollywood and media corporations felt that they had to jettison abusive men who made money for them was not only a big deal in terms of female empowerment but a contradiction of the notion popular among oligarchs that the short-term bottom line is the only thing that matters.

I am disappointed at the persistence of racism and sexism in society and the continued influence in corridors of power of the amoral materialism championed by Ayn Rand. (Republican House Speaker Paul Ryan told the *Weekly Standard*, "I give out *Atlas Shrugged* as Christmas presents, and I make all my interns read it.") However, for all of the moral failings of America in the Trump era, I do not believe that "we failed."

In the early seventies, Ram Dass was told by his guru to "love everybody." Despite the fact that his political beliefs have always been on the left, the spiritual teacher includes a photo of Donald Trump on his puja table alongside that of his guru and other saints. His frequent postelection message was: "Resist with love."

Sharon Salzberg, a Buddhist teacher who is also a protégé of Ram Dass, told me in early 2018 that among her students demoralized by Trump, "There have been two kinds of reactions: those overwhelmed by a sense of anger or fear, whom I've tried to guide to channeling those feelings into doing something constructive for someone else, even if it feels very small; and those who are exhausted by their own reactivity, for whom I've talked about remembering the good. I have compassion for that exhaustion and feelings of futility—I've been there. Yet I also believe that we can be energized by love."

On a Facebook page called "The Hippies Were

Right," a photo was recently posted showing a bearded man holding a protest sign that reads: *What Do We Want? Time Travel. When Do We Want It? It's Irrelevant.* Peace and love transcend time.

In the last speech of his life on April 3, 1968, Dr. King said, "I've seen the Promised Land. I may not get there with you. But I want you to know tonight that we, as a people, will get to the Promised Land." He didn't say when.

Danny Goldberg
May 2018

1967 TIMELINE

JANUARY 1—New Year's Eve at the Fillmore in San Francisco, CA, featuring the Grateful Dead and Jefferson Airplane

JANUARY 5—Ronald Reagan is sworn in as governor of California

JANUARY 14—Human Be-In in San Francisco, CA

JANUARY 15—First Super Bowl: Green Bay Packers defeat Kansas City Chiefs, 35–10

FEBRUARY 1—*Surrealistic Pillow* is released, making Jefferson Airplane pop/rock stars

FEBRUARY 5—*The Smothers Brothers Comedy Hour* premieres on CBS

FEBRUARY 11—A.J. Muste dies at age eighty-two

FEBRUARY 11—Around three thousand WBAI listeners congregate for a "Fly-In" at JFK Airport, on one of the coldest days of the year

FEBRUARY 13—Perception '67 Conference in Toronto, featuring the Fugs, Allen Ginsberg, Richard Alpert, Marshall McLuhan, and Paul Krassner

FEBRUARY 17—Ed Sanders of the Fugs is featured on the cover of a *Life* magazine issue about "Happenings"

FEBRUARY 17—The Beatles release "Strawberry Fields Forever"/"Penny Lane"

FEBRUARY 18—J. Robert Oppenheimer dies

FEBRUARY 22—*MacBird!* premieres in New York, NY

FEBRUARY 25—Sonny & Cher's "The Beat Goes On" peaks at #6 on *Billboard*'s Hot 100 chart

FEBRUARY 28—Henry R. Luce dies

MARCH 1—Adam Clayton Powell Jr. is denied a seat in Congress (Arthur Kinoy represents him in court)

MARCH 6—Lyndon B. Johnson announces draft lottery

MARCH 20—Obscenity trial for Peace Eye Bookstore, New York, NY

MARCH 26—Easter Be-In, Central Park, New York, NY, and at Elysian Park, Los Angeles

APRIL 4—Martin Luther King Jr. announces opposition to Vietnam War in speech at Riverside Church, New York, NY

APRIL 7—Underground radio host Tom Donahue begins broadcasting on KMPX

APRIL 11—Adam Clayton Powell Jr. reelected

APRIL 15—Forty thousand (or more) march and protest as part of the Spring Mobilization to End the Vietnamese War at Kezar Stadium, San Francisco, CA

APRIL 20—US bombs Haiphong for the first time

APRIL 28—Muhammad Ali refuses induction into the US Army

MAY 12—H. Rap Brown replaces Stokely Carmichael as chairman of the Student Nonviolent Coordinating Committee (SNCC)

MAY 18—Andrei Voznesensky performs with the Fugs at an antiwar event at Village Theater, New York, NY

MAY 25—John Lennon's psychedelically painted Rolls-Royce is delivered

JUNE 1—*Sgt. Pepper's Lonely Hearts Club Band* is released

JUNE 2—Race riots in Roxbury, MA

JUNE 5–11—Six-Day War in the Middle East

JUNE 7—Haight-Ashbury Free Clinic opens

JUNE 11—Race riots in Tampa, FL

JUNE 12—*Loving v. Virginia* strikes down state bans on interracial marriages

JUNE 13—Thurgood Marshall is nominated to the Supreme Court by President Johnson

JUNE 16–18—Monterey International Pop Festival, Monterey, CA

JUNE 19—Paul McCartney reveals in *Queen* magazine interview that he has taken LSD

JUNE 20—Muhammad Ali is convicted in Houston, TX, for violating the US Selective Service law

JUNE 22—The *San Francisco Chronicle*'s front page reads, "Hippies Begin Their Summer of Love," and a phrase is coined

JUNE 25—The Beatles perform "All You Need Is Love" live on international TV

JUNE 26—Race riots in Buffalo, NY

JUNE 27—Celebration of Peace Eye Bookstore acquittal, New York, NY

JUNE 28—Community Defense Fund benefit at Village Theater, New York, NY, featuring the Mothers of Invention, the Fugs, Allen Ginsberg, and emcee Bob Fass of WBAI

JULY 4—Freedom of Information Act becomes official

JULY 5—Electric Circus opens in New York, NY

JULY 12—Race riots in Newark, NJ

JULY 15–30—The Congress on the Dialectics of Liberation (for the Demystification of Violence), London, England

JULY 17—John Coltrane dies

JULY 19—Race riots in Durham, NC

JULY 23–27—Race riots in Detroit, MI

JULY 28—Johnson forms National Advisory Commission on Civil Disorders, knows as the Kerner Commission, to study race riots

JULY 30—Race riots in Milwaukee, WI

AUGUST 2—The film *In the Heat of the Night* is released

AUGUST 3—President Johnson announces 45,000 more troops will be sent to Vietnam

AUGUST 13—The film *Bonnie and Clyde* is released

AUGUST 24—Abbie Hoffman and others release fistfuls of money onto the floor of the New York Stock Exchange

AUGUST 25—The Beatles attend a seminar in Wales by the Maharishi

AUGUST 30—US Senate confirms Thurgood Marshall, making him the first African American Supreme Court justice

SEPTEMBER 3—General Nguyen Van Thieu is elected president of South Vietnam

SEPTEMBER 9—*Rowan & Martin's Laugh-In* pilot airs on NBC

SEPTEMBER 11—*The Carol Burnett Show* premieres on CBS

SEPTEMBER 21—The Diggers' Free Store opens on the Lower East Side, New York, NY

OCTOBER 3—Woody Guthrie dies

OCTOBER 6—The Diggers' Death of Hippie march and ceremony takes place in San Francisco, CA

OCTOBER 7—James "Groovy" Leroy Hutchinson and Linda Fitzpatrick are murdered in New York, NY

OCTOBER 7—Trial begins for Deputy Sheriff Cecil R. Price and eighteen others in Philadelphia, Mississippi, for the killing of three civil rights workers in 1964

OCTOBER 8-9—Che Guevara is captured and executed in Bolivia

OCTOBER 11—Yoko Ono's solo art show opens at the Lisson Gallery in London, sponsored by John Lennon

OCTOBER 17—The musical *Hair* has its off-Broadway debut

OCTOBER 21—Around 100,000 people march on the Pentagon in an anti–Vietnam War rally, including Norman Mailer, who loosely based his 1968 nonfiction "novel," *The Armies of the Night*, on the march

OCTOBER 27—Blood is poured onto Selective Service records in Baltimore, MD, by Philip Berrigan and others

OCTOBER 28—Huey P. Newton, cofounder of the Black Panther Party, is arrested for murder in Oakland, CA

OCTOBER 30—Charles Manson arrives in Topanga, CA, from Haight-Ashbury

NOVEMBER 7—President Johnson signs bill establishing the Corporation for Public Broadcasting

NOVEMBER 7—In Cleveland, Ohio, Carl Stokes becomes the first African American mayor of a major city

NOVEMBER 9—Debut issue of *Rolling Stone*

NOVEMBER 21—President Johnson signs the Air Quality Act

NOVEMBER 27—The Beatles' *Magical Mystery Tour* is released

NOVEMBER 29—Robert S. McNamara announces he is stepping down as secretary of defense to become the head of the World Bank

NOVEMBER 30—Senator Eugene McCarthy announces his campaign to oppose President Johnson for the 1968 Democratic nomination

DECEMBER 5—Allen Ginsberg and Dr. Benjamin Spock are arrested at a Vietnam War protest in New York

DECEMBER 10—Otis Redding dies

DECEMBER 12—Timothy Leary and Rosemary Woodruff's wedding ceremony in Millbrook, NY

DECEMBER 22—The film *The Graduate* premieres

DECEMBER 27—Bob Dylan releases *John Wesley Harding*

DECEMBER 31—The Youth International Party, a.k.a. the Yippies, is founded by Abbie and Anita Hoffman, Jim Fouratt, Stew Albert, Jerry Rubin, Nancy Kurshan, and Paul Krassner

DECEMBER 31—Jefferson Airplane and Big Brother play at the Winterland Arena, San Francisco

SOURCES

The following is a list of key sources I used in my research while writing this book:

Books:

Growing Up Underground by Jane Alpert

The Cause: The Fight for American Liberalism from Franklin Roosevelt to Barack Obama by Eric Alterman and Kevin Mattson

The Summer of Love: Haight-Ashbury at Its Highest by Gene Anthony

And a Voice to Sing With: A Memoir by Joan Baez

A Blue Hand: The Beats in India by Deborah Baker

Forward Through the Rearview Mirror: Reflections on and by Marshall McLuhan by Paul Benedetti and Nancy DeHart

Witness to the Revolution: Radicals, Resisters, Vets, Hippies, and the Year America Lost Its Mind and Found Its Soul by Clara Bingham

Muhammad Ali's Greatest Fight: Cassius Clay vs. the United States of America by Howard L. Bingham and Max Wallace

Rolling Thunder by Doug Boyd

White Bicycles: Making Music in the 1960s by Joe Boyd

At Canaan's Edge: America in the King Years, 1965-68 by Taylor Branch

Sometimes Brilliant: The Impossible Adventure of a Spiritual Seeker and Visionary Physician Who Helped Conquer the Worst Disease in History by Larry Brilliant

Boom! Talking About the Sixties: What Happened, How It Shaped Today, Lessons for Tomorrow by Tom Brokaw

The Hare Krishnas in India by Charles R. Brooks

Country Joe and Me by Ron Cabral and Joe McDonald

Never Stop Running: Allard Lowenstein and American Liberalism by William H. Chafe

White Hand Society: The Psychedelic Partnership of Timothy Leary & Allen Ginsberg by Peter Conners

The Dialectics of Liberation by David Cooper

The Rainman's Third Cure: An Irregular Education by Peter Coyote

Sleeping Where I Fall: A Chronicle by Peter Coyote

Long Time Gone: The Autobiography of David Crosby by David Crosby and Carl Gottlieb

The Pied Piper: Allard K. Lowenstein and the Liberal Dream by Richard Cummings

American Gandhi: A.J. Muste and the History of Radicalism in the Twentieth Century by Leilah Danielson

America, the Vietnam War, and the World: Comparative and International Perspectives by Andreas W. Daum, Lloyd C. Gardner, and Wilfried Mausbach

Loose Change: Three Women of the Sixties by Sara Davidson

Slouching Towards Bethlehem: Essays by Joan Didion

Timothy Leary and the Madmen of Millbrook by Theodore P. Druch

Trashing by Ann Fettamen (a.k.a. Anita Hoffman)

Fortunate Son: My Life, My Music by John Fogerty

Revolution for the Hell of It by Free (a.k.a. Abbie Hoffman)

The Norton Anthology of African American Literature by Henry Louis Gates Jr. and Valerie Smith

GINSBERG: India Revisited by Allen Ginsberg

Howl and Other Poems by Allen Ginsberg

Indian Journals by Allen Ginsberg

Journals: Early Fifties, Early Sixties by Allen Ginsberg

The Sixties: Years of Hope, Days of Rage by Todd Gitlin

The Whole World Is Watching: Mass Media in the Making and Unmaking of the New Left by Todd Gitlin

Live at the Fillmore East and West: Getting Backstage and Personal with Rock's Greatest Legends by John Glatt

Music in the Air: The Selected Writings of Ralph J. Gleason by Ralph J. Gleason

American Veda: From Emerson and the Beatles to Yoga and Meditation: How Indian Spirituality Changed the West by Philip Goldberg

New Reformation: Notes of a Neolithic Conservative by Paul Goodman

Here Comes the Sun: The Spiritual and Musical Journey of George Harrison by Joshua M. Greene

Swami in a Strange Land: How Krishna Came to the West by Joshua M. Greene

Bear: The Life and Times of Augustus Owsley Stanley III by Robert Greenfield

Timothy Leary: A Biography by Robert Greenfield

Callus on My Soul: A Memoir by Dick Gregory and Sheila P. Moses

Nigger by Dick Gregory

Ringolevio: A Life Played for Keeps by Emmett Grogan

Dreams Die Hard: Three Men's Journey through the Sixties by David Harris

Hell No: The Forgotten Power of the Vietnam Peace Movement by Tom Hayden

The Long Sixties: From 1960 to Barack Obama by Tom Hayden

Reunion: A Memoir by Tom Hayden

'Scuse Me While I Kiss the Sky: Jimi Hendrix: Voodoo Child by David Henderson

Follow the Music: The Life and High Times of Elektra Records in the Great Years of American Pop Culture by Jac Holzman and Gavan Daws

The Doors of Perception by Aldous Huxley

This Timeless Moment: A Personal View of Aldous Huxley by Laura Huxley

354 🌵 Danny Goldberg

America Divided: The Civil War of the 1960s by Maurice Isserman and Michael Kazin

Heads: A Biography of Psychedelic America by Jesse Jarnow

Abbie Hoffman: American Rebel by Marty Jezer

Blues People: Negro Music in White America by LeRoi Jones

American Dreamers: How the Left Changed a Nation by Michael Kazin

Allen Ginsberg in America by Jane Kramer

Confessions of a Raving, Unconfined Nut: Misadventures in the Counterculture by Paul Krassner

How a Satirical Editor Became a Yippie Conspirator in Ten Easy Years by Paul Krassner

Hip Capitalism by Susan Krieger

Radio Waves: Life and Revolution on the FM Dial by Jim Ladd

Flashbacks: An Autobiography by Timothy Leary

The Psychedelic Experience: A Manual Based on the Tibetan Book of the Dead by Timothy Leary

Look Out, Whitey! Black Power's Gon' Get Your Mama! by Julius Lester

The Armies of the Night: History as a Novel, the Novel as History by Norman Mailer

The White Negro: Superficial Reflections on the Hipster by Norman Mailer

What the Dormouse Said: How the Sixties Counterculture Shaped the Personal Computer Industry by John Markoff

The Selling of the President 1968 by Joe McGinniss

The Gutenberg Galaxy by Marshall McLuhan

Understanding Media by Marshall McLuhan

Hippie by Barry Miles

Jack Kerouac and Allen Ginsberg: The Letters edited by Bill Morgan

The Selected Letters of Allen Ginsberg and Gary Snyder edited by Bill Morgan

The 60s: The Story of a Decade by the New Yorker magazine and Henry Finder

Dream Time: Chapters from the Sixties by Geoffrey O'Brien

2Stoned by Andrew Loog Oldham

Dawning of the Counter-culture: The 1960s by William L. O'Neill

The Leading Man: Hollywood and the Presidential Image by Professor Burton W. Peretti

The Haight-Ashbury: A History by Charles Perry

No Simple Highway: A Cultural History of the Grateful Dead by Peter Richardson

The Rolling Stone Encyclopedia of Rock & Roll by the editors of Rolling Stone

Memoirs of an Ex-Hippie: Seven Years in the Counterculture by Robert A. Roskind

The Making of a Counter Culture: Reflections on the Technocratic Society and Its Youthful Opposition by Theodore Roszak

Do It! Scenarios of the Revolution by Jerry Rubin

The Catcher in the Rye by J.D. Salinger

Franny and Zooey by J.D. Salinger

Fug You: An Informal History of the Peace Eye Bookstore, the Fuck You Press, the Fugs, and Counterculture in the Lower East Side by Ed Sanders

Orange Sunshine: The Brotherhood of Eternal Love and Its Quest to Spread Peace, Love, and Acid to the World by Nicholas Schou

Dharma Lion: A Biography of Allen Ginsberg by Michael Schumacher

Living with the Dead: Twenty Years on the Bus with Garcia and the Grateful Dead by Rock Scully

The Haight: Love, Rock, and Revolution by Joel Selvin and Jim Marshall (photography)

Monterey Pop by Joel Selvin and Jim Marshall (photography)

Summer of Love: The Inside Story of LSD, Rock & Roll, Free Love and High Times in the Wild West by Joel Selvin

Raga Mala: The Autobiography of Ravi Shankar by Ravi Shankar

Somebody to Love? A Rock-and-Roll Memoir by Grace Slick and Andrea Cagan

Love Needs Care by David E. Smith, MD, and John Luce Smith

The I Ching: A Biography by Richard J. Smith

Owsley and Me: My LSD Family by Rhoney Gissen Stanley and Tom Davis

Edie: An American Biography by Jean Stein and George Plimpton

Lowenstein: Acts of Courage and Belief by Gregory Stone and Douglas Lowenstein

The Untold History of the United States by Oliver Stone and Peter Kuznick

Prime Green: Remembering the Sixties by Robert Stone

Women Strike for Peace: Traditional Motherhood and Radical Politics in the 1960s by Amy Swerdlow

Got a Revolution! The Turbulent Flight of Jefferson Airplane by Jeff Tamarkin

Black Power: The Politics of Liberation by Kwame Ture and Charles V. Hamilton

From Counterculture to Cyberculture: Stewart Brand, the Whole Earth Network, and the Rise of Digital Utopianism by Fred Turner

Bobby Kennedy: The Making of a Liberal Icon by Larry Tye

We Are the People Our Parents Warned Us Against: The Classic Account of the 1960s Counter-Culture in San Francisco by Nicholas von Hoffman

The Making of the President 1968 by Theodore H. White

The Electric Kool-Aid Acid Test by Tom Wolfe

Autobiography of a Yogi by Paramahansa Yogananda

Troublemaker: A Memoir from the Front Lines of the Sixties by Bill Zimmerman

Magazines:

Crawdaddy

Dissent

East Village Other

Nation

New Republic

Newsweek

Ramparts

Realist

Rolling Stone

San Francisco Oracle

Time

Village Voice

Online Articles/Websites:

Abrams, Cary and Kroeger, Brooke. "Anatomy of the Great Banana-Smoking Hoax of 1967," *East Village Other* (blog). http://eastvillageother.org/recollections/bananas.

"The Archive," *The King Center*. http://www.thekingcenter.org/archive.

Batura, Amber. "How Playboy Explains Vietnam," *New York Times*. February 28, 2017. https://www.nytimes.com/2017/02/28/opinion/how-playboy-explains-vietnam.html.

The Beatles Bible (blog). https://www.beatlesbible.com/.

"Category Archives: Oscar Janiger," *Psychedelic Salon* (blog). http://psychedelicsalon.com/category/people/oscar-janiger/.

"The Communication Company Archives," *The Digger Archives* (blog). http://www.diggers.org/Communication-Company-Archives/index.html.

DeLong, Doug. "What Really Happened to Diane Linkletter?" *Blog Critics* (blog). July 27, 2007. http://blogcritics.org/what-really-happened-to-diane-linkletter/.

Electri Pipe Dream (blog). http://electripipedream.tumblr.com/.

Ledbetter, James. "The Day the NYSE Went Yippie," *CNN Money*. August 23, 2007. http://money.cnn.com/2007/07/17/news/funny/abbie_hoffman/.

Levi, Charles. "Sex, Drugs, Rock & Roll, and the University College Lit: The University of Toronto Festivals, 1965-1969," *Historical Studies in Education*. Autumn 2006. http://ojs.library.queensu.ca/index.php/edu_hse-rhe/article/view/348/423.

Love Serve Remember Foundation. https://www.ramdass.org/.

"Martin Luther King Jr. and the Global Freedom Stuggle," *King Institute Encyclopedia*. http://kingencyclopedia.stanford.edu/.

McDonald, Joe. "The Banana Affair," *Country Joe's Place* (blog). http://www.countryjoe.com/banana.htm.

McLuhan, Marshall. "This Is Marshall McLuhan: The Medium is the Message." NBC, 1967. McGraw-Hill Book Co., video, 51:55. https://archive.org/details/thisismarshallmcluhanthemediumisthemessage.

Shafer, Jack. "The Time and Life Acid Trip," *Slate*. June 21, 2010. http://www.slate.com/articles/news_and_politics/press_box/2010/06/the_time_and_life_acid_trip.html.

ACKNOWLEDGMENTS

2018 PAPERBACK EDITION

THANKS TO: Kay Goldberg and Max Goldberg, for encouragement, insight, and inspiration; Sid Blumenthal, Hendrik Hertzberg, Joyce Linehan, Ami Bennitt, Pamela Des Barres, Joel Selvin, Eric Alterman, and Dennis McNally, for your generosity and support; Patty Nasey and my Fieldston classmates, for the warmth and solidarity; Sharon Salzberg, for last-minute wisdom; and Peter Simon, for his prodigious talent and generous friendship.

2017 HARDCOVER EDITION

THANKS TO: Laura Nolan, who started all of this and held my hand throughout; Steve Wasserman, for encouragement when it meant the most; Johnny Temple, for taking the plunge and for his friendship; also thanks to Johanna Ingalls, Ibrahim Ahmad, Aaron Petrovich, Alice Wertheimer, and Susannah Lawrence at Akashic Books; Evan Malmgren, for research assistance; Steve Earle, for continual inspiration; my colleagues at Gold Village, Jesse

Bauer, Cyndy Villano, and Shelby McElrath, for putting up with this; Warren Grant and Lori Ichimura, for looking after me all these years; Raghu Markus, for his support and for the example he sets; Hilda Charlton, across many dimensions; David Silver, for walking on so many paths with me; Margery Tabankin, for her radiant spirit and friendship; Eric Alterman, for very helpful notes and emotional support; Michael Simmons, for going above and beyond and saving my ass repeatedly. Love and thanks to the late Jack Newfield, Stanley Sheinbaum, Tom Hayden, Tim Leary, and Allen Ginsberg, for letting me into their lives.

Gratitude to my Fieldston friends, who helped me remember how we felt in high school: Joel Goodman, Peter Kinoy, Susan Solomon, Joshua Greene, Laura Rosenberg, June Christopher, and the late Gil Scott-Heron.

Thanks for talking to me: Lou Adler, Rosanna Arquette, Heather Booth, Joe Boyd, Denardo Coleman, Robbie Conal, Peter Coyote, Sara Davidson, Pamela Des Barres, Jodie Evans, Jim Fouratt, Todd Gitlin, Barry Goldberg, J.J. Goldberg, Nigel Grainge, Gary Greenberg, David Henderson, Earl Katz, Paul Krassner, Zach Leary, Elliot Mintz, Mtume, Ram Dass, Glenn Silber, Grace Slick, Andy Stern, Wavy Gravy, Cora Weiss, and Bill Zimmerman.

Thanks to Dr. Michael Eigen, for the encouragement.

And thanks especially to Karen Greenberg, whose love, intelligence, and patience nurtured every moment of the process and to whom no amount of thanks is sufficient.